T0381548

COMPLETE TEACHINGS OF WICCA

BOOK ONE: THE SEEKER

THE WITCH OF OZ

BALBOA
PRESS
A DIVISION OF HAY HOUSE

Balboa Press books may be ordered through booksellers or by contacting:

Balboa Press
A Division of Hay House
1663 Liberty Drive
Bloomington, IN 47403
www.balboapress.com.au
1 (877) 407-4847

Because of the dynamic nature of the Internet, any web addresses or links contained in this book may have changed since publication and may no longer be valid. The views expressed in this work are solely those of the author and do not necessarily reflect the views of the publisher, and the publisher hereby disclaims any responsibility for them.

The author of this book does not dispense medical advice or prescribe the use of any technique as a form of treatment for physical, emotional, or medical problems without the advice of a physician, either directly or indirectly. The intent of the author is only to offer information of a general nature to help you in your quest for emotional and spiritual well-being. In the event you use any of the information in this book for yourself, which is your constitutional right, the author and the publisher assume no responsibility for your actions.

Any people depicted in stock imagery provided by Thinkstock are models,
and such images are being used for illustrative purposes only.
Certain stock imagery © Thinkstock.

Print information available on the last page.

ISBN: 978-1-5043-1175-5 (sc)
ISBN: 978-1-5043-1193-9 (e)

Balboa Press rev. date: 12/29/2017

TABLE OF
CONTENTS

FOREWORD

WHO IS THE WITCH OF OZ?

Lady Tamara Von Forslun (The Wicce of Oz) has been involved in the Craft and teaching Wicca and Witchcraft (read Wiccecraft) for over 40 years, she is considered one of the world's respected Wiccan Elders and is the Founder and Creator of "The Church of Wicca" (Australia 1989), and was the Arch Priestess of the Aquarian Tabernacle Church in Australia (1991). Lady Tamara started her involvement in Satanism as a teenager at the age of 14 till she was 15, leaving the group because she found it was not for her. At the time all books related Witchcraft to Black Magick and Satanism, of which she eventually found out that they are completely different and have no similarities whatsoever.

Lady Tamara then at the age of 16 met a gentlemen at the "Mediterranean Restaurant" in Subiaco, where she worked, his name was David and he had a Coven in the foothills of Perth and invited her to attend. She did attend their Festivities and found it was exactly what she was looking for; also the people were exceptionally friendly and helpful in her endeavours. Lady Tamara remained and was Initiated into this Coven of Draconis by David the Fifth who was the High Priest and his High Priestess Lady Margaret who was a Blood Wicce or better known as a Hereditary Witch, where Wiccecraft had been in her family for several generations back in Great Britain where she came from, her daughter Layla and I became the best of friends. After a couple of years of being with this Coven David got terribly ill and eventually passed into the Summerlands.

Lady Tamara was then in a documentary with her best friend and fellow Wicce Astra, as they were both professional dancers. They did the documentary and were approached by an Alexandrian High Priest named Simon Goodman, they met with him and were invited to attend their circle, of which Lady Tamara accepted, but Astra declined due to the fact she did not like him at all. So again Lady Tamara met with the fellow Coveners especially their High Priestess, Michelin. Lady Tamara absolutely loved this Lady and respected her immensely as a Spiritual Wiccan Mother figure. Lady Tamara was Initiated into this Coven of the Acorn at the age of 18 years of age, and started on her training as an Alexandrian Wicce. But due to politics and the non disclosure of many questions that were asked but never answered Lady

Tamara along with a few other Wiccans started up her own Coven with her High Priest Lord Imhotep in North Perth just out of the Perth city. It was small but a happily working group. Lady Tamara then purchased her first property in Mundijong, a small farm that was perfect for her lifestyle and her Coven to grow and learn.

Both Imhotep and Lady Tamara worked together for many years until it became too far a distance for Imhotep to travel due to illness. They did continue working together with Lady Elizabeth and David as a group for about nine years working on High Magick, separate from their individual covens.

Lady Tamara started working alone without a High Priest and after a lot of money, legal endeavours and many years of trying to legalise Wicca as a religion in Australia, Lady Tamara Founded and had legalised it at a federal level as Australia's first legal Neo-Pagan Church, The Church of Wicca. This was a great transition as it meant that Wicces could not be prosecuted in Australia anymore, as it was still illegal in certain parts of Australia especially Queensland and Western Australia.

Through Lady Tamara's ambitions to make it recognised both federally, and by local authorities she endeavoured on having more and more contact with the media due to the help of her friend Terry Willesee of the Willesee family. Where she did several documentaries, and hundreds of interviews on TV shows and at least one interview a week on radio. Through this media connection she had contacts Australia wide and met up with fellow High Priestesses from other states who wanted to be a part of the Church of Wicca, and so several Churches were set up in Queensland with Lady Brianna, New South Wales with Lady Mara, Victoria with Lady Mystl and in Western Australia eventually many High Priests and High Priestesses who hived off and formed their own individual covens. Lady Elizabeth, Lord Ariston, Lord Richardt, Lady Sharadon, Lady Tree, Lord Pilgrim, Lady Kundra, Lord Petrus, and many dozens of Ordained Priests and Priestesses.

Lady Tamara also became the first and only legal Wiccan Marriage Celebrant in Australia, and was always travelling interstate marrying Wiccan couples and also non-Wiccan couples who just loved her ceremony. Also as an Arch Priestess of The Aquarian Tabernacle Church (ATC) she became a Chaplain at prisons and hospitals around Australia and would venture to those who asked for her services, she became quite recognisable as a marriage celebrant and officiated at hundreds of weddings and just as many funerals.

Lady Tamara had a successful two-storey Wiccan and New Age store in Fremantle, Western Australia, (The Alchemist) which was also the largest organic herbal store in Australia. With all alternative medicines and much, much more. Lady Tamara funded and supported financially The Church of Wicca through its complete life cycle, by running many training nights such as Outer Courts, Festivals and also has a published magazine called The Spirit Earth Magazine which was distributed Australia wide and became quite popular.

Due to politics and deceitful people trying to bring down Lady Tamara, she eventually sold her shop in Fremantle and handed over the Church of Wicca to Lady Amaris, her last High Priestess. She felt that her legacy was in safe hands and with new blood, would flourish and bring newer connections to modern Wicca and those that were in search of the Goddess and God and the mysteries that Wicca teaches.

But, alas, it was also too much for her and she closed down the Church of Wicca, and went back to the old ways of having just a small suburban coven in a backyard, with no concern for those who need that contact. Lady Amaris had her reasons, and hopefully somewhere out there is a new soul who can commence with a new legal authority like the Church of Wicca as a guiding beacon for those seeking Wiccan Truths and to vanish foolhardy ignorant untruths about Wicca, Wiccecraft and its followers. On that day she will rejoice and be a part of that Truth as an active Elder of Wicca and Wiccecraft.

Lady Tamara through her myriad travels worldwide has learnt from the likes of Alex Sanders, Lady Margaret a Hereditary Wicce, David the 5th a traditional Wicce, Lady Elizabeth a Traditional Witch, Stuart Farrar and Simon Goodman as Alexandrian Witches, Pete Pathfinder a Gardnarian Witch and Founder of the ATC, Velvet Reith a Voudoun Priestess, Jubabe a Shaman from South America, and most importantly her mother Valma who was a Love Goddess and loved everyone and everything.

Lady Tamara thanks all of these teachers especially her latest teachers such as her High Priest Lord Asherah and Tarquin both true devout Priests of the Goddess. Lady Tamara also wishes to thank Pachamama, the Earth Mother for all her lessons that were heard and unheard.

Lady Tamara's series of books disclose everything that she has ever learnt at great depth along her very long and hard life. Along the way all that she has learnt, she has passed on freely to those who would listen and learn. Her classes, teachings, Outer Courts, Facilitations at Universities around the world, were teaching the truth about Wiccecraft. Lady Tamara, now at the end of her life, as a teacher reveals all she has ever learnt as a student of Magick, Wiccecraft, Shamanism, Wicca and Herbal Medicine in her series of books titled "The Complete Encyclopaedia of Wicca". If you wish to know all about Lady Tamara's life, read her autobiography titled "The Witch of Oz" autobiography. Hope you enjoy the writings of Lady Tamara as I have.

Lady Arwen - Grandmother of the Circle of Boskednon.

WICCA

INTRODUCTION FOR THE TRUE SEEKER

Since the beginning of time, man has been in awe of the Universe and everything that it offers. Our ancient ancestors never had names for their differing belief systems; they just existed in harmony with nature, ultimately being called Pagans (the ways of the land). In so many differing lands and countries they all held the same similar beliefs that were taught to them by their Mothers and Fathers, and passed down by word of mouth to their children's, children's, children. But in truth it was the first Mother and Father that taught man the mysteries of Magick. Man learnt all their lessons by watching and listening to Nature, who was our greatest teacher. She still is our greatest classroom but students are few these days, and do not listen in the stillness, we need to listen to the words that travel on the winds of time.

Man has stopped listening to Nature and thus stopped believing in Magick, that is why Magick does not exist for so many people. Man looks at things differently these days, we see things with the eyes of pain, and uncertainty, of doubt and confusion, and of disbelief instead of just being in touch with Nature and listening to Her story. Yes, She (Nature) has a story, Herstory not history. Maybe the greatest story that has ever been told! The names have changed but the essence will always remain the same.

There has always been Wiccecraft in the world, but today in the 21st Century it has changed about 80%. Let me explain my remarks throughout this series of my books which in total I call "The Epagomenes", (The secrets of the Pentagram of the Wicce). We need to awaken our inner self and realign with our planet and each other and listen to what Nature is telling us.

Wiccecraft has been in every land that had an Earth based belief system; Africa with its ancient dark mysteries, their Shaman was called a Sangoma. Egypt had a more celestial Wiccecraft taught by the Priests and Priestesses, especially those of Isis and the Priests of Saiss. The same with Rome, Greece, Babylon, Assyria, and India. Great Britain had the Samethoi, the original Wicces; Tibet, China, Native American Indians, the Indigenous Australian Aboriginal, Mesopotamia, Scandinavia, The Netherlands, Incans, Aztecs; all had their Shamans or Shamanka, and many hundreds of more cultures with their own Magick and knowledge of this Earth and the Universe both within and without.

To believe in, and to know REAL Magick, we must firstly believe in ourselves, and know how to be at One with all things. In doing this we must bring all things into balance, before we can create a balanced world outside of ourselves, we must know and create a complete balance within. This is the Principal of Equilibrium and total Harmony. Written on the Emerald tablets by Hermes Trismegistos (the Greek name for him) but more correctly known as The High Priest "Thoth", where he wrote and said; *"As Above, so Below, as Within so Without"*, we cannot remove ourselves from the truth but embrace and awaken it within us the very microcosm of the macrocosmic Universe, even if it does not agree with us.

Life is a great classroom, but we have forgotten how to see and really look; listen and hear; sense and openly feel. I am hoping that my Series of books, where I have over 50 years of learning, training and teaching hundreds of Seekers, will open your eyes, ears and soul to the truth of the Universe so you can learn and know just a small fragment of what Magick is really about. It does not matter about your religious background, what matter's is that you come into Wicca with an open mind and a non-judgmental attitude. Acceptance and tolerance is the key to truly being a Wicce. We have to remember the winner has always written history, and we know who won, although it was through lies, misogyny, fear, and ignorance. We do not proselytize, and try not to tell you what to do or think or feel, or what to believe, for the Goddess reveals herself to us in many ways. I am only here to help you find a better understanding of the big Pagan picture. What I share with you, are my thoughts and feelings, which are shared by the majority of likeminded knowledgeable Wicces in the world, especially true dedicated Wicces.

I am the Founder and Creator of the Church of Wicca, which was Australia's first legal Neo-Pagan Church; it took me many years to eventually have it legalized in 1989. It was the only officially accepted Wiccan or Pagan Church with registered Ministers of Religion, and legal Wiccan Marriage Celebrants and Chaplains. I was the Arch Priestess, but I stepped down and handed over the reigns of the Church to our new High Priestess, Lady Amaris, whom I had great faith in. I stepped down because it was time for new blood and new ways at looking at things, for the modern audience. I believe that lady Amaris had that insight to take The Church of Wicca to the next level.

The Magick that I hope to show you is Self Love, and a deep connection to the Goddess and those around you. Ours is a spiritual training that trains and educates the mind, body and spirit of the Seeker, and that is who you are at this time, Seekers. It is a training that needs self-truth, self-respect and self-discipline in many areas of your life, not just your Magickal. It is therefore essential that in order to develop to the full your abilities and powers, when eventually you will work within the Magick Circle. That you commence in the study and training known as the Outer Court. Most Covens around the world have Outer Courts; these are pre-training for the Seeker who is commencing on their journey of Wiccecraft or Wicca. This Outer Court includes much of the Secret Lore of Wiccecraft. And I believe as I have for the past 40 years that the time is now to open the coffers and share our sacred knowledge and to help others in finding their own truth and destiny to whichever path this journey takes them. And hopefully at the end of this book will make you one of the Sacred Children of the Goddess and God!

What follows is a related form of theory and practice which conditions and trains the mind of the body, and opens up the Inner Spiritual Being so as to understand not only yourself but understand all this beautiful world around us, that we as humans take for granted, and that we should respect and call Mother! We use to be called the Hidden Children of the Goddess, because of the period known as the Burning Times, but no more! For now we can stand tall without fear of persecution from the ignorance of mankind and be proud of our heritage and share our truth openly with love in our hearts to all those who seek to know the Magick of the Wicce within. Their will always be ignorance and persecution but we must rise above this uneducated and ignorance that is destroying our freedom of Truth.

Think inwardly, Wiccecraft is a community of love and generosity, it is a philosophy and a religion of Nature, and it is a way of life. I believe that life IS indestructible energy, perpetually cast in a container, a body be it that of man or animal. Wicca is inward communication, reincarnation and Deity as a balance of masculine and feminine, with the feminine being the principal aspect of our faith. We follow the laws of the land, we tolerate the establishment, we don't break any rules, and we don't necessarily live by them. I believe in freedom of individual's rights, and everything is acceptable as long as it does not hurt nor hinder anybody, neither anything nor create hang-ups.

I claim to use my knowledge of the Ancient Arts of Wiccecraft for personal benefit not for personal gain. I help rather than exploit, as it is often the want of the practitioners of Black Magick; which has always been confused with Wiccecraft They are not the same and NEVER CAN BE.

Satanism/Black Magick is a cocoon; a dimensional shelter for introverts, and is greedy and shallow, and very much anti-Christian. It is a creation of Christianity, whereas Wiccecraft is not anti anything, except maybe anti-anti. It is open and honest. Black Magick and Christianity both thrive on Mystery and Ritual, and in both sex has played a big role at many times in history. Christianity is open prudery, this is why Satanism always tries to be exactly the opposite, and leans towards sexual excess. Both Christianity and Satanism have sexual hang-ups, but Wiccecraft treats sex as a normal, natural and a pleasurable experience. Sex and all religions, in hundreds of different cults and beliefs, they vary but are what we always question. Birth and Death are the two main reasons, which have always intrigued man, and in his search for the answers he has embraced sex with religion. Whereby man assists God in the Creation of Life. We don't exactly know how the essence or spark of life is created, but we do know that a man and a woman are drawn together in a moment of ecstasy, and thus a new life is created. During the moment of orgasm, the two lovers are elevated briefly from the Mundane Plane to the Fool Stool of the Gods.

Wiccecraft is a fertility religion and this does not mean that we have sexual orgies to better our sexual pleasures. Quite the opposite, sexuality is very private, and I believe that it should be kept very private and personal between the two consenting adult lovers, but at home and away from the Circles of Wiccecraft (which has since the early 1950's been called Wicca) has always been a fertility religion, when man first realized the Power of Creation through the sex act. Where he can actually associate himself with God as in the Creation of Life. This is why in most Eastern countries, the men have harems or many wives, especially if he is king or someone of great importance, (or someone who thinks he is important) and it shows his masculine power.

Our system hopefully can help you in:

1. Providing a true background of the Wiccan system of belief.
2. Relate a person's spirituality to the big picture.
3. Encourage you to look into areas that are off limits to lay people in mainstream religions.
4. Provide you with Elemental Tools in Self-exploration.
5. Set the record straight with regard to humanity's treatment of Wicces.
6. To help in grounding you and making you aware of your own truth.
7. Prepare you for a Path of which you might at the end of these books take fully and eventually be Initiated into Wiccecraft or Wicca and become a Wicce, it may help you to search and find a coven.

So let us together go on a journey that will hopefully educate you and take you on a Path to self-discovery, and the discovery of the true and real Magick, which is called Wiccecraft and Wicca.

Like anything in life you only get out of your study exactly what you put into it. I have known many that claim to have studied and learnt much, but when it comes down to the basic essence of what the Craft is all about, many do not know nor understanding the many varied details and what it takes to be a good Wiccan. If you wish to go further in the endeavours and one day become a Wicce, then your studies are quite immense, and your commitment to all the areas are the intrinsic value of what being a Wicce is all about, you must study not only the physical training of being a Wicce, but the mental aptitude, the psychic training and skills, and also be in true oneness with your Higher Self and become the Spiritual person you know you need to be, your Higher Self.

Just because one is interested in Wicca does not mean they need to dedicate their life or commit to the path of the Wiccan or the Wicce, it is all up to one's own choices and that deep inner connectedness that one seeks with the Goddess and God. Because the deeper you invest in your Spiritual Being the closer you will not only come to know your true self, but the nearer you become with all of Nature, and thus be at One with The Goddess and God.

WICCAN POINTS
TO REMEMBER

PERFECT LOVE AND PERFECT TRUST:

This is a term frequently used within the Craft as a statement of trust, that members will not betray the other. This probably originated back in the Burning Times, when the slip of the tongue could see whole families destroyed at the hands of the Inquisitors and not so nice neighbors.

BLESSED BE!

This is a shortened version of the ancient Saracen's Kiss, which has become known among Initiates as the Five Fold Salute. It is an act of humility presented by Wiccans to their sisters and brothers of the Wiccan Community. It is our term for greetings and partings, as we do not say hello (hell—o) or goodbye (good—bye), but instead Blessed Be!

MERRY MEET AND MERRY PART!

This is also a shortened version of the High Priestesses blessing to all her Coveners, where she says; "I give thee my hand, and I give thee my heart, Merry we Meet, and Merry we Part, and Merry we shall Meet again." We also say this instead of hello or goodbye.

AS ABOVE, SO BELOW: AS WITHIN, SO WITHOUT!

It is a simple statement called the Hermetic Principle, named after our greatest of teachers Thoth, or also known by his Greek title Hermes Trismegistos, meaning (Hermes Thrice Blessed). It is where Wiccans put forth their belief in the Nature of balance. An example of further intuitive thinking on this statement relates to the Magick Circle, which is in reality a Magickal Sphere, the microcosm of the macrocosm.

DIVINE LOVE!

Is a reality of Truth, a feeling of ultimate giving without expectations of return (wants instead of needs) In essence it is a Divine Love, which is unconditional.

BLESSED BE!

And we all know what that means! As we always respond in like. When you go to any Wiccan Magick Circle, always be respectful. Always bring a small plate of food to share, as this is called Agape! You should also offer your services to help clean up afterwards and be a thankful servant of the night, which means we will all humble ourselves in turn in duties with tea, coffee etc. This shows our host or hostage how much we appreciate them offering their home for our trainings and festivities!

Blessed Be!

MY TRUTH OF BEING

"In the beginning; the God/dess, and within the infinite stillness of the Unformed and Unmanifest, a note was sounded. The tone issued forth an endless vibration besetting countless other tunes in support, of the mind of the Goddess, and through Love the Image was given Life. And the Spirit of the Goddess was given dominion as the Creative Principle of all that is and was to come for all eternity. Creation continued, and this Omnipresent image of the Goddess, the Mother/Father of Creation began to contemplate itself as Individual Being, and sparks of Celestial Fire were thrown throughout the boundless Universe, forming centres of Light, of Spirit Consciousness. I was one of those Firelights, point of Individual Awareness in my Omnipresence. I knew myself to be the Goddess. I knew myself to be me!

Creation continued, and I sought to express the fullness of my Being… Conceived in Love the precious idea of my Self in expression comes forth into Manifestation as a living soul… I am… I am… I am… In time, a part of my Self-expression descends into the dense lower world for the experience of it… I let myself play with Creations and I identify with them… I am descending, deeper and deeper into materiality… Mother, help me! My consciousness of you is fading… Father the Light is gone… There is darkness… Where am I? Who am I? What is the purpose of my life? I am a far country… I have spent all in search of meaning and I am in want… I have come under the bondage of others and I feel the swine in the fields… And the Angel of the presence says; *"You are so much more than you think you are… stand up and seek the Mothers Kingdom… much more than you think you are… stand up and seek the Mothers Kingdom… your true estate… begin the journey home now!"*

I turn within and seek my self… through the tunnel of mind I travel moving across the emotional sea of my subjective world… Be still! I speak… let the troubled waters be as glass… reflecting only the memories of gladness, ecstasy, jubilation and joy… Let all others be dissolved… and my fading nature responds and joins me on the journey to the Light… There is a door before me… and I sense with mind and heart that it is the way to the Chamber of Truth… Slowly I reach out and open the door, and suddenly I am engulfed in a blazing golden Light… Above me, below me, behind me, beside me, through me is the Light of Spirit… Oh beautiful me, abundant me, the harmonious me, the glass me, the forgiving me, the creative me, the whole me, the perfect me… Slowly this Higher Self fills my consciousness with itself and my awareness of two separate entities is fading away… Now there is only the single I, and from the I a voice speaks:

"I am with you always… all that I am you are… all that I have is yours… Speak now with authority, the Truth of your Being!"

And I respond; "I am Love, I am Wisdom, I am Power, I am Joy, I am Strength, I am Beauty, I am Abundance, I am Harmony, I am Gladness, I am Forgiveness, I am Creativity, I am Wholeness, I am Perfection, I am the Spirit of the Goddess, and beginning this day I will think and speak as the Goddess thinks and speaks, I will act as the Goddess acts, and from this moment on I shall remain in the Secret Place of Oneness with Spirit, and I will see only with the High Vision of Spirit. The dynamic Will of the Goddess is now made manifest on Earth as it is in Heaven. I am now in the glory that I was in the Beginning and shall be at my end!"

I find that when I am really down emotionally or very negative, saying this aloud in the mirror and looking at myself saying it several times, helps me to lift my spirits and remember exactly how wonderful this world really is, and how we truly are.

MEDITATION

Meditation is a means of achieving an Inner Peace, a transcendental experience, a deeper insight, which can help in daily life, and in the search for meaning. The technique of Meditation was devised and still exists to assist man individually, to uncover within themselves that deeply hidden centre of the One Creative Life, that is the birthright of every man and woman. From that centre, much can be understood that is obscure; and from that level much can be done for the world.

Meditation is a means to create a man of conscious enlightened WILL. Meditation is not an exercise in itself but a means of achieving a higher use of consciousness through commitment.

Meditation is composed of several activities:

RELAXATION   The ability to just be in the now and quiet your mind to a state of calm.

BREATHING   Breathing helps take us to different level of being away from the normal to the Spiritual.

FILTRATION   Filtering outside thoughts, feelings and pictures so the mind becomes a blank canvas.

COMMITMENT   regular times of meditation and relaxation.

The following points aid meditation:

Avoid answering questions automatically with solutions from memory rather rely on meditation.

Avoid disputes only leading to form, instead of idea and formation.

Train you in the perception of the invisible within the visible.

Search for analogies and comment on their broadest sense.

Always, seek knowledge of harmony, and fineness of form - the Arts are very ideal for this purpose.

Anyone can meditate, even you. Its not a secret arcane science, nor is it a mysterious esoteric process, although some of you may have heard that it was. It does not involve a lot of discipline or a lot of discomfort. All it takes is a little commitment and a little practice, and a little perseverance to learn to use the fundamental tool for self-expansion and personal growth.

Meditation is easier than walking through a meadow, easier than driving a car, or even easier than cutting a sandwich in half. All of these things and everything else we do require an incredibly complex degree of coordination between mind and body. Millions of neural, muscular and cellular connections must be made, and maintained. And the degree of energy control and precise channeling of your life force into action is almost impossible to imagine. Yet we have learned to do everything that we do, almost automatically without even thinking about it.

To meditate, you don't have to do anything; you simply just have to be in a settled and quiet state. In fact, the whole idea is to stop doing whatever you are doing, consciously or unconsciously and focus completely on the subject of your meditation in a relaxed, flowing and non-controlling way and relax your breathing until it actually becomes you. That is all meditation is. It's the most natural thing in the world, and you are not strangers to it as you have been meditating for most of your life. Although you may not have realised, that this was what you were doing.

For instance, when you watch TV, and drift into the scene, or lose yourself in a spontaneous race between two drops of rain sliding down a windowpane, you are meditating. In each case, you are submerged in a process that takes you out of yourself and your normal stream of consciousness and beyond your ordinary sense of time, thought and space.

The problem is what you meditate on, which can profoundly influence, program and direct your energy, your life cycle and all the space around you. So when you focus on your breath, a leaf, a stone, a crystal, and a candle flame; a sound or a positive thought; you end the experience feeling more perceptive and more alert. And when you focus on your energy and state of being you re-enter completely refreshed, revitalized and recharged.

In the beginning when you were a baby, you spent all of your time meditating on your growth and development and expansiveness. That is why time was so much more timeless then. You were in a state of harmony with the universe all around you, so when you focus on needing something, you knew just how to materialize it, but since being a baby we have forgotten how to breathe properly and just be.

You begin to lose your meditational harmony as you began to develop your sense of Self, your Ego, which separated and differentiated you from everything else, and you lost even more of it as you developed a rational analytical ego, which kept you trying to find logical ways to shield and protect you from your inner sense, alienation and dissociation from everything else that is; and which hooked you into books, TV, computer games, computers, Facebook, internet, newspapers, teachers, and other authorities as the only way to gain knowledge and understanding of yourself, your world and your Goddess and God.

As far as creature-hood goes, on a physical level, life ends when growth ends. The point is, that now you have grown separated from your macrocosmic universe, as you are in the next phase of growing, which needs to include reintegrating and re-harmonizing yourself with all that is around you. Opening channels to that process, gaining intuitive knowledge and inner understanding, and creative expansiveness out of anxiety and chaos through meditation are the results you can expect from further study and training in this field. We need to do this to widen out connection with the universe and everything in it, or we just become selfish, fearful creatures on a self-delusional path to nowhere.

Taking it a further step, meditation is the word that describes your state of consciousness, when you have become so totally emerged in an object, an event or thought in a relaxed manner. You become so completely involved and centered in what and where you are, that your mental chatter fades away your body tension, emotional anxieties disappear and time flows at an altered rate of speed. As you begin to more fully experience who you are, how you are feeling, where you are tense and blocked, and what you are asking for out of life, you will develop more and more control over your health, over your wants, over your creativity and self expansion, and over your actual physical involvement. The more a harmonious meditative relaxed state you are in the more connected and the more creative you will become.

By practicing meditation often not just spasmodically when time allows, and being completely who you are, you will become more than who you are now, you will be able to cross the next evolutionary bridge, being able to develop the full potential of your creature hood. It is the most exciting journey there is, and hopefully I can make it easier, by helping you discover the inner avenues that can take you all the way you choose to go. From wherever you are coming from, to here and to now, and to what lies beyond.

Beginning Meditation!

To meditate you need only two things that are essential outside yourself, a place and a time. Everything else in the Outer World is optional. From time to time you may choose an external object, person or event as a meditative subject. But for now, the right place and the right time will start you on your right way. At this stage, the right place will be anywhere your little heart desires, any place you like and feel relaxed and away from being disturbed.

If you have made yourself an Altar or Shrine to the Goddess, or even a Temple at your home, or even a Magick Circle; any of these places are perfect for your meditative adventures. In that place you might like to include a chair or a large cushion, a soft rug, or whatever warms your spirit. Like a candle, a flower, crystal, familiar, or favourite object, or a picture, or as I said before, even an Altar with a statue of the Goddess and God on it.

Whenever you choose to turn inward. At this stage the right time will be any time that you specifically set aside for meditation only. Between 10-30 minutes every morning and night before or long after meals will be ideal. You will not need to be rigid about it, and you don't have to meditate the exact time every day, whether you choose to use it or not. Other than the place and time, everything else you already have is on the inside of your very being.

Alignment

When you are in alignment with the magnetic axis of the Earth, you will yourself flow more freely with the space around you. Getting aligned is easy; always meditate facing North, like a needle of a compass you use to check your direction. Magnetic alignment is the Path of least resistance to meditating, and to interphasing your life energy with the energies around you, on a microcosmic and macrocosmic level.

(Record your Progress and exercise in your Magickal Diary)

STANDING IN PENTAGRAM

For thousands of years the Pentagram Position has been the primary posture for energy exchange and for recharging and rejuvenating your body. In his sketches, Leonardo da Vinci immortalized it. In your meditation place, it can immortalize you, by helping you maintain a radiant inner glow and an easy access to complete meditation.

Stand with your spine straight, your pelvis aligned under you, your feet further apart than your shoulders or as far as you can place them without locking your knee's. Tip your head slightly back, keep your eyes open for balance, but allow your gaze to lose focus. Raise your arms keeping them straight until your elbows are just above your shoulders, and your hands are in line with the top of your head. Turn your left palm down and your right palm up. Breathing deeply into your diaphragm, and experience filling your lungs to capacity then overflowing with newfound energy.

(Record your Progress and exercise in your Magickal Diary)

MEDITATION POSITIONS

Any position that keeps the right and left hand side of the body in equal balance, and that you maintain comfortably without moving for the length of your meditation, is the right position for you. But always keeping your back and neck straight. Of course make sure that you are totally comfortable and relaxed. You are constantly taking energy in from your universe, storing it, and discharging it back into the universe again. Converting energy into life and matter, and life and matter into energy is every creature's fundamental role.

When you meditate, the energy exchange is amplified and greatly heightened. Which explains why complete meditation is so truly enlightening and invigorating. To smooth out the energy amplification and make it easier on yourself, your meditation position must ultimately allow you to lose whatever sense of separation or alienation you experience in your universe. That is why you keep both sides of your body in balance. By not crossing one leg over the other, and not folding your arms protectively in front of you. That is also why as you harmonise yourself within your space through your position and your breath, you expand your personal energy and your inner power base to remarkable degree's. Experiment with the meditation positions to find the one's that help you flow into expansiveness with a minimum of effort.

SITTING POSITION

My favourite traditional position for meditating is sitting. Sitting in a straight-backed chair, or on the floor. In a chair, sitting erect with your spine straight. Keep both feet on the floor a comfortable distance apart. It is better to remove your shoes, loosen your collar, your belt or anything else that prevents you from breathing freely, easily and naturally, and deeply into your diaphragm and abdomen. If you have a robe then wear this. Allow both hands to fall loosely on your lap. Tilt your head slightly back so that your neck and spine form one continuous vertical line.

Then close your eyes gently and look up at the inside of your forehead. For now just experience how it feels to sit like this. Notice where you are touching the floor and where you are not. Sense the floor under your feet and the solid support it offers. Connect with the sensuality of the Air Element on your skin, experience it, that's all, and just experience it!

(Record your Progress and exercise in your Magickal Diary)

LYING DOWN

Let your legs spread slightly apart with your toes and feet hanging loosely from your ankles. Let your hands fall to your sides, palms up. Sense how straight your spine is, notice what parts of your body are in contact with the floor, and what parts are holding up, like the small of your back, just lie there and feel the Air moving over, around and throughout your body. As you breathe deeply and quietly into your diaphragm! I dislike this position for some people as they can get too relaxed and fall asleep. Snoring can be a problem if you are in a group.

(Record your Progress and exercise in your Magickal Diary)

CREATIVE VISUALIZATION

Creative Visualisation is the technique of using your imagination to create what you want in your life. This chapter is about learning to use your natural creative imagination in a more conscious way. As a technique to create what you truly want; such as love, fulfillment, enjoyment, satisfying relationships, rewarding work, self-expression, health, beauty, youth, whatever your little heart desires.

In Creative Visualisation you use your imagination to create a clear image of something you wish to manifest, seeing the end result not the process. Then you continue to focus on the idea or picture regularly, giving it positive energy until it becomes objective reality. In other words, until you actually achieve what you have been visualising. Creative Visualisation is Magick in its truest and highest meaning of the word. It involves understanding and aligning yourself with the natural principles that govern the workings of our universe, and learning to use those principles in the most conscious and creative way.

FOUR BASIC STEPS TO MAKE IT EFFECTIVE ARE:

Set your goal.

Create a clear idea or picture.

Focus on it often.

Give it positive energy, continuously.

You do have to make an effort, for creative visualisation to work effectively, you simply put it out clearly to the universe where you would like it to go, and harmoniously let the flow of the river take you there. Visualisation is very important in magick and Wiccan rituals and ceremonies, as we need to see the end result to make it manifest into reality.

We will now do a simple visualisation technique, designed to get energy flowing, to dissolve any 'blocks', worries, etc., and to keep you firmly connected to the physical plane so that you don't space out during meditation and get to light headed.

MEDITATIONAL EXERCISE

SIT COMFORTABLY WITH YOUR BACK STRAIGHT... EITHER IN A CHAIR OR ON THE FLOOR... CLOSE YOUR EYES AND BREATHE SLOWLY AND DEEPLY...

COUNTING FROM TEN TO ONE, UNTIL YOU FEEL DEEPLY RELAXED... IMAGINE THAT THERE IS A LONG CORD ATTACHED TO THE BASE OF YOUR SPINE... AND EXTENDING DOWN THROUGH THE FLOOR AND WAY DOWN INTO THE EARTH... IF YOU WISH, YOU CAN IMAGINE THAT THIS IS LIKE A ROOT OF A TREE... GROWING DEEPER AND DEEPER INTO THE GROUND... THIS IS ALSO CALLED THE "GROUNDING CORD".

NOW IMAGINE THAT THE ENERGY OF THE EARTH IS FLOWING UP THROUGH ALL PARTS OF THIS CORD... AND UP THROUGH YOUR FEET... AND FLOWING UP THROUGH ALL PARTS OF THE BODY... OUT AND THROUGH THE TOP OF YOUR HEAD... PICTURE THIS UNTIL YOU REALLY FEEL THE FLOW WELL ESTABLISHED...

NOW IMAGINE THAT THE ENERGY OF THE COSMOS IS NOW FLOWING IN THROUGH THE TOP OF YOUR HEAD... YOUR CROWN CHAKRA... THROUGH YOUR BODY AND DOWN YOUR GROUNDING CORD, AND YOUR FEET INTO THE EARTH... FEEL BOTH THESE FLOWS GOING IN DIFERENT DIRECTIONS AND MIXING HARMONIOUSLY IN YOUR BODY... WHEN YOU HAVE DONE THIS... JUST RELAX...

(Record your Progress and exercise in your Magickal Diary)

THE NEXT FORM OF MEDITATION IS DESIGNED TO KEEP YOU BALANCED

BETWEEN THE COSMIC ENERGY OF VISION, FANTASY AMD IMAGINATION, AND THE STABLE EARTHY ENERGY OF THE PHYSICAL PLANE... A BALANCE THAT WILL INCREASE YOUR SENSE OF WELL-BEING AND YOUR POWER OF MANIFESTATION... ONE TECHNIQUE THAT I FIND VERY EFFECTIVE IS TO CREATE A SANCTUARY

WITHIN YOURSELF... WHERE YOU CAN GO ANYTIME YOU WANT TO... IT'S AN IDEAL PLACE OF RELAXATION, SAFETY AND HEALING, AND YOU CAN CREATE IT EXACTLY ANYTIME YOU WANT TO...

KEEP YOUR EYES CLOSED AND RELAX IN A COMFORTABLE POSITION... IMAGINE YOURSELF IN SOME BEAUTIFUL NATURAL ENVIRONMENT... IT CAN BE ANY PLACE THAT APPEALS TO YOU... A MEADOW... ON A MOUNTAIN... IN A FOREST... BESIDE THE SEA... IT COULD EVEN BE UNDER THE SEA OR ON ANOTHER PLANET... WHATEVER IT IS, IT SHOULD FEEL COMFORTABLE, PLEASANT AND PEACEFUL WITH YOU... EXPLORE YOUR ENFORCEMENT... NOTICE THE VISUAL DETAILS... THE SOUNDS... THE SMELLS... ANY PARTICULAR FEELINGS OR IMPRESSIONS YOU GET ABOUT IT... NOW DO ANYTHING YOU WANT TO DO TO MAKE IT MORE HOMELIKE AND COMFORTABLE... AN ENVIRONMENT FOR YOU... YOU MIGHT WANT TO BUILD SOME TYPE OF HOUSE OR SHELTER... OR PERHAPS CREATE A TEMPLE DEDICATED TO YOUR GODDESS AND GOD... OR CREATE A LARGE STONE CIRCLE... OR PERHAPS JUST SURROUND THE WHOLE AREA WITH A GOLDEN LIGHT OF PROTECTION AND SAFETY...

CREATE AND ARRANGE THINGS THERE FORE YOUR CONVENIENCE... AND ENJOYMENT... OR DO A RITUAL TO ESTABLISH IT AS YOUR SPECIAL PERSONAL SANCTUARY... MAYBE YOU COULD DO THE LESSER BANISHING RITUAL OF THE PENTAGRAM OR A SELF BLESSING RITUAL...

FROM NOW ON THIS IS YOUR OWN PRIVATE SANCTUARY... TO WHICH YOU CAN RETURN AT ANYTIME JUST BY CLOSING YOUR EYES AND DESIRING TO BE THERE... *YOU WILL ALSO FIND SPECIAL POWER FOR YOU... AND YOU MAY WISH TO GO THEIR EVERYTIME YOU DO CREATIVE VISUALISATION... YOU MAY MAKE CHANGES AND ADDITIONS TO IT AT ANY TIME... BUT JUST REMEMBER TO RETAIN THE PRIMARY QUALITIES OF PEACEFULNESS AND A FEELING OF ABSOLUTE SAFETY AND HEALING... EACH OF US HAS ALL THE WISDOM AND KNOWLEDGE WE EVER NEED RIGHT WITHIN US... SOMETIMES WE FIND IT DIFFICULT TO CONNECT WITH THIS PART OF OUR MIND... BUT ONE OF THE BEST WAYS OF DOING SO IS BY MEETING AND GETING TO KNOW OUR INNER GUIDE... OUR INNER GUIDE IS A HIGHER PART OF OUR SELF... THIS FOLLOWING EXERCISE WILL HELP YOU MEET YOUR INNER GUIDE... STILL WITH YOUR EYES CLOSED AND RELAX AGAIN DEEPLY... GO TO YOUR INNER*

SANCTUARY AND SPEND A FEW MINUTES THERE, RELAXING AND GETTING ORIENTED...

NOW IMAGINE THAT WITHIN YOUR SANCTUARY YOU ARE STANDING ON A PATH... AND AS YOU DO SO, YOU SEE IN THE DISTANCE A FORM COMING TOWARD YOU RADIATING A CLEAR BRIGHT LIGHT... AS YOU APPROACH EACH OTHER YOU BEGIN TO SEE WHETHER THE FORM IS MALE OR FEMALE... HOW THEY LOOK... HOW OLD THEY ARE... AND HOW THEY ARE DRESSED... ARE THEY YOUNG OR OLD... GREET THIS BEING... AND ASK HER/HIM WHAT THEIR NAME IS... TAKE WHATEVER NAME COMES TO YOU FIRST AND DO NOT WORRY ABOUT IT!

NOW SHOW YOUR GUIDE AROUND YOUR SANCTUARY AND EXPLORE IT TOGETHER... YOUR GUIDE MAY POINT OUT SOME THINGS THAT YOU HAVE NEVER SEEN BEFORE... OR YOU MAY ENJOY JUST BEING IN EACH OTHERS COMPANY... ASK YOUR GUIDE IF THERE IS ANYTHING SHE/HE WOULD LIKE TO SAY TO YOU... OR ANY ADVICE TO GIVE YOU AT THIS MOMENT... IF YOU WISH, YOU MAY ASK SOME QUESTIONS... YOU MAY NOT GET AN ANSWER IMMEDIATELY, BUT IF NOT, DON'T BE DISCOURAGED, THE ANSWER WILL COME TO YOU IN SOME FORM LATER... WHEN THE EXPERIENCE OF GETTING TO KNOW ONE ANOTHER AND BEING TOGETHER IS COMPLETE... THANK YOUR GUIDE AND EXPRESS YOUR APPRECIATION... AND ASK HER/HIM TO COME AND MEET YOU IN YOUR SANCTUARY AGAIN... OPEN YOUR EYES AND RETURN TO THE OUTSIDE WORLD, AND RECORD YOUR PROGRESS AND EXPERIENCES IN YOUR DIARY...

(Record your Progress and exercise in your Magickal Diary)

Do not worry if you did not perceive and see your guide precisely and clearly. Sometimes they remain in the form of a glow of light, or a blurry, indistinct figure. The important thing is that you serve their power, love and their importance. Especially their presence, if your guide should come to you in the form of someone you know then that is fine, unless you do not feel comfortable. Do not be surprised if your guide seems eccentric or unusual in some way, the form in which they don't express themselves in words, but instead through feelings or intuitive knowledge. She/he may even change form at some time, or may stay the same for years to come. Whatever, as long as you feel safe and comfortable, there is no need to think you are doing something wrong. Because it stems from your own mind, then how can it be wrong? Your guide is there for you to call upon anytime you need.

This last form of Creative Visualisation I wish to discuss is a very simple, but wonderful technique. It is called the "Pink Bubble Technique" and is designed to start you off slowly in the Art of Creative Visualisation, and to lead you into more and more effective and better things. I have thought that sometimes the simplest things are often the most effective, like this exercise. It does no one harm to become stronger and much more adept with more complicated techniques, which I will cover at a later date.

SIT COMFORTABLY AND CLOSE YOUR EYES AND BREATH DEEPLY… SLOWLY AND NATURALLY… GRADUALLY RELAX DEEPER AND DEEPER AND IMAGINE SOMETHING THAT YOU WOULD LIKE TO MANIFEST… IMAGINE IT HAS ALREADY HAPPENED… PICTURE IT AS CLEARLY AS POSSIBLE IN YOUR MIND… NOW IN YOUR MINDS EYE, SURROUND YOUR FANTASY WITH A PINK… BUBBLE… PUT YOUR GOAL INSIDE THE BUBBLE… PINK IS THE COLOUR ASSOCIATED WITH THE HEART…

AND IF THIS COLOUR VIBRATION SORROUNDS WHATEVER YOU VISULAISE IT WILL BRING YOU ONLY THAT WHICH IS IN PERFECT AFFINITY WITH YOUR BEING… THE THIRD STEP IS TO LET GO OF THE PINK BUBBLE AND IMAGINE IT FLOATING OFF INTO THE UNIVERSE… STILL CONTAINING YOUR VISION… THIS SYMBOLISES THAT YOU ARE EMOTIONALLY 'LETTING GO OF IT'… NOW IT IS FREE TO FLOAT AROUND THE UNIVERSE ATTRACTING AND GATHERING ENERGY FOR ITS MANIFESTATION… THERE IS NOTHING MORE YOU NEED TO DO… WHEN YOU HAVE DONE THIS… GET BACK INTO YOUR NORMAL BREATHING AND SLOWLY OPEN YOUR EYES AND ALWAYS REMEMBER:

(Record your Progress and exercise in your Magickal Diary)

"THE DIFFERENCE BETWEEN POSSIBLE
AND IMPOSSIBLE IS ONE'S WILL!"

SENSING GROUP ENERGY

The energy that we talk about in Wiccecraft is real, a subtle force that we can all learn to perceive right now, as we are sitting in a Magick Circle, be aware of the energy level in the group. Do you feel alert? Aware? Excited? Inquisitive? Calm? Anxious? Tense? Or Relaxed?

Energy travels up and down the spine, this is called Kundalini or serpent energy, but before we do any forms of Meditation or Magickal work, we must first Earth or ground ourselves, this will be done now. Please close your eyes... focus on your breathing and relax with each breath... completely relax... imagine a warm energy glow at the base of your spine... feel it growing like a root from a tree searching deep down into the Earth for water...but yours is searching for the Earth force... feel it stretching down deep into Mother Earth... deeper and deeper and deeper... Now just Ground yourself and feed from the life-force of the Earth... just sit there as erect as you can without straining...just notice how the energy level has changed... do you feel more alert... more aware... more nourished... more at peace...

Your breath moves energy in and out of your body... it awakens your body's centers of power... so take a deep breath... breathe deeply... breathe all the way down and breathe from your diaphragm... from your belly... from your womb... loosen your pants or belts if you need to... fill your belly with breath and feel yourself relaxing... recharging...

Now notice how the energy of the group has changed... now let's reach out and take hands still keeping your eyes closed...with your right hands facing up and your left hands facing down (this is called the serpent hold) ... linking ourselves together around the Circle... it may seem like a subtle tingling... or a low heat... or even a sensation of cold... or a bright whirling light of energy circling around and around and around.

(Record your Progress and exercise in your Magickal Diary)

THE TREE OF LIFE MEDITATION

Now begin by sitting erect and breathing deeply rhythmically in a 4 x 4 breath… as we breathe remember to sit erect but comfortable… and as your spine straightens feel the energy rising… imagine that your spine is the trunk of a giant Tree… and from its base are roots extending deep down into the Earth… into the centre of Mother Earth Herself… and you can draw up power from the Earth… with each breath… feel the energy rising… like Mana or sap rising through a tree trunk… feel the power rise up the spine… feel yourself becoming more and more alive… with each breath…

And from your Crown Chakra at the top of your heard… you have branches that sweep up and back down to the Earth like a Weeping Willow… feel the power burst from the Crown Chakra… and feel it sweep through the branches until it touches the Earth again… making a circle… making a circuit… returning to its source… and breathing deeply, feel how all our branches intertwine… and the power weaves through them… and dances amongst them like the wind… feel it moving…

Now just focus on your breathing as you inhale in that energy… and as you exhale make a sound you like… a moan, a sigh, hum, vowel, note, etc.… and continue this for a few moments.

(Record your Progress and exercise in your Magickal Diary)

21

MEDITATION QUESTIONNAIRE

(Try not to look at the Chapter for your answers, meditate on them)

Time it took to do Questionnaire: _____

Date: _____

What Research was used: _____

1. What is the purpose of Meditation? _____

2. Why do you need to Meditate? _____

3. What is meditation composed of? _____

4. What is the best position for meditation and why? _____

5. Why is the Pentagram Position so powerful? _____

6. What is Grounding and why is it important? _____

7. What is Visualisation? _____

8. What is an Inner Guide, and do you have one _____

9. Name two different types of meditations _____

10. Why is a Sanctuary important and explain your Sanctuary _____

11. Explain your pink bubble experience? _____

12. How often should you meditate and how long and Why? _____

13. How often do you meditate and how long and why? _____

14. How do you feel after a good meditation and why? _____

15. How do you feel after a bad meditation and why? _____

THE CHAKRA'S

Chakras are your psychic centers, or energy centers. The word Chakra is Sanskrit, meaning "**WHEEL**". The Chakra's are power centers, which gather and attract energy and information within the body. This is associated with the Endocrine Glands, and the nerve plexus. By the Indian Mystics it is often referred to as "Organs of Psychic Perception" or even "Etheric Organs". The Chakra's serve as Channels for our Spiritual and psychic information. So wherever we find a major gland in our body, there is a nerve plexus, and one of the Seven Major Sacred Chakra's. I wish to also advise you that although the Chakra's are associated with the Endocrine System, they are not to be confused with the actual physical organs of the body.

The First Chakra (Root or Base Chakra): This is at the base of the spine, at the tailbone or anus, and has a direct relationship to the ovaries and testicles, which is called Kundalini. The first Chakra also has to do with SURVIVAL. All survival data and genetic information necessary to keep the body alive is found at this psychic centre. It also tells you what you need for survival in an individual, the proper foods, shelter, rest, exercise, sexuality, etc.! The question here is do you allow yourself to have physical and material pleasures such as joy, happiness, sexual fulfillment; and do not deny ourselves these things. The problems in this Chakra are usually apparent when we have grounded or earthed ourselves properly at all. This sometimes occurs when you focus on *another's survival and needs and neglect your own*. This Chakra also gets overloaded if you are trying to keep two bodies alive, in this case you will tend to get very ill. As maintaining another life is only good with children, or in an immediate life or death situation. It is wise to question yourself. *"Am I trying to prove myself, by keeping another alive?"*

The Second Chakra or Sacral Chakra: This is located just below the naval, and has a direct relationship to the Pancreas. This Chakra is related also to CLAIRSENTIENCE, which is the feelings and emotions of other people, it picks up all the vibrations, sometimes it can even duplicate their emotions. Reflected here is the degree of your own personal reality. This Chakra also governs the erotic world, it rules sexuality, sensuality and desire and even lust. Problems usually occur in this Chakra when you are too open to the feelings of others, when this happens there is a tendency to duplicate their emotions, and enter into a sympathetic state of anger with them, rather than just being and having empathy for their feelings. If you allow yourself to be invaded by another's feelings then your body is alive via the stimuli of another - which is an unhealthy state.

The Third Chakra - The Solar Plexus: This Chakra is located at the Solar Plexus and has a direct relationship to the Adrenal Gland. It governs energy distribution and distributes vital energy throughout the body; it is your CONTROL AND POWER CENTRE. Through this Chakra you can regulate and balance your own energy, by learning when to give and when to take energy. The problem associated with this Chakra occurs when you allow your energy to be given away, giving in the demands of people. *"Give me your energy, I want your energy and support. I control you."* You must know why you choose this, and why you agree to give up or take too much energy, control or be controlled. It is this contrast between you as a spiritual being and you as a physical body, and consequently this is how you operate. When you allow others to hook into your energy or even when you try to control the energies of others, you do not own your own power, and therefore cannot trust it. Being hyperactive and sending energy all over the place indicates that the Solar Chakra is too open causing depletion of your own energies; the draining feeling. When tension in the Solar Chakra occurs, ask if your energies have been where you want them, or if you have given too much away. To rid yourself from outside energies from others that drain your own, it is important to always ask yourself; *" Why you agree to these situations and what are you getting from it."*

The Fourth Chakra - The Heart Chakra: This is located under the ribs at the Sternum, and has a direct relationship to the Thymus Gland. The Heart Chakra has to do with affinity, your ability to love and to enter into a state of oneness with yourself (self love) with another person, or a group. It is the centre of your Path and your goals. Every thing is usually found around this Chakra, as it is the meeting between your being and your 'body'. It is the inner you that does know.

The problems in the Heart Chakra occur when we are out of affinity with ourselves or when we are operating with others on a pure affinity level. If we cannot look at ourselves, or when we are operating with others on a pure affinity level. If we cannot look at ourselves with love, we cannot accomplish very much. In order to manifest your body in the most capable positive, joyful, and loving way, you must have love and affinity for it. When you are out of the present time occurrences re-stimulate past pictures or incidents, which say; " Nobody likes me!" This relationship doesn't work, so I am no good! Then you are kept from affinity with yourself. It is difficult to have to ask you but you must always ask yourself where and why you stopped being close to yourself. Realise your Goddessness and who and what took your right away, who played one-upmanship with you, and who placed judgments on you.

If people around you cannot be themselves, and you cannot be yourself, then get rid of them, so be it, I did and I have. You do not have to play games with other people; you do not need other people laying their trips on you. Push out the dark pictures and the negative energy of others. Return it to neutral or send it back without malice. Energy that is not yours in your Heart Chakra should be pushed out to enable you to have affinity with your SELF.

The Fifth Chakra - The Throat Chakra: This is located at the cleft of the throat and is connected to the Thyroid Gland. This Chakra is COMMUNICATION - which is the vehicle with which we communicate as beings. It helps to give us the ability to express what we feel, verbalize clearly, communicate clearly with other people. It is your inner voice. It gives you communication between your personality and your soul. It is your most vital and rapid form of growth. You learn through words, "Heal the Words, and receive the words." Problems occur in the Heart Chakra when your communication with others is not very clear and direct an honest. We always grow through words and we learn from each other with words. But it is important to find out whose words you are using and you're expressing what needs to be said.

We must let go of unfinished conversations whether an hour ago or ten years ago for these keep us out of the present time. The programming of others can also cause frozen energy in the Throat Chakra that you should say things in a certain way you cannot say what you feel and you cannot express your emotions in a certain way. You cannot get good grades in English etc. Such programming keeps away spontaneity, which prevents you from being in the present time and thinking about yourself in new terms. Ask yourself: "Who won't let me say my feelings are hurt; who won't let me be angry; tell someone I love them, verbalize affection and healing? Who blocks or blocked me from using communication in the best way possible? Who told me I didn't have anything to say, wasn't important enough to speak and express my thoughts and feelings?"

Eliminate all the inner voices from those people who prevented you from speaking up. Do you have pictures that say; if you don't have something profound to say, don't speak! If you can't say something nice, don't say it at all. KNOW you have the right to express what you want to express. It might not be good insight but get it out. If others can't effectively incorporate what you have said, then that is their problem. If you choose not to say it, write it, get it out of your system in order to keep the Throat Chakra clear. You cannot deal with any problem until you have made it real by either writing it or verbalizing it.

Be aware of heat in the back of the neck and let go of all unspoken thoughts and unexpressed emotions and send them back. Those conversations are over - finished. Rid yourself of self-judgments that say; "I don't know how to say it right, others express themselves better. I don't have creative dialogues. Nobody listens to me anyway." Also be aware of people who 'demand' that you hear them. They are trying to plug your fifth Chakra without equal communication.

The Sixth Chakra - The Third Eye Chakra: This is located between the eyebrows and is connected to the Pituitary Gland and is the Sixth Chakra which is the Third Eye, the centre of the individual CONSCIOUSNESS, consciousness defined as SOUL quality. It has to do with CLAIRVOYANCE, which is the ability to see the invisible within the visible: such as Auras, levels of energy and pictures, also the Spirit World. It is also the ability to arrive at a concept without going through rational processes, i.e. abstract intuition. Through the Third Eye, individual consciousness is expanded into Universal Consciousness. By this, you reach up into the Manifested Universal Mind. The problems associated with the Sixth Chakra occur in two ways. The first is that people want you to see the world in their way (Conditioning). This clogs your own intuitive sense of things, and if you are not aware, cautious, you will respond to the data and see the world their way. When their more permissive data prevents you from acting on your own data, we begin to operate off of their people's pictures. It becomes difficult to distinguish what is the real us, from their pictures of us. The result can be a feeling of craziness, headaches and confusion. The second way the Brow Chakra becomes jammed from people plugging into it is trying to see where you are at or wanting your validation. (I want to see you; I want you to see me). This creates enormous tension.

Get rid of people with whom you have tried to share your reality, but who were incapable of recognizing it. Another thing to be aware of in this Chakra is pressure behind the eyes. When this happens, you may be trying to visualize what you are seeing or perceiving with your Third Eye through your physical eyes. Be aware of this, and redirect your energy.

The Seventh Chakra - The Crown Chakra: This is located at the top read of the head. It is the soft spot on a baby's head. This concerns KNOWINGNESS, the ability to sit still and know. It is the controller of all the other Chakra's, the centre of Cosmic Consciousness or Spirituality. It is supreme consciousness, eternal peace, eternal knowledge, etc.! It connects humans with the infinite. The problems of the Seventh Chakra come from people trying to own you or run you, trying to manipulate you. Such situations block communications between the being and the body.

Someone is trying to communicate with your body.

This ownership message is: *"You don't have a thought or desire of your own"*. Because this Chakra is the ultimate control of the other Chakra's, people who desire to own you, plug in there. When this happens you must ask yourself why are you willing to play the victim game? Ask what the agreement is, the key picture of what is holding them there. It's not trusting your knowingness, not taking time to be still enough to touch with your spirituality and feel the Oneness with all creation? Try to get rid of energy that is not your own. Tell yourself that you want Cosmic Consciousness to meet your body and be responsible for what happens to your body. Situations, where someone speaks of someone as my woman, my man, are not ownership qualities if the agreement is to work together. However, having a pattern of having men in control or vice versa in a relationship is one of ownership.

SELF-BLESSING
RITUAL

The Self Blessing Ritual is an activity, which many Wiccans do less and less as time goes by. In the times of our ancestors, everyone did some form of Self-Blessing To be in touch with your true Inner and Higher Self. You should do this ritual every morning and evening. With SELF-EMPOWERMENT central to ritual and to your own spirituality, the Self Blessing Ritual is very simple, beautiful and a powerful cleansing process. The High Priestess usually leads but you can do this on your own. This one I wrote in 1976, and use it every day.

Touch the Crown Chakra:

"BLESS ME MOTHER, FOR I AM YOUR CHILD, AND I AM PART OF YOU!"

Touching the Third Eye:

"BLESS ME MOTHER, THAT I MAY SEE MY WAY CLEAR, AND SEE YOU IN ALL THINGS!"

Touching the Throat Chakra:

"BLESS ME MOTHER, AND BLESS MY WORDS, THAT I MAY SPEAK CLEARLY AND TRUTHFULLY, WITH LOVE AND POWER!"

Touching the Heart Chakra:

"BLESS ME MOTHER, AND BLESS MY HEART THAT IT BE OPEN TO ALL LIFE, AND FILLED WITH COMPASSION AND STRENGTH!"

Touching the Solar Plexus Chakra:

BLESS ME MOTHER WITH DIVINE LIGHT AND ENERGY, AND ALLOW MY DIVINE LIGHT TO TOUCH OTHERS IN YOUR NAME!

Touching the Sacred Chakra:

"BLESS ME MOTHER, AND BLESS MY BEING WITH THE POWER TO HEAL ALL WOUNDS AND THE EARTH!"

Touching the Base Chakra:

"BLESS ME MOTHER, AND BLESS MY SEXUALITY, THE GATEWAY OF LIFE AND DEATH, AND TEACH ME TO FEAR NEITHER!"

Touching the Souls of your Feet:

"BLESS ME MOTHER, AND BLESS MY FEET THAT HAVE BROUGHT ME ALONG THE PATH THAT LEADS TO YOU AND JOY DIVINE!"

Touching the Palms of your Hands: (with fingers of opposite hand touching palm)

"BLESS ME MOTHER AND BLESS MY HANDS THAT THEY MAY DO YOUR GREAT WORK, TO HELP ALL OTHER LIFE!"

Stand in Pentagram Position with head tilted back:

"BLESS ME MOTHER IN THE RADIANCE OF YOUR MAGICKAL SIGN, FOR I AM YOUR CHILD NOW AND FOREVER BLESSED!"

Chakra Questionnaire:

Time it took to do Questionnaire: _____ Date: _____

What Research was used: _____

1. What does the word Chakra mean and why? _____

2. What Chakra is related to the Colour red and why? _____

3. What objects contain the spectrum of the rainbow and why? _____

4. Which Chakra governs the erotic world and why? _____

5. Do our Chakras need to be opened or closed, explain answer? _____

6. What are some other terms used instead of the word Chakra? _____

7. What Chakra do you relate to and why? _____

8. Which Chakra do you feel tension and why? _____

9. Which Chakra is related to the Pituitary Gland and why? _____

10. Which Chakra is the spiritual Chakra and why? _____

11. Names the colours in order from the base Chakra to the Crown Chakra? _____

12. Which Chakra is the mediator of all the others and why? _____

13. Can our Chakras get blocked, explain answer? _____

14. How many Chakras are there? _____

15. Which Chakra is associated with healing and why? _____

16. Which Chakras are feminine and which are masculine? _____

17. What are the colours of the rainbow from top to bottom? _____

THE ELEMENTS
AND THEIR
ELEMENTALS

There is so much to learn about the Elements, especially the areas of your life that they control, as this is an important step in your spiritual development as a Wicce. Once you begin to work with and understand these individual Elements they will begin to help you harmonise with yourself and the Magickal Forces of Nature in balance. This will also help aid you in you choosing the right Goddess and God, picking personal symbols and also determining the best time to work for total spiritual fulfillment. It is very difficult to be 100% Spiritual if you are overwhelmed with passion, inflamed with anger or given to flights of fancy.

Besides being good for controlling emotions, the Elements are associated with almost everything we come in contact with. The Elements also correspond to the Seasons, different times of the day and night, Elementals, herbs, plants, planets, spirits, teachers, zodiacs, tree's, runes, parts of the body, stones and crystals, religions, archangels, traditions, Ladies and Lords, Watchtowers, Compass Points/Quarters, Goddesses and Gods, etc. They also represent Astrological Zodiacs, which help us to understand different personality types, and differing modes of expression. Without a doubt the Elements are one of Natures greatest contributions. They are a wondrous storehouse of knowledge and wisdom just waiting to be tapped into by the Wicce within you.

THE ELEMENT OF FIRE

THE PRINCIPLE OF FIRE:

The basic qualities that we associate with the Fire Element are heat expansion and light. Because every Element has two polarities or two ways in which it can act. For example when the Fire Element is in its Active or Positive mode it is constructive and creative; when it is in its Negative or Passive mode it is dissecting and destructive. There is a certain Magickal Force, which is similar to electricity in many ways, and for want of a better term, we call it "ELECTRICAL FLUID", and note that it relates to the expansion of Fire. Fire is the Element in the South quarter of the Magick Circle, and is the power of the noonday Sun, it rules the Season of Summer, and thus we celebrate the Midsummer Solstice on December 22nd of each year. The colours associated with this Element are reds, oranges, and gold's. It is also the realm of the Heart Chakra, the Power of Man, and represents action. When using the Book of Life, also known as the Tarot Cards, it is where you would place the Swords or Athame's/Daggers.

The Elemental creatures are Salamanders and Dragons, and the ruler of these Elementals is the Archangel Michael. The Kabalistic God name we invoke is Adonai. The Quarter is also called the Realm of Briah - which is the Creative World.

Fire is transformation, the life giving generative powers of the Midday Sun. This is also emblematic of the Father God in many cultures, and is the Element of fervent intensity, aspiration, and personal Power. Fire is the force, which motivates and drives all living organisms. Fire along with Air creates energy. Gets us going and produces stamina. "What the mind can imagine (Air), the Will (Fire) can create".

Fire is bright, brilliant and flamboyant and unfortunately neither stable nor logical. Fire leaps intuitively to grasp the moment with little regard for what is around it. Fire is very reckless, seeking, and passionate and knows only itself.

Fire is also unique because in order for it to create, it must first consume or destroy. This concept is plainly exhibited in the bush fires. The Fire burns, consumes and destroys, and the trees and underbrush of the forest, which in time will produce new growth. Fire is the active Element within all of us, and it pushes towards the new by getting rid of the old.

For Fire to be used constructively it must first be contained. When Fire is contained its energy can be used and directed towards a desired purpose, such as heat or light. It is the same way with the personal forces it dominates such as passion, anger and aggression. When these emotions are controlled and their energy channeled in a constructive manner, they bring about reconstruction. We all know what happens when our feelings go unchecked, just like Fire; they wreak havoc, and bring destruction and create chaos.

The Element of Fire is Spirituality brought to us by the supreme commander of Light, Michael. This illuminating agent of Divine Light, whose name means "Perfect of God", is the Guardian of the South. He is also visualized as a Roman soldier dressed always in reds and gold's, and ready to do battle against all evil. The best way to describe a Fire person is that they are the essence of passion, and I don't just mean sexual desire but rather all-powerful emotions.

FIRE CORRESPONDENCES:

Colour:	-	Reds, orange as in flames, amber, blues and gold's.
Archangel:	-	Michael
Elementals:	-	Salamanders and Dragons
Southern Wind:	-	Notas
Chakra:	-	Heart and Solar Plexus
Symbols:	-	Triangle, lightning, flames, Salamanders, Sword, Man.
Tools:	-	Sword, Athame, Fire Pot, Double headed Axe.
Tarot:	-	Swords or Daggers
Plants:	-	Basil, Blood Root, Dragons Blood.
Stones:	-	Flint, Topaz, Sunstone, Amber, Obsidian.
Places:	-	Volcanoes, ovens, and fire places, hearths, Bale Fires, deserts.

Zodiacs:	-	Aries, Sagittarius, Leo.
Time:	-	Midday and summer
Direction:	-	South
Process:	-	Passion, anger, quick, active, energy, power.

The Element of Air

The Element of Air is related to Fire and Water, and in fact is the mediator or balance between the active and passive qualities between them. The Air Element has the dryness of Fire and the Humidity of Water. This is the direction of the Rising Sun; all masculine energy comes in through this direction. The colours associated with this Quarter are blues, whites and gold's. It is the realm of the Head, the intellect of man with horns, it also represents change, it is the Element of Air and when using the Tarot Cards for meditation, ritual or divination, as it is where we place the Wands or Rods or Staff's. The Season is spring, and the time for rituals is Sunrise or just prior to the rising Sun. It is the Astral and Mental World, and its Elementals are Sylphides, Faeries, and The Pegasus. And its ruler is Euras. The Archangel is Raphael. The Kabalistic God name associated with this Quarter is Yod-Heh-Vau-Heh; this Realm is also called Yetzirah—the Astral Plane. The Zodiacs for Air is Libra, Aquarius and Gemini.

Air speaks to the intellect and brings forth the true essence of the individual through the creative imagination. It also represents new beginnings and all thoughts. Air speaks to the intellect and helps to bring forth the true essence of the individual through the creative imagination. The Air Element has always been associated with breath, which is synonymous with the 'Spirit" or 'Soul' of all living creatures, this dates back to the time of Matriarchal rule, as it was the women, after giving birth who would gently breathe into their child's mouth Initiating the breathing process. In Greek mythology the female Air Soul was 'Pneuma', which means breath, or the Muse who always brought inspiration, giving poets and seers the Power of understanding.

Breathing is paramount to life itself and enters the body at birth and withdraws at death. It was for this reason, in the past, that mirrors were held close to the mouth of a dying person in hopes of capturing their Soul in the mirror. This belief came about through old folklore, which spoke of mirrors being traps, and the Realm of the Dead as being the Hall of Mirrors. Air is the bridge between Spiritual inspiration and the conscious projection of ideas. Fresh clean Air is exhilarating, it is movement, and it inspires creativity. Air is the tie that binds us together through conversation, intellectual sharing and the endless seeking of knowledge.

AIR CORRESPONDENCES:

Colours:	-	Blue, silver, white, gray.
Archangel:	-	Raphael
Elementals:	-	Sylphides and Faeries
East Wind:	-	Euras
Chakras:	-	Throat and Heart
Symbols:	-	Circle, birds, feathers, fans, bells, Sylphides, flutes, chimes, clouds.
Tools:	-	Wands, Rods, Staff, Scepter, Roade.
Tarot:	-	Wands and Staffs or Spears
Plants:	-	Almond, Broom, Clover, Eyebright, Lavender, Pine.
Gems:	-	Amethyst, Sapphire, Citrine, Azurite.
Places:	-	Sky, Mountains, treetops, bluffs, airplanes.
Zodiacs:	-	Gemini, Libra and Aquarius
Time:	-	Dawn and Spring.
Process:	-	Thinking, reading, speaking, praying and singing.
Direction:	-	East

THE ELEMENT OF WATER

THE PRINCIPLE OF WATER:

The basic qualities that we associate with the Water Element are coldness and shrinkage. When the Water Element is in its active or positive mode it is life giving, nourishing and protective. In its passive or negative mode it is dissecting, fermenting and dividing.

There is another Magickal Force associated with this Element and is similar in many ways to Magnetism, and for want of a better term we will call it Magnetical Fluid.

This Element is situated in the Quarter of the West, and our oceans of whence all life came. It has the power of Sunset, and all feminine and psychic energy comes in through this direction. The colours associated with this Realm are greens and blues. It is the realm of the Womb, the Cauldron, the Realm of Fertility in life and love. When using the Tarot Cards, it is where you find the Cups or Chalices - these representing the Womb and the Tomb, or the cradle and the coffin. It is the Season of Autumn. It is the Spiritual or Divine world called Atziluth, and its Elementals are called Undines, Water Maidens, Water Sprites, Mermaids, etc. The Archangel is Gabriel; the Lord of the Elementals is Zephyrus. The Kabalistic God is Eh-he-heh.

Water is the third basic Element and the most primary form in which liquid can exist. Water is passive and receptive and has long been seen as the source of all potentialities in existence. It is associated with the Great Mother, the Universal Womb, birth and fertility. Water I also emblematic of the life giving and life destroying abilities of the Universe. Water is used to cleanse or purify physically as well as psychically.

Where Air is the intellect, Fire the energy or drive, Water is the emotional response to situations, fluid, responsive, and giving. Water is sensitivity and emotion. Water is like the Great Mother and when heated by the Fire God's passion, life is brought forth, but when cooled by the midnight Air, silence and death are eminent. This is why so many religions use immersion in Water to symbolize the return to a primordial state of purity. In essence, the Wiccaning or

Wiccan Baptism, or dunking of an individual in Water signifies death and rebirth of both body and the Spirit. The Element of Water is both detached and willful as it flows freely. However there are times when Water will allow itself to be contained. Water is a gentle Element and it inspires intuition and the desire to worship.

The Element of Water is truly linked to, and part of the Goddess which is within all of us. Water is also remembering the past and foreseeing the future.

WATER CORRESPONDENCES:

Colours:	-	Greens and Turquoises.
Archangel:	-	Gabriel
Elementals:	-	Undines and Mermaids
West Wind:	-	Zephyrus
Chakras:	-	Sacral and Base
Symbols:	-	Crescent, shells, Chalice, Cauldron, anchor, Cup,
Tools:	-	Vessel, Holy Grael, Chalice, Cauldron.
Plants:	-	Aloe, Cucumber, Dulse, Gardenia, Lily, Lotus, Willow.
Gems:	-	Aquamarine, Chrysocolla, Moonstone.
Places:	-	Oceans, Seas, rivers, streams, lakes, caves, waterfalls,
Zodiac:	-	Cancer, Scorpio and Pisces.
Tarot:	-	Cups or Chalices
Time:	-	Sunset and autumn
Process:	-	Love, nurturing, sensitivity, psychic ability, healing.
Direction:	-	West

THE ELEMENT OF EARTH

THE PRINCIPAL OF EARTH:

The Earth Element is related to Air, Fire and Water, and in fact involves all three in a solid form. The properties of the Earth Element are heaviness, solidarity and closeness. Since the Earth Element combines Air, Fire and Water, we may consider that fluid to be in its vicinity to be Electro-Magnetic.

This is the Realm of the North, and of the Ancient Ones, all balanced energy and power enters here. The colours associated with this realm are browns and russets. It is the world of Solidarity and Intrigue. It is ruled by the Elementals, which are called Gnomes, and they are ruled by the Northeast wind Bureaus. The season is winter and the power time is midnight. It is the material of the Physical World and is called Assiah.

The Archangel of this Quarter is Auriel, and the Kabalistic God name we intone is Agla. Earth has the vibrational frequency, which forms a solid quality, it is considered to be Passive in Nature, and negative in polarity. The Earth symbolically represents both the Womb and the Tomb, that which brings life forth and that which takes it away or reclaims it. However unlike Water, and Earth is stationary and does not create actively as it is seen mystically as the final outcome. It does provide the other three Elements with a place to physically make manifest a desire. Earth is our base of operation where we exhibit the final product of our imagination. Earth is also related to the flesh and all physical matter and it holds, nourishes and affirms. Earth sees, smells, senses, and feels; it is both sensual and practical. It can be stubborn as well as generous and has instinct rather than feelings for the cycles and seasons of time. Earth is slow, steady and ever changing whilst remaining the same.

EARTH CORRESPONDENCES:

Colour:	-	Yellow, brown, green, russet.
Archangel:	-	Auriel
Elementals:	-	Gnomes and Dwarves
North Wind:	-	Bureaus
Chakra:	-	Root
Symbols:	-	Square, Cornucopia, Spindle, Scythe, Salt.
Tools:	-	Shield, Pentacle, Pentagrams, Scourge, Horn.
Tarot:	-	Pentacles
Plants:	-	Alfalfa, Cotton, Oats, Patchouli, Vetivert, Wheat.
Gems:	-	Moss Agate, Jasper, Malachite, Peridot, Tourmaline.
Places:	-	Caves, Forests, fields, gardens, canyons.
Zodiac:	-	Capricorn, Virgo and Taurus
Time:	-	Midnight and winter
Process:	-	Responsible, practical, organized, steady, and grounded.
Direction:	-	North

BEING IN BALANCE

THE HEAD: The forepart is electric, the back of the head is magnetic and so is the right side; the left side is electric and so is the inner of your being.

THE EYES: The forepart is neutral and so is the background. The right side is electric and so it is with the left side. The inside is magnetic.

THE EARS: Forepart neutral, back-part also. Right side magnetic, left side electrical, inside neutral.

MOUTH AND TONGUE: Forepart neutral, back-part as well as right side and left side both neutral, inside magnetic.

THE NECK: Forepart, back part, and right side magnetic, left side and inside electrical.

THE CHEST: Forepart electro-magnetic, back part electrical, right side and inside neutral, left side electrical.

THE ABDOMEN: Forepart electrical, back-part and right side magnetic, left side electrical, the inside neutral.

THE HANDS: Forepart neutral, back part also, right side magnetic, left side electrical, the inside neutral.

THE FINGERS OF THE RIGHT HAND: Fore and back part neutral, right side electrical, left side also the inside neutral.

THE FINGERS OF THE LEFT HAND: Fore and back part neutral, right side electrical, left side as well, the inside neutral.

THE FEET: Fore and back part neutral, right side magnetic, left side electrical, inside neutral.

THE MALE GENITALS: Forepart electrical, back part neutral, right and left side also, the inside magnetic.

THE FEMALE GENITALS: Fore part magnetic, back part, right and left side neutral, the inside electrical.

THE LAST VERTEBRA TOGETHER WITH THE ANUS: Fore and back part neutral, right and left side as well, the inside magnetic.

Exercise: 4 x 4 breathing

(This is where you breathe in to the count of 4, then hold to the count of 4, then exhale to the count of 4. Keep this up for at 5-10 minutes)

WICCA AND
WICCECRAFT

WICCA THE WAY POEM

Wicca the Way, the Powers that be,

for the young and the old, the bold and the free.

The Path is to know, the Path is to see, the way of the Ancients, as it used to be.

All be Earth's children of Sun and of Moon,

down through the ages we've danced to the tune.

The flow of all life through Goddess and God,

none shall forsake thee, the Sword and the Rod.

Holy the Star that is worshipped in Truth, Morgaine and Merlin forever in Youth.

All is the Horned One, Fertility Rite, and Blessed Be Diana, in Love and in Light.

Candles and Incense and Tools of the Trade, for Magus

and Wicce Queen all debts shall be paid.

Praise is the Elements Fire, Earth, Water and Air,

Celebrations and Sabbats you will find us there.

Blessed be the Power, and Bind ye the Cord,

Blessed is the Union, and Love the reward.

The song of the Ages it echoes again, Blessed is the knowledge, long may it reign.

The Path of the Wicca, the Path of the Wise, in Power and Glory, all Truth shall rise.

We stand United, through Ages long past, the Truth that is Wicca, forever shall it last.

Gathered together those of the Kin, in freedom and Love beyond any sin.

Merry Meet, Merry Part, tis Union for all,

Blessed the Fellowship that answers Her Call!

1977

Join Wicca See The World As She Really Is!

You probably haven't seen any posters around spouting off about how great it is to be Wiccan or a Wicce. As in being Wiccan is a personal choice, and no one has ever been pressured into becoming a Wiccan. There are no threats of Hellfire or damnation. There is no retribution for not practicing Wicca, although most Covens do prefer their members to honor a commitment, once it is made. You can be a Pagan without being a Wiccan; and you can be a Wiccan without being a Wicce. Wicca does not brainwash or mind bend people, nor does it ask for 3/4 of your salary to pay for gaudy shrines or the like. Wiccans do not recruit new members or run missionaries, or even go 'witnessing'. Wiccans believe; that no one religion is right for every one.

In the Gospel of Sri Rama Krishna, the Indian Mystic he expressed this quite beautifully when he said:

"God has made different religions to suit different aspirants, times and countries.
All doctrines are only so many paths; but a path is by no means God he or herself.
Indeed, one can reach God if one follows any of the paths with wholehearted
devotion. One may eat a cake with icing either straight or sideways, and it will
taste sweet either way".

There are so many Seekers searching for the answer to their own personal questions on life and the hereafter. In their journey they have tried Christianity; they have tried as Muslims, Hindu's, Buddhists, Spiritualists, they have tried LSD, Speed, Soap Opera's, Donahue and Oprah Winfrey. Many have also tried Wicca, and found it not for them. As most groups go, there never use to be a large turnover of members but these days with more and more public notoriety, people are searching out the Craft, and today it is the fastest growing religion in the history of the world. Neophytes are rare as it takes a lot of testing and training, questions and answers before a new Wiccan passes into the Inner Sanctum of the deeper Mysteries of Wicca, its rituals and worship.

All members must be comfortable with the new Neophyte, and she with them. Should the Wiccan community not be compatible with the new Neophyte, she may get a reference, maybe not. We today have many Circle's, Covens, and this series of Outer Court Lectures put into a book is created to rightly educate and to help facilitate its members to where is appropriate for them to belong.

So it is like an introduction course, where at the end we introduce you to other Covens, and then you can select where is appropriate. For those that have been Initiated and eventually leave the Inner Sanctum, and usually for a good reason, go with Perfect Love and Perfect Trust, and are welcome to return if they desire. This rule varies if they need a break, and this is usually a maximum of three months.

Now Wicca is not a financial institution as such and does not have ambitions in that regard. Seekers do not have to pay for Initiation into the Mysteries, unlike some organizations that ask for thousands of dollars for a course of saunas and salads. Small fee's, where they exist are similar to dues required at clubs to help pay for running costs etc.! We do not rule out tithing as this is always a welcomed gesture of the heart but is personal. Wiccans practice in their own way along with a few likeminded others. Wiccans are aware of the ultimate good of all religions. UNION WITH DEITY! We do not brandish and put down other paths because they are different to ours, and we do not mock their ways. We accept them as an integral part of spiritual progression for each individual for whatever level of their spiritual growth they are at.

One of the oldest Tablets found says:

FOR IN THE BEGINNING DID THE HOLY VOID ISSUE FORTH FROM THE STARS, AND BREATHE LIFE INTO THE COSMOS; FOR IT IS WRITTEN:

"SANAT KUMARA OF THE THIRD RACE. (THE MIOCENE AND EARLY PLIOCENE PERIOD) THIS PERIOD WAS THE GOLDEN AGE OF MAMMALS AND COVERED A SPAN OF ABOUT 70 MILLION YEARS FROM 26 MILLION BC. GEOLOGICALLY SPEAKING THIS TIME WAS ONE OF GREAT MOUNTAIN BUILDING; THE HIMALAYA'S, THE ALPS AND THE ANDES WERE FINALLY ELEVATED. THE CLIMATE WAS SPEEDILY COOLING AND CULMINATED INTO AN ICE AGE. THERE WAS NOW PLENTIFUL FAUNA AND MANY LKARGE ANIMALS INCLUDING APES AND ELEPHANTS. THE CONTINENT OF LEMURIA COVERED THE PACIFIC OCEAN AND EXTENDED ACROSS SOUTH AFRICA INTO THE ATLANTIC OCEAN. EUROPE,

NORTH AMERICA AND NORTHERN ASIA WERE ALMOST ENTIRELY UNDER THE SEA, WHILST AN ISLAND EXISTED NEAR THE AZORES. ON THIS CONTINENT LIVED THE THIRD RACE, AND BY NOW THEIR BODIES HAD BECOME MATERIAL. THESE WERE BEING

COMPOSED OF THE GASES, LIQUIDS AND SOLIDS WHICH CONSTITUTE THE THREE LOWEST SUB-DIVISIONS OF THE PHYSICAL PLANE, BUT THE GASES AND LIQUIDS STILL PREDOMINATED, FOR AS YET THEIR VERTEBRATE STRUCTURE HAD NOT YET SOLIDIFIED INTO BONES, AND THEY COULD NOT YET STAND ERECT. AT FIRST THE BONES WERE AS PLIABLE AS THOSE OF A NEW BORN INFANT, AND IT WAS NOT UNTIL THE MIDDLE OF THE LEMURIAN PERIOD THAT MAN DEVELOPED A BONY STRUCTURE. THE FIRST RACE WAS SEXLESS, AND THE SECOND RACE WAS CALLED THE SWEAT BORN AND BONELESS, WHICH HAD THE FIRST GERM OF AWAKENING SEXUALITY. THEN CAME THE ANDROGYNES, THE EARLY THIRD RACE. THUS WE COME TO THE CRUCIAL POINT IN THE EVOLUTION OF THE HUMAN RACE -- THE DATE OF THE SEPARATION OF THE SEXES, WHICH WAS ABOUT 18 MILLION YEARS AGO."

For the secret doctrine states: "THE THIRD RACE SEPARATED INTO THREE DISTINCT DIVISIONS, CONSISTING OF MAN DIFFERENTLY PROCREATED. IN THE FIRST TWO OF THESE DIVISIONS MEN WERE EGG-BORN (OVIPAROUS). THE EARLY SUB-RACES WERE ENTIRELY SEXLESS, BUT THOSE OF THE LATER SUB-RACES WERE BORN AS ANDROGYNES. SO FROM BEING A-SEXUAL, HUMANITY BECAME DISTINCTLY HERMAPHRODITE OR BI-SEXUAL, AND FINALLY TO DISTINCT MALE FROM FEMALE."

Just before the division of the sexes began, and certainly connected with the evolutionary impulse which brought it about. There came to this rainbow planet that we call Earth, certain spiritually advanced beings. Man has called them Angels, but to the Wicca, we know them as the Ancient One's or Shining One's, known under the stars as Hertha, Morgana and Merrdyn, led by one known as Sunat Kumara, 'The Solitary Watcher'.

These powerful Initiates greatly speeded up the evolution of mankind and became the disciples of the Goddess and God, and the spiritual teachers and guides to humanity, forming the basis of the spiritual hierarchy, which watches over the evolution of the races upon our planet. They were and still are our Greatest Teachers and Mentors, even though man has given them many names, but to us The Children of the Old Religion, no matter what name or title they will always remain the Wise Ones of Wicca.

No matter where you go in this world, you will hear the marvels of the greatest Magician the world has ever known, and that name is Merlin, the secret advisor to King Arthur. Now everyone has heard of the old legends filled with the knights and the Holy Grael, and the Magick of Merlin. In the ancient times of Avalon and all of Britain, all Magician Priests were called Merlin. Yet who shall hear a much older tale, and tale older by far which tells of the first Merlin of Avalon; that came to the Blessed Isles, and the first Arthur the King. In these times it was not Mary, the Virgin Mother of Jesus that was the Goddess of her people but the ancient Morrigan, She who was the greatest of Earth Goddesses, She who was the Great White Mother known in every ancient land by different names. But to the people of Wicca, it was the ancient Morrigan who was the Mother Goddess to our people.

She was worshipped as Nature and the Moon, and neither was She distant from us, but forever existed within our very being, She dwelt in the very heart of every man, woman and child, and In the ancient legend of Arthur and Merlin, at the end of their lives, they return to the land of Mists, the land of the Fae, the Faerie from which they came originally, the sacred land of Elphane.

Where was this Mystical place? Well it was near the Summerland's of Lyonesse, a place of Mists and Magick called Avalon. This place was only open to those who had the secret keys that could unlock its great deep, and the true Mysteries and Secrets. This land was also known as Tir-nan-Og, Eden, and lately was called Atlantis, where the Great Mother had Her strongest power. This was the homeland of all the greats like Merlin and Thoth, who maybe were one in the same.

Now the sacred peoples of Avalon had two great Mysteries, one was for the men and of the Sun, and the other was of the women and of the Moon, the older of these two religions, and existed side by side for thousands of years as the religion of the women, and of the night. Here the Great Mother was also beneath their feet, and in the heavens she had given birth to both the Sun and the Moon to be our guiding lights, so that we shall always know that in the darkness, there is always a guiding light for us. To our Earth, these two symbols became the essence of all our new religions which mankind could grow and aspire. Even today the Christian Madonna is pictured standing on the Crescent Moon, to show from where She originated, she is also donned in the blue robe of purity of the Goddess Morrigan.

In the beginning our ancestors of Atlantis had risen up within their spirits, and yearned to be like the Sun, and they yearned that their souls should shine with the rays of the Great Lord of Light, Ra. But as their knowledge grew it surpassed their spiritual evolution, and their ways became corrupt as they turned from spirituality to Sorcery and power, rather than wisdom. They also enslaved the lesser races and created monsters by the use of alchemy. The God's of old saw this and were angered, and so in council decided to destroy these people who had so defiled their Mothers lands. And they created a resonance of pure sound and that vibration would cause the Earth to shake and the lands to rise and fall, and then sink deep beneath the seas of time and space, and obliterate their memory forever.

So here again the great wheel of our God's of evolution was drawing to a close and with it a land, a science, and a Magick with their people. But when the Great Mother heard this, She was set to tears, for no matter what Her children had done, they were still Her children, and She could not let their memory die, how could it die?

She was the eternal Promise of Immortality? And so out of all Her children, She had to select a chosen few who were learned in their special endeavors and chosen because of their knowledge and their spiritual progression. These learned people would transmit their wisdom to the new younger races of this land, and so She warned them of the upcoming disaster. She told them to prepare themselves so that they may escape and take their Arcane sciences with them, and hopefully educate the younger races of man so they may not befall the same hand of the God's.

They built and sailed in Seven Great Ships to the great lands of the Earth; to Egypt they went, to Greece, Rome, South America, Britain, Scandinavia, and India. Here they Founded the great Mystery Schools, so where they went they built great Shrines and Temples of dedication that were in accordance with the people that they had encountered. The Pyramids, which are found all over the world, are some of their handiwork, and so are the great Stone Circles of Britain. These were of our ancient Craft, and they were from Atlantis, and so from this ancient land, knowing of the intended disaster, left their homeland to preserve the ancient Mysteries and our Sacred Lore. The members of these Divine Mystery Missions were picked according to their sacred knowledge and their esoteric Craft; first a great King who was to represent the visible Sun who was surrounded by his men at arms, which represented the Sacred Epagomenes of the Magick Circle, these were called "The Days of the Year".

The second was a Great Magician, he was the Merlin and represented the Invisible within the Visible, and he was the Hidden One, versed in esoteric Lore and the ancient Arts. He was to be the Merlin who would lead all through the Labyrinthine Ways of Annwyn (The Underworld) in search for the Holy Grail of Immortality. The Merlin was to be the source of all life, and from which shines the essence or Aura of the eternal hidden Sun, which we now call the Spirit, which is the true self, the Higher Self of the Initiated Wicce. Such a man was this Merlin, whose name means literally "Man of the Sea". He had no name, but was honored by his title as the Great Merlin.

Thirdly there was the incarnation of the Great Mother Goddess, the High Priestess, the Wicce of Old, and to her was allocated all the powers and Magick of the Universe. She was the Great Oracle and Medium by which all priesthoods took form. She was associated with the Moon, and the tides of the oceans, and especially the aspects of birth, life and rebirth. These Magickal people came to the Blessed Isles carrying Arthur, the Merlin and Morgaine (Woman of the Sea) the High Priestess.

Here they arrived on the shores of Wales and started to establish the culture that we now know as Wiccecraft, or later in the 1950's called Wicca, due to the Burning Times where Witchcraft became the most hidden and secretive religion in the history of mankind.

Merlin's life shows in the patterns of a Wiccan Initiation. 1. His life on Atlantis, *governed by the ancient Morrigan, the Crone aspect of the dying Mother*: 2. Merlin's crossing of the water, (*the first death)* and his teachings of the *Sacred Mysteries with the chaste Morgaine*; 3. His eventual *marriage to Ellen*, (the *subsequent disillusionment)* and 4. Finally *his enchantment with the Faerie Vivienne*, the Lady of the Lake, who shows us that Atlantis is not dead but lives on in a body much younger and far more beautiful than our dreams could ever behold. With his Mission now achieved, Morgaine tricks him out of the sacred word of power, that is life itself, and wherefore his spirit returns once more to the land of the West, where all souls find their resting place. This is the land known as Avalon and is no more, but we still go they're in our dreams, and with death our souls listen to the footsteps of the Crone as She nears, and we then again tread the ancient Pathways to the Goddess, whom they thought forgotten. It will always be the Faerie Vivienne who will raise the sacred Sword of Endeavor above the Waters that cover up the past, and to Her it will be returned when all is done, for She is the Spring of Eternal Youth that shall come again and again, until the end of all time. For She is the Secret and Holy Grail that is, and will never be empty.

It was the teaching of Wiccecraft that the Pathway of the Initiate was to descend into the darkness of Annwyn, beneath the waves in search for the Holy Grail. The Initiate must open their Inner Vision, and they will truly see many things, and hopefully learn many secrets. But the Initiate must remain silent or he/she will be trapped forever, and unable to return to the World of Men (Abred).

If he/she follows the instructions of the High Priestess, he/she will find the Grael from which is the Secret of Life, the legacy's of the amassed experiences of the previous millennium. Having searched hard and eventually finding the Holy Grael, he/she must drink from the Waters of Life, and thus return from Annwyn to Abred to do his/her Will among mankind, and the Faeries. He/she may not incarnate for many cycles to come, but his teachings have lived for all of time and they are for us, the most sacred. Even though forms may be different, the Spirit will always be the same. We must Endeavor to be as Merlin, and live our lives accordingly with the respect of others and ourselves. We must accept the things we cannot change, and change the things we cannot accept. There are so many barriers and challenges in life that we are meant to face, as these will make us the better person.

We must not judge another because of their differences, diverseness and strengths. For we are all linked one with the other, and if we judge each other, then we only judge that which exists within our very selves, and our spirit. We must learn to love unconditionally and through this selfless act we become closer to deity. For if we judge anything or anyone, then we are judging the Goddess who created them, and this is definitely not our goal!

WHAT IS WICCA?

Wicca has two main components "hands-on" participation in both areas. In common with most areas of Theological study, we have the Theoretical and ideological aspects, and we have the practical or ritual aspects. The ideological Tenets that form the Wiccan philosophy are really quite simple. They are the basic premises that the individual can examine, research, test and eventually satisfy his/herself that Wicca is or is not what they are seeking to help them answer the ultimate question.

The practical or working aspect employs the use of natural Tools and the focusing of psychic energy to achieve an end that is related and bound by the theoretical aspect.

A Wiccan Believes:

- Worship of twin Deities; a Goddess and the Horned God.
- In Reverence for the Earth.

- Controlled and responsible use of Magick.
- Reincarnation as a Natural evolution.
- Love unto all beings, unconditionally.

It should be noted that these points are not the whole story. They are better perceived as the prime difference between Wicca and the Mainstream Religions. Another major difference between Wicca and the religions of the Book is that Wicca has very little Dogma. It is a living religion, which belongs to the present. In Wiccan Philosophy, that 'present' is ever becoming or ever moving and this allows Wicca to evolve. Consequently, we have no Bible, instead we have our Book of Shadows, which is hand written as a journal of the Wiccans experiences within the Craft. In it working rituals are recorded and these may be different from rituals designed for the same end by group Church Elders, because the Church of Wicca can and will change as interpretations are modified. Wicca is not cast in stone!

What is required in Wicca is a simple belief that the consciousness of man is not restricted to the body. But can extend beyond the limits of the sensory world and the life force should be revered. One of the main reasons people join Wicca, the Occult and other spiritual systems is to gain an insight, a deeper understanding of themselves which will give them power over their own lives.

The saying "KNOW THYSELF" bears mentioning, as this is also one of the main aims of Wicca. The Traditional "Tenets" that I wrote for the Church of Wicca and the Aquarian Tabernacle Church is as follows:

THE TENETS OF
WICCECRAFT

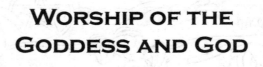

WORSHIP OF THE GODDESS AND GOD

I feel that Western Religions are out of balance, being concerned primarily with the masculine personification named God-Allah, Buddha, Jesus and Krishna, etc. God the Father, and male Saviors abound, and in imitation of the Pantheons, male Priests and Ministers.

Wiccans are different; we believe a male Deity revered without a female Deity counterpart is only half effective. Hence modern worship usually revolves around both, not one or the other. While this is unique today for the masses, ancient faiths have survived, unadulterated by well-meaning Missionaries. The Goddess and God are still worshipped as they have been for Millennia.

Wicca asks you to awaken your own feelings and desires, we do not tell you what to believe in nor what to do, nor how and when to do it. With Wicca, you are free to think for yourself, and are not treated like sheep; instead you are treated as the Sacred Children of the Old Religion, and its Goddesses and Gods with total respect and Perfect Love and Perfect Trust.

REVERENCE FOR THE LIVING EARTH

Our planet is revered and respected as a manifestation of the Goddess and God, and Nature signifies the processes and wonders of the Earth that's undetermined by humans. The Earth is a living organism, a direct gift from the Goddess for us parasites. Many other religions preach that the Earth is a tool for humans to dominate, subdue and master.

Many Wicces are practising Conservationists to varying degrees, as we are concerned about our planets welfare. Many rituals involve projecting our thoughts, prayers and energies into the Earth to lend even a minute amount of energy to aid in Her recovery from the ravages of man; this is done usually at every Full Moon.

"Planet earth is 4,600 million years old. If we condense the inconceivable time span into an understandable concept, we can liken the Earth to a person of 46 years of age. Nothing is known about the first seven years of this person's life, and whilst only scattered information exists about the middle span, we know that only at the age of 42 did the Earth begin for flower! Dinosaurs and the great reptiles did not appear until one year ago, when the planet was 45. Mammals arrived only 8 months ago; and in the middle of last week man-like apes evolved into ape-like men, and at the weekend, the last Ice Age enveloped for 4 hours.

During the last hour, man discovered agriculture. The Industrial Revolution began a minute ago! During these 60 seconds of biological time, modern man has made a rubbish dump of paradise. He has multiplied his numbers to plague proportions, caused the extinction of 500 species of animals; ransacked the planet for fuels, and now stands like a brutish infant, gloating over his meteoric rise to ascendency on the brink of war to end all wars, and of effectively destroying this oasis of life in the Solar System".

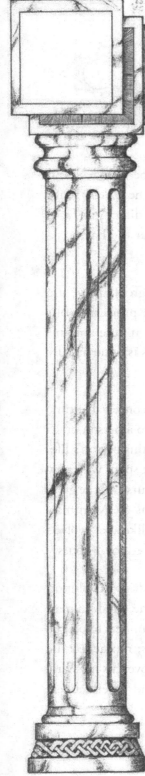

ACCEPTANCE OF MAGICK

Magick is Cause in Effect by effort of one's Will. Magick plays some role in most religions, though they would not call it so; rather call it be miracles etc. With Wicca know that it is not a Religious Magick, nor is it a Magickal Religion; know that it simply embraces Magick as an opportunity to attune with the Divine, Earthly and human energies.

Because Wicca is truly a Religion of Nature, Magick takes on a secondary role in our practises. Even if the Rite is performed for a specific Magickal end, the Goddess and God are always invoked before power is raised and sent. In most other religions, only the Priests or Saviours are believed to be able to channel Divine Energies.

Wicca is not so exclusive, and views Magick as a normal natural part of our life and Religion, and its availability to all with just one cause.

Know also that to be the most powerful Wicce, is to be the most Natural Wicce

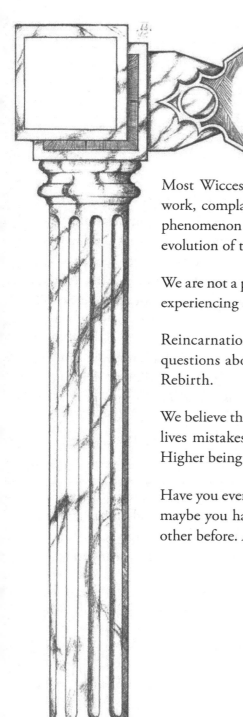

REINCARNATION

Most Wicces accept Reincarnation as a reality. We are not just born, live, work, complain, pay taxes, and die. The ancient Doctrine of Rebirth is the phenomenon of repeated incarnations in human form to allow for the natural evolution of the sexless, ageless human soul.

We are not a physical body experiencing a spiritual life; we are a spiritual body experiencing a physical life.

Reincarnations is not an exclusive Wiccan concept, but answers the many questions about our daily life and the Mysteries of Birth, Life, Death and Rebirth.

We believe that we are here to learn, evolve and hopefully correct our previous lives mistakes, and to take up where we left off to progress in becoming a Higher being and closer to the Goddess and God and our Truth of Being.

Have you every wondered or thought: *"Have I been a Wicce in a past life."* Well maybe you have and maybe we were all sitting in a circle and learning from other before. As I believe that once a Wicce always a Wicce.

RESPONSIBILITY FOR ONESELF

Before the time of courts and man made laws, Nature had her own laws and rules, and man lived by following them without question. Living in comfort with Her ways, and the ways of respect and tolerance. For this was the time when man was totally responsible for oneself and ones actions. But times have changed and now we are told that we are not allowed to be responsible for ourselves. We grow up hearing terms like "Grow up and act your age, and be responsible!"

But Freedom has been taken away from us by a system of Patriarchy, which wishes to remain in control and be dictators telling us like children what to do, believe, think and feel. This is on all levels. It is a time for us to accept our own lives and that it offers as a learning step to our true spiritual beings that we are. To be responsible and to stop placing the blame on others, especially external figures such as the Tempter, the Devil, and Satan etc.!

All things that happen to us on our journey are signs and obstacles that we must learn from, through faith and perseverance to overcome and understand their true meanings. When we hurt ourselves, the lesson is not the pain, but how we react, and how we learn from it. These days anybody can sue anybody for almost any reason. They see it as an end to a means.

NO DEVIL

Since the beginning of the Craft Movement we have been accused of worshiping such Christian heresies such as the Devil. This is absolute rubbish as we do not even have a concept of this entity as it is Christian not Wiccan. To believe in the Devil or Satan you must be a Christian, it is their abomination that they created to put fear into their congregations so that they always had the fear not to leave their churches, in fear of damnation.

We take no credit for this Christian Myth creation, it is their own darkness that they have created, as they must face their own fears and face themselves. I believe that light and dark are a true balance, and we do not have the right to hate something, let alone try to destroy it. If we destroy one of these, then we also destroy the other.

For they are a perfect harmonious balance and compliment each other, and need each other to exist in harmony. To understand something, is better than destroying or hating it. It is like the Goddess and God, remove one, and the other is incomplete and ceases to exist, which places the whole of life, as we know it out of balance.

If you think of the Devil, then you feed that very aspect within yourself, and are therefore running in fear of the Shadow, and can only ever see the light from a distance like being in a tunnel with the light at the end. I teach people to be one with the Shadow, embrace it, understand it and except it, as a part of your Truth, and all will reveal itself in time. Do not look for the Light at the end of the tunnel, be engulfed in the Light!

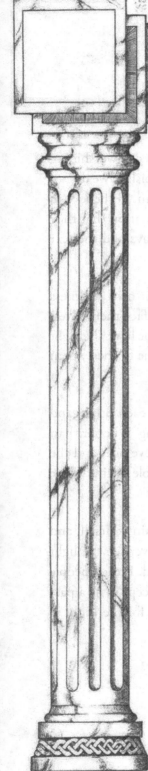

AN IT HARM NONE, DO WHAT YOU WILL

In order to help bring the ways of Light, Love and Truth to the entire world, our secrets, once so closely guarded out of dire necessity, are becoming secrets no more. With changing times, secrets and knowledge belongs to no one person. If we do not share our knowledge to the right people, then when we die, that knowledge dies with us.

Our Credo, "AN IT HARM NONE, DO WHAT THOU WILT" is the fundamental basis of our faith. The Goddess matters not what we do in life, as long as we harm no one, nothing in Nature, and especially ourselves. This includes human, animal, insect, tree, rock, and gems, as all are sentient beings that are Different to us but still living entities of Creation.

This credo does not give us license to run willy-nilly, but teaches us to stop long enough to think and respect every action BEFORE we do it. And now in full;

"EIGHT WORDS THE WICCAN REDE FULFILL,
AN IT HARM NONE, DO WHAT THOU WILT,"

Non-Proselytization

No person has ever been pressured into becoming a Wiccan. There are no threats of hellfire or brimstone, no retribution for not practicing Wicca. In fact Wicca can be a very personal faith, with many, as there are many solo practitioners around the world within the Craft. Our Goddess and God are not jealous deities, for Wiccans believe that the Goddess is many-named, one of which is Mary (the mother of Jesus), and the Old God is likewise many named and is also called by some simply God, Allah, or Jehovah.

Initiates are not brainwashed, badgered or subdued. Wicca is not a human controlling cult, masquerading as a religion. There are no Missionaries or Witnesses. We earnestly believe that no-one religion is right for everyone. I do not think that we a better than others, for each religion has its place in the divine drama, and for those who are seeking that spiritual Oneness with Deity, no matter what form, name, title or path.

If the Goddess and, or God has called you, for they are all the same but different. For the last thousand years, the Old Religion has been persecuted, and because of this we went underground and became the most hidden and secretive religion in the world until 60 years ago.

This persecution began with the "Burning Times" because of fear, greed and ignorance, where an estimated 9 million men, women and children were slaughtered in the name of Jesus Christ. We are still persecuted today, it may not be as ugly, but it is still rampant. Stupid ignorant people are brainwashed with lies about Wicces and Wiccans. They all believe in the writings of a book written a thousand years ago by bigots, misogynists and celebrant Patriarchal Priests who were sheepish fools.

Today the Judaic and Christian faith are panicking because their churches are emptying, and their flocks are leaving and returning back to their ancestral ways and traditions. The Old Goddesses and Gods have awakened, and are awakening the soul of mankind, their sacred Children are remembering and re-seeking their Truth. Hopefully through this remembrance we can once again find the "Garden of Eden" and create a new Golden Age of Enlightened Beings on Earth.

WORDS OF THE MIGHTY ONES!

Keep your silence amidst the noise of the world, for there is my peace in that silence.
Keep peace between yourself and all other beings, and listen to all of mankind,
For even the ignorant among mankind may perceive a truth you do not see.

Surrender, not your Spirit to any other, yet seek not battle,
But rather seek to avoid those who spread vexation about them.
Seek not ambition too closely!
For the most humble work must also be done, this pleases the Goddess and God.

Those of the Wicca are as your Sisters and Brothers.
Speak not of the Craft to the Outsider, for the world is plagued with misunderstanding.
Remember that the world also has its right to seek for Deity.

Strive to be gentle and understanding with your fellow man, and be tolerant of their
emotions, even if you do not understand them. And regard the passing of years
without sorrow, for age shall bring you deeper wisdom and greater understanding.
Study then the secret ways and cultivate the Spiritual strength
to shield you in unexpected misfortune.

Seek not to harm your own body, or the body of any man, or woman, or child or animal, for
all bodies is made of the substance of the Earth, and ye shall not harm the Earth Mother.

Therefore, care for your body, keeping it clean and healthy, disgrace not the Craft before
your fellow man, and bring not disrepute upon its followers. Remember that you have
walked this world before and you shall walk it again in time, you may have filled this
world with broken dreams and sadness, and these shall stay with you for many lifetimes.

Yet this world is beautiful, though you are blind to its true beauty!
Therefore be careful, Seek and be happy, and you shall find the
Path of Truth which is the Path of Perpetual Happiness.

WICCA QUESTIONNAIRE

Name: _____

Time it took to do the Questionnaire? _____ Date: _____

1. What was the Beginning? _____

2. Who was Sunat Kumara? _____

3. What does the word Androgyne mean? _____

4. What is Lyonesse? _____

5. What is a Neophyte? _____

6. Where is Lemuria? _____

7. What does the word Oviparous mean? _____

8. What does the name Merlin mean and why? _____

9. Who was the Visible Sun in our Mythology? _____

10. What does Abred Mean? _____

11. What is the Holy Grael? _____

12. Why do we revere the Earth? _____

13. How old is the Wiccan Religion? _____

14. What are the 5 Tenets of Wicca? _____

15. Why are we called The Old Religion? _____

16. When did the Burning times Begin and end? _____

17. What does the word Pagan mean and why? _____

18. What is the Wiccan Rede? _____

19. What does the word Occult mean? _____

20. When was the Wiccan religion legalized and Founded in Australia and who was its Founder? _____

THE GODDESS
AND THE
HORNED GOD

Christianity at first brought none to little change, as people saw in the story of their Jesus, only a new version of their own ancient tales of the Mother Goddess and Her Divine Child, who is sacrificed and reborn. Same story, just different names and times. Country Christian Priests, who were mostly drawn from the peasant class, usually led the dance at the "Sabbats". The Covens, who preserved the knowledge of the subtle forces, were called Wicce (weesh), from the Anglo-Saxon root word meaning "to shape and bend". They were those who could shape the unseen to their Will. The Healers, Shamans, Teachers, Poets, Minstrels, Midwives, Priests and Priestesses, Herbalists, Alchemists, they were the central figures of every village and community of the time.

Persecutions of the Inquisition from the Roman Catholic Church began slowly in the 12th and 13th centuries, which saw a revival of aspects of the Old Religion by the traveling Troubadours, who wrote love poems to the Goddess under the guise of living noble ladies of their times and ladies of great importance. Magnificent Cathedrals were built in honor to the Virgin Mary, the Mother of Jesus, as She had taken over many aspects of the ancient Goddess, blending the old to create the new. All they did was take a statue of the Goddess and don her with the same blue garbs and call her Mary. Wiccecraft was declared a heretical act. In 668 A.D., where the Archbishop of Canterbury ruled that "People who ate and drank in heathen Temples, or who wore the heads of beasts, should do three years penance". Wicces continued to use the Stag Horns (which were a symbol of the Horned God and of fertility), however their only concession was to hold their Sabbats secretly, on the Moors or in lonely dark forests, away from the gaze of the ignorant converted people.

In 1324, an Irish Coven led by Dame Alice Kyteler was tried by the Bishop of Ossory for worshipping a pagan Horned God, she was saved only because of her rank in society, but 23 of her followers were tortured and put to death. Since then, Wars, crusades, plagues and peasant revolts raged over Europe in the next centuries. Joan of Arc' was loved by the French peasantry because she was a Pucelle and called the "Maid of Orleans", she led armies of France to victory, and she was burned at the stake for what she was, a "Wicce", but by the English not the French. The word Maiden is a term of high respect in Wicca, and all loved Joan of Arc because she was a true leader of the Old Religion. The stability of the Roman medieval church was shaken. Messianic movements and religious revolts swept the Christian world, and the church could no longer calmly tolerate any rivals of any sort especially by a mere girl of 19 years of age, a Pucelle with such power and foresight who followed the Old Religion.

In 1484, Pope Innocent VIII put his Seal on the Bull that unleashed the power of the Inquisition against Wicces for interfering with Nature and fertility. Two high members of the Inquisition were Dominican Monks, Kramer and Sprenger, with the full approval of the Pope; who wrote and published in 1486 the "Malleus Malificarum". This book had run to 14 editions by 1520, and confirmed popular belief and misconceptions with immense hostility towards Wiccecraft. The Persecution was mainly directed against women as well as children, especially young girls who were believed to inherit evil from their mothers. The ascetics of early Christianity, which turned its back on the world of flesh, had degenerated, to some of the quarters of the church into hatred of those who brought that flesh into being. Misogyny (the hatred of women) had become a strong element in Medieval Christianity. As was stated in the Malleus Malificarum *"ALL WITCHCRAFT STEMS FROM CARNAL LUST, WHICH IS IN ALL WOMEN, INSATIABLE."* At the start of the terror, the Inquisitors looked for the 'Mark of the three nailed claw", known as the Wicces Mark'. Other marks looked for were warts, tumors or protuberances. These marks meant certain death to their owner, for any such blemish was automatically regarded as the devils mark—used by a Wicce to suckle her familiar. But when a Wicce' was warned that she might be arrested, she would amputate any potential markings with a knife, which eventually became a symbol to each Wicce and is called the "Athame". She preferring death from hemorrhage or blood poisoning to that of extended torture and ultimately death.

Once denounced by anyone from spiteful neighbors to an angry child, for any reason at all, a suspected Wicce was arrested and not allowed to return home until proven innocent, which was very rare, as a guilty prisoner was more valuable. In Britain, they forbid legal torture, but the Wicce could still be tested. The suspected Wicce was stripped naked with her arms crossed and thumbs tied to her big toes; she was flung into the nearest deep water. If she sank, she was innocent. But they were usually dead by the time they were hauled out. If they could swim or float, it was certain proof of their guilt and would be taken and hanged or beheaded.

Suspects could also be deprived of sleep and subjected to slow starvation before hanging. In Europe, the full rostrum of the Inquisitions horrors was applied. The accused were tortured until they signed confessions prepared by the Inquisitors admitting to consorting with Satan, to dark and obscene practices that were never true nor part of the Craft. But the accused were tortured until the name of a full Coven quota was given. Confession earned a merciful death, usually strangulation before the stake. Suspects who maintained their innocence after and through horrendous torture were burned alive.

The Wicce trials offered great opportunities for the male medical fraternity to stamp out midwives and village herbalists, and for others to rid themselves of many Heretics or peasants who walked a different religious path. Very few of those tried during the "Burning Times" were actually Wicces at all, maybe one to every thousand. The victims were usually elderly, the senile, the mentally ill, the homeless, women whose looks were not pleasing or who suffered from some handicap, village beauties who bruised the ego's by rejecting advantages by local priests, or who aroused lust; in the hundreds of victims who were put to death by hanging in a single day. In the Bishopric of Trier, in Germany, two whole villages were left with only a single child inhabitant apiece after the trials of 1585.

Wicca went underground, and as already stated became the most secret of all religions. Traditions were passed down only to those who could be trusted absolutely, usually to members of the same family (Hereditary or Blood Wicces). Communications between Covens were severed, no longer could they meet on the great Festivals to share their knowledge and exchange the result of their Spells and Rituals. Part of the Tradition became lost and forgotten. Yet somehow in secret, in the silence over glowing coals and behind closed doors, and encoded as Faery Tales and Folksongs, or hidden in the subconscious memories, the seed was passed on always between the hands of the Lunar Children of Wicca, known as "The Hidden Children of the Goddess".

Holland, Denmark, Sweden and Norway were slow in taking on the Inquisition, but were quick to realise that such practices as the Inquisition were non conducive to trade or business. Those who could do so, escaped to lands where the Inquisition did not yet reach. The last person to be publicly and legally hanged by the law in England for being a Wicce was Alice Mallard of Exeter in 1684. Her descendant Andrew Mallard in the 1990's was falsely accused, persecuted and jailed for 12 years in Western Australia's prisons as a murderer but released from prison for an offence he did not commit.

In 1736 the Act of James 1, was repealed. It now became illegal to prosecute for Wiccecraft, Sorcery or Enchantment. Instead, anyone claiming to be able to work Magick by Wiccecraft could be sent off to prison for a year, during which they had to spend a whole day per quarter in the Pillory of the nearest market square. The legal repeal in 1951 of the Old Witchcraft Act, releasing Wicces from fear of persecution did much to bring Wicces out of the 'Broom Closet" so to speak, so we can counter the imagery of evil with Truth. The word Wicce carries so many negative images that many people wonder why we use the word at all. Yet to reclaim the word 'Wicce' is to reclaim our right; as women to be powerful, and as men to know the feminine within as Divine, also to right the many incorrect wrongs that have been done to our Faith and culture over millennia by a greedy, ignorant and misogynistic new religion.

To be a Wicce in the 21st Century is to reclaim our right to identify with over 9 million victims of bigotry, hatred, ignorance, superstition and greed, and to take responsibility for shaping a world in which prejudice claims no more victims. A Wicce' is a shaper, a creator who bends the unseen into form, and so becomes one of the Wise (eventually and hopefully), one whose life is infused with Magick and the Goddess. Wiccecraft has always been a religion of poetry, not theology. The myths, legends and teachings are recognized as metaphors for 'that which cannot be told', the absolute reality that our minds can never completely comprehend. The Mysteries of the Goddess can never be explained - only felt or intuited.

Symbols and ritual acts are used to trigger altered states of awareness, in which insights that go beyond words are revealed. When we speak of "the secrets that can never be told", we mean that the inner Truth literally cannot be expressed in words, as true Spirituality is very personal. It can only be conveyed by experience, and no one can legislate what insight another person may draw from any given experience.

The primary symbol for "that which cannot be told" is the Goddess. The Goddess has infinite aspects and thousands of names. She is reality behind metaphors of the manifest Deity that is Omnipresent in all life including us. The Goddess is not separate from the world; She is the world and all things in and on it. The Moon, Sun, Earth, Stars, stones, seed, flowers, flowing rivers, wind, waves, leaf, branch, bud, blossom, fang and claw, man and woman, heaven and earth. In Wicca Spirit and Flesh is One! The Goddess religion is unimaginably old, but contemporary Wiccecraft can just as accurately be called the Religion of the New Age, for the Craft today is undergoing more than a revival, it is experiencing a renaissance, a re-creation.

The Christian religion is Patriarchal and does not speak to female needs and experiences. It also tends to make appear right and fitting the suppression of women. The oppression of men is not so apparent, men are encouraged to identify with a model no human being can successfully emulate. They are at war with themselves. In the West to 'conquer' sin, and in the East to 'conquer' desire or ego, and so lose touch with their true feelings and their bodies, becoming successful male zombies. The symbolism of the Goddess is not structured same as the symbolism of God the Father. Every individual can know the Goddess internally in all Her incredible diversity, and She does not legitimize the rule of either sex by the other, and lends no authority to rulers of temporal hierarchies. In Wicca, each of us must reveal our own TRUTHS. Deity is seen in our own forms, whether male or female or both, because the Goddess has Her male aspects as well.

Sexuality in Wicca is a SACRAMENT. Religion is a matter of reconnecting with the Divine within and with Her outer manifestations in the entire human and Natural world around us.

Our patriarchal models have also conditioned our relationships to the Earth and the other species that share it.

The image of the Goddess as outside of Nature has given us rationale for our own destruction of the Natural order and justified our plunder of our Mother Earth's resources. We have attempted to conquer Nature as we have tried and failed to "Conquer" sin.

The models of the Goddess who is immanent in all of Nature, fosters respect for the sacredness of all living things. Wicca can be seen as a religion of ecology. Its goal is harmony with Nature, so that life may not just survive, but THRIVE! Ancient civilizations were one hundred percent polytheistic; they had a multitude of Goddesses and Gods. The Mystical processes of Nature were assigned a figurehead. After all, the wind, tides, Moon, Sun, birth, death, love, war, of all of these events or processes could not be random acts. Some body have created and have must control over them?

The spread of domestication and civilization led to the establishment of many Pantheons throughout the world. In Great Britain there were the Celtic, Samethoi and the Druids, and also the Gaelic families. The Roman Pantheon was also quite extensive, as was the Greek and Nordic. Egypt spawned its own eternals, as did the Indians, Persians, Etruscans and the numerous other tribes on the other continents. The advent of Christianity and later Islam; led to the wholesale subjugation of polytheistic religions in favor of the one masculine God who did everything.

(Given at Rome, at St. Peters on the 9th December of the year of the Incarnation of our Lord, one thousand four hundred and eighty four, in the first year of our Pontificate.) These were the words of the Pontiff giving orders to his soldiers.

When the Inquisitors were told of a twin town called Triers in Germany, they asked the Pope; "Excellency upon arriving in this land of heretics of so many, how do we tell them apart?" The Pontiff replied: "It matters not, destroy all, destroy the disease, and let God decide and judge at the Gates of Heaven."

The Goddess and Horned God Questionnaire

Name: _____

What Research did you use: _____

Time taken to do Questions? _____ Date: _____

1. When was Wiccecraft declared a Heretical Act?_____

2. In 1324 the Bishop of Ossory tried someone for what reason? _____

3. Who was the Pope that unleashed the Inquisition? _____

4. What were the names of the Dominican Inquisitors? _____

5. What is the Malleus Malificarum? _____

6. Who was the last person to be legally hanged? _____

7. Who was the last person to be burnt at the Stake and where? _____

8. How many victims of the Burning Times? _____

9. What is a Sacrament? _____

10. What are our views on sexuality? _____

11. Who and what is Merlin? _____

12. Where do Wiccans come from? _____

13. Who are the Mighty Ones? _____

14. Who are Jehovah and what does this name mean? _____

15. What is the newest religion? _____

16. When is the Golden Age? _____

17. Why is Self-Awareness so important? _____

18. What is the symbolism of Stonehenge? _____

19. What is the purpose of a Magick Circle? _____

UNDERSTANDING
THE GODDESS
AND GOD

We are all familiar in the Western World with the creative concept of a male God or savior, whether the idea comes from Christianity, Judaism, or Islam. When we think of God, at the back of our minds is a picture of an old gray haired and bearded man in the sky, or on a hilltop or in a cave who has a certain set of laws; rules and regulations that we must all obey at every cost. If we follow his rules we will be loved and accepted by God, our Father, but if we disobey, we will be condemned and punished, (thanks dad).

Even today when the power of this belief has been weakened, and many do not even believe in a God at all, the image of Jehovah from the Old Testament is still very strong though we may consciously reject this view of God, subconsciously and within the structures of our society, this idea exists. When we feel guilty or unworthy in some way, and expect punishment. It is so ingrained in us, that to a large extent the "Jehovah" figure is the only way we can envisage God. We appear to have only two choices; either this male God exists or there is no God at all?

Jesus Christ, through his teachings of the New Testament, tries to offer us an alternative, by describing a God of Love, who loves all, no matter what we do or who we are. Unfortunately, even though Christianity attempts to uphold Jesus' teachings, we find when we discuss the Nature of God with many Christians, that they will and are still heavily influenced by the Jehovah of the Old Testament, and see God as wrathful, judgmental and punishing unless you 'get it right'.

However, in the second half of the 20th century, another concept of God has appeared. This time God is not male, but female. Her devotee's talk about the Great Goddess or the Great White Mother, who existed in our ancient World long before the domination and take-over of male centered religions and before Christianity achieved its dominance of the world. Many books have been written on the need for our society to turn towards the Great Mother Goddess who has been forgotten and ignored for millennia. She was one part of the divine duo throughout all of history as the most potent and well loved of all religious paths. On the face of it, assessing the idea of a female Creattrix, is a purely intellectual way, it seems quite ridiculous. Why should it matter whether God is male or female? Surely a supreme deity is beyond gender at all.

Eastern religions like Buddhism and Taoism already accept the genderlessness of God. In Taoism, we are presented with the concept of the "Tao", which means "The Way". There is no entity or image which can be worshipped or appealed to, Buddhism is similar, but since its ideas were taught by an historical man Gutama Buddha, he is the one worshipped, despite the fact that he insisted he was not a God.

If we were assessing the Nature of God in an entirely logical way, the concept of "Tao" would be the true representation, since it perceives a supreme entity as pure energy, beyond all ideas of human form and character. The trouble with this idea is that human beings find it hard to grasp what the Tao is really like. It is ever mysterious and beyond the comprehension of our limited minds. We need an image that we can relate to, that we can understand in human terms, so give it a human appearance, but the truest representation of God which we can grasp and which fits in with our growing ideas of deity, is of God as the Great Mother. A masculine God is omnipotent, but judges us, condemns and gives only limited love if deserved. His power is used to punish transgressors and reward the faithful and obedient. Man does the same.

However, when you think of a Mother, the picture is different. An ideal mother gives her children unconditional love which never waivers nor lessens no matter what her child does, it will always be loved, supported in its growth, and nourished by the Mother. Even if the child abuses her, or commits horrendous crimes within society, this love never alters and changes. A wise mother obviously encourages loving behavior, and discourages mistakes, but her love never changes. When we think of the Great Mother, we are thinking of a Mothering entity that will unconditionally love us all, forever, whether we believe in Her or not is not relevant, as She believes in us; Because we are Her creations, Her children, the Children of the Gods, to use the Earthly metaphor. This is a completely different picture from the one drawn by the belief in a male God, which relies on the threat of punishment, or withdrawal of love and rewards to keep us in line and afraid, and in control. Since it is now time for the Matriarchal side of our Creator to be accepted and valued by mankind, it makes sense to worship a Female Goddess. Only in this way will we begin to balance our imbalanced society, which has denigrated and denied the Great Mothers gift for millennia, we will raise the Mother but also honor the Great Father as in a balance needed to this time of equilibrium.

As we all aware in our society there are many people who do not obey the rules of the Christian faith, and still seem to escape any and all punishment. Some of them seem to flout all the laws of society and religion, and yet still prosper and thrive, laughing at the laws of God. Others obey all the rules, behave in a very humble and loving way, constantly devout in the behavior yet seem to receive no reward for their actions. They are often despised and taken advantage of because of their weakness.

The Christian Church avoid the implications of this by stating that such people are rewarded in Heaven, and the others will go to hell. Since this is only a speculation, and not a **FACT,** it is of little physical help to those suffering on Earth in the present. The priests of the One God can only offer a better life when we are dead - Heaven after Earth. In contrast to this, the Devotee's of the Great Mother can promise peace, joy, and Paradise on this Earth as in Heaven, while we are living. To be in Paradise does not require us to be disciplined and sacrificial for the sake of future rewards; all it requires is a small change in attitude.

In the world of the One God, whether it is one reflected to us through Christianity, Judaism, Islam or Science (which is our latest religion) we are offered a Patriarchal world of conflict and fear. We have to accept the masculine world of aggression and conquest, whether it is conquest of others or ourselves. We as individuals have also become more aggressive and frightened in our present world. All harmonious ideas of Joy and happiness are looked down upon, as impossible, or just too hard, leaving us with only suffering as the route to all our salvation.

In this ignorant worldview, we learn to succeed only through struggle and pain, so it becomes an inevitable and necessary part of life. When we look to the feminine and the Great Mother, there is a different perspective, one of ease and comfort. The Great Mother will always look after us, no matter what we do and no matter what we believe, say or think. There is no requirement to subscribe to a particular religion or way of behaving to "Earn" Her love. She shows us all equally no matter. The feminine is a concept of harmony, of bringing together Joy and Peace. The priests of the One God see a world that is out of harmony with itself, where only the strongest survive and the weakest fail, this is not necessary.

The Mother worldview shows us harmony in everything on Earth, and in the whole of creation. This idea is the essential harmoniousness of all creation and was recently brought out very clearly in the book "Gaia" by James Lovelock. His book is named after the ancient Earth Goddess, who was worshipped as the original Earth Goddess. Though She was eons ago acknowledged as the first to emerge from the primordial state of chaos. Later male-dominated cultures devalued Her and placed sky God's like Uranus and Zeus above Her. The Truth of existence is how we see the Earth that we live on, and our fellow man that shapes our lives. Our desires and fears, act as magnets, drawing towards us the reality which we feel is the "True" one, (Like attracts Like). If we believe in this conflict and limited love, if we do not behave in a certain way we will not be loved or rewarded, then this will be the reality that we create. We will become aggressive or defensive to words and ways of other people because we expect them to hurt or exploit us. This in turn like a magnet attracts us to the very aggression we fear and confirms our beliefs, just look at ISL, their destructive and murderous path founded by the very belief.

Mankind seem to believe that the strongest, most powerful and the most ruthless continue to survive, and somehow it is by divine order, in believing this we have no problems in exploiting everything in and on this world, especially the very earth we live on and our fellow man. But we know that deep within the hollows of our mind we have the fear that there will always be someone stronger and more ruthless that can literally take everything we own away from us.

In living like this, and allowing ourselves to judge others by seeing them as higher or lower, stronger or weaker, then we will continue to live in fear of us always being judged ourselves.

This new religion has created a god who does this at the end of our life when we die, sending only a few chosen to heaven and the rest as sinners to their hell, based on their scale of balance judging our very worth, devoutness and being told what to do and believe. The sad history of our patriarchal and indoctrinated species for the last two thousand years has been centered on being controlled and living with fear and conflict. Our stupid idea of 'Right' is always based on patriarchal power and force. Just look at the situation with North Korea and America, two stubborn leaders who believe they are right because "might is right". Each of them individually believing that they are right, and nothing can sway as the rest of the world are ignorant morons who do not have a clue as the realities of what is going on. Cause we know what's going on we have all grown up in schools with bullies, this is no different. Each side of this conflict believes that justice will prevail and is on their side, but we all know that it is superior strength that will prevail, but to what extent. Remember they each have their finger just above a red button that may see the demise of mankind and the end of our planet, as we know it.

It is always about people crossing boundaries, about wealth, and differences of beliefs and opinions, and it is the people who suffer the most because of this brutish ideology. We all know that the unwritten law is that the more powerful you are the more you can ignore the rights of others who are less powerful. Look at the worlds most powerful countries USA, China and Russia, they have each accumulated such incredible wealth and power by their use of aggression, and so too has the Roman Catholic Church through two thousand years of aggression in the name of love, created armies of powers, a wealth beyond ridiculous, and the total control and domination over a billion souls continuing to fill their coffers. The silly thing is that the British Commonwealth actually has and owns over a third of the world through their domination, even though they are one of the smallest nations in the world, yet the most powerful.

In such a sad and frightening world, we wake up each and every day worrying about the events of the day, thinking that we have to go to work to pay the bills, we have to pay the bills, we have to except the very world we live with all its factories that are destroying our Natural worlds environment, we are afraid of being alone, of losing what we have. Instead we should be happy to go to work, happy to pay our bills, happy to be loved, and happy at what we have in this world, by acknowledging it all and trying to better ourselves, and our very world we live in, with a positive attitude to starting each day as an adventure to find Light and Truth at the end of our journey.

In a Matriarchal world there would be absolutely no reason for anyone to feel unworthy, because we know that no matter what we are and will always be loved by the Great Mother Goddess. Even though our lives are filled with mistakes and errors, Our Great Mother will change Her unconditional love towards us Her children. As She is always prepared to help, defend, protect and support us at any cost. Being at one in a Matriarchal world means there should be no more inner conflicts, regrets, remorse, fear, distrust, and inner torment. As Her Light gives us peace in this life, but sadly we have only ever known a patriarchal world in our recorded history, but there is evidence and documented proof that an ancient civilization known as the Golden Age existed with a complete Matriarchal society which were guided by women. All knowledge of these existences shows a world of harmony and tolerance. But this was later wiped out and destroyed by the patriarchal ruling world as it grew and changed.

The power of the dominating male structures changed the world to what we see and know today. But we again in this changed and enlightened world of the 21st century can lift the Veil and welcome our Mother back home, we can again have the true Garden of Eden, and a Golden Age of Matriarchy filled with peace, harmony, tolerance, beauty, understanding, contentment and the removal of fear. There would be no place for conflict, nor any rules, except the laws of the land and Nature. Today we are again changing, and slowly waking up to the reality that the true spirituality and faith of the world lies in an ancient concept of what is termed religion today. If we bring to birth this Matercentric society filled with unconditional love of the Great Mother darkness will surely fade and Light will engulf the world and our lives.

There are many who believe that the ideal society is one in which both men and women rule and are equal. But this is NOT POSSIBLE, even if we could define what the word 'equal' means. As recent research has shown (in "Brain Sex", by Anne Moir and David Jessel), "there is a fundamental difference between the male and female brain, which manifests itself in the way men and women think and feel. Whilst men can ignore their feelings and rely on 'logic' to make decision, it is necessary for our evolution to move into a female—centered society, one in which men can learn to care for others. It is probable that in the far future we will have societies in which neither sex is dominant, but at our present stage of evolution to move into a matriarchal centered society, one in which men can learn, and it is spiritually necessary and inevitable that we move into a Matercentric society, as I will explain at a later date. This will benefit both men and women. At the moment our patriarchal society, with its rules and regulations, intolerance and aggression, gives immense advantages to men, because it reflects their way of being masters of the world.

There is no real way that women, or men for that fact, can achieve equality in such a society. We are seeing a drive for freedom within many countries of the world, and a growing acceptance of others ways of living. Many patriarchal structures, which restrict freedom, are being eroded or destroyed slowly. In this climate, women will be far less advantaged than before, because they have to be able to use aggression and logic in the same ruthless way they are accustomed to.

As men see that women's ability to mobilize both intellect and feeling in decision making leads to a greater stability, they will no longer wish to develop and dominate. They will see clearly that they will be happier directed by women than by other men, and gladly allow them to guide society. Women can rule as a mother figure but not by taking on masculine though processes to control, in a butch attitude or way. Women have become more masculine in their views in our world because of having to be heard, the sad thing is that men have also become softer and more feminine in their world views, this is not balance but disharmony of the Natural order. Both men and women have their powers of attainment and authority, when in balance will create a harmony the world needs before it is too late."

CERRIDWEN AND CERNUNNOS

A great powerful Enchantress from Welsh mythology, Cerridwen was regarded as a woman of incredible power and Magick. She overshadows both Welsh and Irish culture as an emblem of all ancient wisdom and rebirth, remaining today as a Wiccan Goddess of the Lair, as well as of inspiration. As a woman of fierce Magickal power and knowledge, the Goddess Cerridwen's story is interestingly less about Herself and more about Her children. Seen by many as a Mother Crone, Cerridwen is driven in the Welsh tales by a desire for her son's success in life. Also the mother of a beautiful young daughter named Creirwy with Tegid Foel, Her boy Morfran with immense physical hideousness. Gaining him a promising future Cerridwen had to counteract his ugliness, so She does so by using her advanced Magick to brew him a potion of mental and spiritual intellect that surpasses all mortals.

The Lady Arwen (inspiration) is the owner of the sacred Cauldron. The Goddess Cerridwen creates a Magickal potion that would give Her son brilliance and power beyond all mankind. This particular Magickal Potion was so special that it needed to boil for a period of a year and day, and to protect Her Magickal elixir Cerridwen ensured that a blind man tended its fires, and that a young shepherd boy named Gwion Bach constantly stirred it. Gwion always so careful but with constantly stirring became tired and accidentally splashes three drops onto his thumb.

Due to the immense heat of the elixir it burnt through his skin, and he without thinking put his thumb into his mouth to suck it to ease the pain, in avertedly taking in the three drops of the elixir. Unbeknown to him, it was these first three drops that held the full Magick of the potion and the rest becomes a toxic poison. But without realizing what has happened he becomes wise beyond his means and he flees in an attempt to escape the wrath of the Goddess Cerridwen. But the Enchantress Goddess can never be fooled, and so She takes on the chase of Gwion across all the lands, and in many Magickal forms (The Chain Dance). Gwion, now possessing Magickal powers of transformation, transforms himself so he can escape the Enchantress Cerridwen as a Hare.

The Goddess Cerridwen immediately transforms into a Bitch Greyhound; now the chase is on both transforming from hare and greyhound, to trout and otter, to hawk and corn. Eventually the Goddess eats Gwion as the corn when She transformed into a hen.

So in truth and the mystical story, in swallowing her enemy, the Goddess Cerridwen accidentally becomes pregnant with him. This making Her more angry and resentful, She decides to murder the baby once it has been born, thinking that She would forever be rid of the shepherd boy her ruined Her son Morfran's life. But when he came into the world, She found him so beautiful that She fell in love with him and could not harm him in any way or form. She could not kill him, but She also could not look upon him. So to relieve Her pain She wraps him in a Magickal woven cloth and throws him into the ocean, and let the tides of life and death take him from Her sight. But instead of dying he was picked up by a prince named Elfin who adopted him and gave him the name Taliesin, who eventually became the Mythical Bard of the Fae.

There became many tales of this Magickal Cauldron of Cerridwen, Cauldron of Arwen, Cauldron of Taliesin, for it became part of the legends of Merlin and King Arthur, and to many was in fact the Holy Grael. The Mystical Cauldron of Rebirth and Inspiration. In the legends of Wiccecraft the cauldron and the Holy Grael are the same, represented by the Element of Water as the Giver of Life.

CORRESPONDENCES:

Archetype: Crone, Initiator, Moon Goddess, Great Mother, and Grain Goddess, Goddess of the Cauldron

Expression: Mother of Inspiration, Mother of Nature,

Time: Full Moon, and midnight.

Season: Harvest and winter

Object: Cauldron and Chalice

Number: Three (combinations of 3)

Colour: Green, blue-green, silver or white.

Animal: Sow, hen, greyhound, otter, and hawk.

Tree: Elder and Yew.

Plant: Patchouli, Corn, Barley, Hellebore, Ivy, and Morning Glory.

Stone: Moonstone, Beryl, and Chalcedony.

CERNUNNOS: (PRONOUNCED KAR-NAY-NA):

The ancient people of the Blessed Isles, known as the Celts, the Druids, and long before them their was the Samethoi, the warriors of old who worshipped the Horned God of the forest and animals called Cernunnos (Karnayna) by the Gaul's, and in old Gaelic literature called Uindos, Herne (Hermes), Hu Gadam, and Hesus (Jesus). He was the most powerful and well loved of all the deities of old. He was so loved that everyone throughout the land knew the name of Cernunnos, the Lord of wild and untamed things. He also hared three sons Toutates, Esus and Taranis who were also known as his doubles.

The name Cernunnos simply means "Horned One" or "He who has Horns". He is seen in artwork and old buildings always depicted with rings of withy on his head and giant antlers growing from his head. Other horned beasts such as rams, goats, stags, and bulls always accompanied him. He is also depicted holding in one hand a Torc and the other the spotted Serpent Worm. The earliest known representation of Cernunnos was found at Val Camonica, in northern Italy, which was under Celtic occupation from 400 B.C. The most recognisable was found on a Cauldron of pure silver known as the Gundestrup Cauldron (pictured on the next page). It was found in Jutland, Denmark and is dated at around 1 B.C.

Ancient descriptions of Cernunnos under the guise of the Irish Uindos, who was the son of the King of Ireland named Lugh. He was a great warrior and protector of the forest; the Gods protected his lands against enchantments for evil purposes. He is also known as Cernunnos the Hunter of the Wild, a poet and is God of all Nature, especially tree's, plants and animals. Here is an image to the left of the God of Etang-sur-Arroux with an obvious depiction of Cernunnos. As a Druidic version and also sitting in a Buddha type style. He wears a Torc at the neck and on the chest with two snakes (worms) with ram heads encircles him. Cernunnos is more than ready to take on anyone who challenges him in battle. But He battles his foes using the Magick of plants, roots and trees, which he controls. Although is seen as a warrior, Cernunnos is actually a very gentle deity and even shows respect to his enemies by playing music when they die by his hands.

CORRESPONDENCES:

Archetype:	Guardian, regenerator, protector. Father God.
Expression:	Father of Life, Father of Nature,
Season:	Summer
Time:	Noonday Sun
Object:	Torc necklace, horns, cornucopia, stang, Stag.
Number:	six
Colour:	Red, orange, yellow, black or brown.
Element:	Fire
Animal:	Stag, Ram, serpent, dog, eagle.
Tree:	Oak
Plant:	Benzoin, Bay, Mistletoe, Orange, Juniper, Sunflower, and Marigold.
Stone:	Agate, Jasper, and Carnelian.

Egyptian Goddess and God Aset and Usir (Isis and Osiris)

We always hear the name Isis, but this is the Greek name for the Goddess Aset, whose name means "Throne" and is the personification of total maternal devotion. She is the Divine daughter of Seb and Nut; wife and sister of the Her Consort, Osiris also correctly named Asar, and She is mother to Horus. She is always depicted as a royal woman, and wears Her seal on Her head, The Throne that is the hieroglyph for Her name. At certain times Her headdress changes to a Solar Disk with Theban horns or even into a vulture's cap.

Ancient facts prove that Aset was a true wife and mother to Her family but also to Her people. When Her husband was slain by His jealous brother Set, where He was killed and cut into 14 pieces and spread across the country and hidden. She spared nothing in finding His hidden body. Aset so in grief searched the lands until She found all the pieces of Her beloved Asar. She then through Her Magick reassembled Him and brought Him back to life, and they made Love, She conceived and gave birth to Her divine son, Horus. Aset was the Mother of the Land and also worshipped and revered as the "Great Magick" who protected not only Her son but also all Her mortal children from predators and dangers, and the very perils of daily life. She later was being so maternal adopted Anubis as Her Divine son.

CORRESPONDENCES:

Archetype:	Mother, Protectress, Goddess of Love, and Goddess of the Moon, Magick and Fertility
Expression:	Mistress of Magick, Goddess of Motherhood, A Member of (Ennead), and Giver of Food.
Time:	New Moon
Season:	Spring or Summer
Object:	Thet (knot or buckle), Scepter, Chalice and Mirror.

Number:	Two or Eight.
Colour:	Sky blue, green, gold, white.
Animal:	Snake, goose, owl, hawk, ram, vulture.
Tree:	Fig, Willow
Plant:	Lotus, Lily, Narcissus, Myrtle, Isis, date.
Stone:	Lapis Lazuli, Aquamarine, and Sapphire.

USIR–OSIRIS

Usir was written as Asar symbolizes God in mortal form. Seen in the cycles of birth, life, death and rebirth Asar is the personification of all these mortal stages right through to the highest ascension of all divine Power. He was the King of the land who brought complete civilization to all the lands of Egypt. By 2400 BCE He had become a dual role as God of Fertility, the Dead and the Underworld. As was stated before he was the husband of Aset, father of Horus and divine son of Seb and Nut. He was tricked and murdered by his brother, Set. Who was seen as the power of all evil and darkness? After Asars resurrection He became God of the Underworld and the judge of all men who have died and enter the Underworld.

He is always depicted holding the Magickal scales of Judgment, when the heart of the deceased is weighed against the feather of the Goddess Maat, and Thoth stands by recording the findings and the eventual verdict. In most of His statues Asar is seen as a mummified bearded man, who wears the white crown of the North, and wears an elaborate pectoral necklace of precious gems, and stands in God Position, which is also called the Menat pose. He is depicted with the Crook of the shepherd that is a symbol of responsibility and sovereignty, and also crossing His chest is the Flail, that is uses to separate the wheat from the chaff. At death all man meets with Asar, and knows that through His grace can be returned to the living world and the world of the next, through one of his descendants. It is through Asar that gives man the concept of Rebirth.

CORRESPONDENCES:

Archetype:	King, Priest. God of Fertility, God of the Underworld,
Expression:	Father of stability and growth, The Resurrected King.
Time:	The Setting Sun

Direction:	West
Element:	Water
Season:	Autumn and Winter
Object:	Djed, Crook, Flail, Menat, Was.
Number:	Seventeen, fourteen and twenty-eight.
Colour:	Gold, yellow, green and white.
Animal	Dolphin, whale, sea snake, and starfish.
Tree	Willow.
Plant	Watercress, Lily, and Lotus.
Stone	Cat's-eye, Gold, Opal, and Moonstone.

Assyro - Babylonian

Ishtar and Tammuz
Ishtar:(pronounced Is-tar)

To the ancient Babylonians the Goddess Ishtar "Light of the World", "Opener of the Womb", "Lady of Battles" and "Great leader of Hosts", was the most fierce and powerful amongst all the Goddesses. Ishtar was Goddess of the Moon, of the star lit night sky, divine personification of the Shining planet Venus. Sacred prostitution was an integral part of Her Temples and her diverse cult. Ancient scripts say that when She descended from the celestial city of heaven harlots, strumpets and courtesans accompanied her. Ishtar had many lovers and indulged in every sexual pleasure that was available, She inspired the young lovers to better their sexual foes. She was not a loyal; Goddess and was also very cruel to those She honored. All of Her affairs with mortals and gods ended disastrously.

Besides all this when She was young, She fell deeply in love with a shepherd boy who was also God of the harvest, sadly it was Her great love for Him that caused His death. She was so filled with grief and anger that She swore to would venture to the depths of the Underworld and bring Him back to the land of the living. When She left the Earth, all Nature died, but when She returned months later all life was returned to the Earth, and everything blossomed with new life. This was the Spring that we all celebrate.

CORRESPONDENCES:

Archetype:	Virgin, Queen. The Goddess of Sex and Power.
Expression:	Divine Harlot, Patroness of Pleasure.
Time:	Full Moon
Season:	Spring
Object:	Bow and Quiver, Moon Sickle

Number:	Seven
Colour:	Green, Aqua, Sapphire Blue.
Animal:	Lion, Fish.
Tree:	Apple and Cherry.
Plant:	Yarrow, Woodruff, Violet, Foxglove, and Rose.
Stone:	Rose Quartz, Pink Tourmaline, Emerald, and Azurite.

Tammuz

Tammuz as we have said was a Shepherd, but he was also a Hebrew King, who was a God of Fertility, and dies a violent and horrific death. Tammuz was a Sumerian God of Nature, vegetation, food, and agriculture. Each Spring He would manifest in the seed of the cornfields. He was well loved throughout the whole of Sumeria, Assyria, Babylonia and Akkad. He represents the Divine Sacrifice, showing the cycle of birth, life, death and eventual rebirth due to the love of Ishtar.

His sacred death brought about the winter of death, which stagnated all life on the planet. But when He returned with His love, the Goddess Ishtar, all life was renewed and sprang into being once again. Tammuz and Ishtar's story is the story of death, loss, grief, and then rebirth through love, where every Spring they return from the Underworld and give life and love to all.

CORRESPONDENCES:

Archetype:	Divine Victim, God of food and vegetation. Father of Animals.
Expression:	King, God of the land.
Time:	Setting Sun
Season:	Autumn and Winter.
Object:	Cross, Scythe, Sheaf, Flute of Lapis.
Number:	Two
Colour:	Gold, orange, brown and green.
Animal:	Lion, Phoenix, Fish.
Tree:	Elder, Yew, and Ivy.
Plant:	Bay Laurel, Corn Barley, Frankincense, and Fumitory.
Stone:	Jasper

Nordic: Freya and Odin

Freya:

The name Freya, means "Lady", She has been since the beginning of the Teutonic kingdoms been the most revered in old Europe. Freya was known by many titles and names; "Faire One", "Great Mother", "Goddess of Love", "Warrior Queen". Freya was famed for her incredible beauty and high intellect; She was a member of the Vanir tribes of the Deities. Freya was a Goddess of love and patroness to all women, especially housewives, mothers, and empowered all women but also was a great warrior and oversaw many great battles, and helped Her people through the hallways of life and death. She carried all noble slain warriors to the Realms of the Gods.

Freya although a great Goddess who rode through the sky always with the Moon behind Her in a Magickal chariot drawn by either sic cats normally but when going to battle it was drawn by a huge olden Boar. She always walked amongst Her people, wearing a falcon plumed cloak of great power, and with it a Magical necklace called "Brisingamen" whose powers were unlimited and desired by many other gods. Freya, Wife to Odin whom She loved and adored above all others, and Priestess to Her people, was the protectress of Marriages, even though She was quite promiscuous and had many lovers, but never loved another. When Odin eventually found out that She was unfaithful He left Her, and She cried for forty days and nights weeping tears of gold. Freya searched for Him through all the Nordic Nine Worlds, and was finally rescued and returned back to the Earth and Her people.

Correspondences:

Archetype:	Virgin, Lover, and Party Girl.
Expression:	Priestess of Love, Life and Death.
Time:	New to the Full Moon.
Season:	Spring to Summer.
Object:	Brisingamen, Feather Cloak, and Wings.

Number:	Five.
Colour:	Silver, Pink, pale blue, and green.
Animal:	Cat, Hawk, and a Boar.
Tree:	Apple and Holly.
Plant:	Cowslip, Crocus, Rose, and Lilac.
Stone:	Blue/pink Tourmaline, Emerald, and Chrysocolla.

ODIN: (WODEN)

The Greatest of all the Norse Gods was Odin; Father of the Gods, also called Woden and Wotan, which mean Master of Ecstasy. Odin was respected for his great-accumulated knowledge and the wisdom to use it. He was the Father of Gods and always shared His wisdom with all who asked. He was the wisest of and respected by all. Being a warrior who was never defeated in battle, and possessed great-unlimited Magickal Powers.

Odin like Freya was of the people, and was always involved in their daily lives. They always helped out with great tasks and feats that mortal man could not resolve. They were sometimes gone years at a time as they traveled their lands and shared exploration and knowledge with their people.

Whenever he wandered the earth he traveled with his companions that were a pair of great ravens, and a pair of wolves. He also rode into battle on His great eight legged stallion named "Sleipner", which was a Faery beast that represented time and space. Odin was always in search for more knowledge, he built great Halls of Libraries that were filled of His travels and the knowledge that He discovered, He treasured Knowledge so highly above treasures and gold, that He gave His right Eye for that knowledge.

CORRESPONDENCES:

Archetype:	Warrior, Father, Healer, Knowledge, Runic Alphabet, Death, and Royalty.
Expression:	Priest, Shaman. Father of Knowledge and Wisdom.
Time:	Sunrise.
Season:	Winter
Object:	Sword, Shield, and Runes.

Number:	One.
Colour:	Gold, Red.
Animal:	Wolf, Raven, Horse.
Tree:	Birch, Oak.
Plant:	Holly, Mistletoe, Juniper, Gum Arabic, Marigold, Angelica, and Mastic.
Stone:	Diamond, Bloodstone, and Garnet.

GREEK: DEMETER AND ZEUS
DEMETER:

The Great Demeter is the Goddess of vegetation, corn, fertility and a bountiful Earth overseeing the fertile fields and grain crops, especially Barley and Corn. Demeter was the original Foundress of all Agriculture; She was also the creator of the Rite of Marriage, as a legal joining of two families. Thesmophoria held every April is Her greatest Celebratory Mystery. The first of all the harvests were taken and given as an offering to her Temples, especially the grains that were made in bread as a sacrificial offering. Demeter never accepted animals as offerings as She loved all life, so livestock became sacred to her.

Demeter being a Greek Goddess chose a few consorts including Zeus and Poseidon. But Zeus desired Her so much that He tricked Her in the form of a Bull, impregnating Her and making Her the Divine Mother of Persephone. Demeter's brother, Hades abducted Persephone and imprisoned Her in the Underworld where He made Her His wife and Lover. Demeter was so heart stricken that She searched the whole world for Persephone, weeping constantly as She did. And like Ishtar the whole world became barren and died, as Demeter ignored Her Earth due to Her despair. The Great God Zeus was so saddened by this that He made an agreement with Hades, that She would return for six months of the year to the living Earth and Her Mother, and for the other six months She would return to the Underworld, and into His arms.

CORRESPONDENCES:

Archetype:	Mother, Fertility, Goddess of Agriculture, and Goddess of Corn.

Expression:	Patroness of the Mysteries.
Time:	Full Moon
Season:	Spring to Summer
Object:	Torch, Scepter, Water, Jar, and Corn Dolly.
Number:	Three and Thirteen
Colour:	Cornflower Blue, Yellow and Silver.
Animal	Horse, Dolphin, Dove, Crane.
Tree	Hawthorne, Hops
Plant	Corn, Barley, Bean, Rose, Narcissus, Sunflower, Poppy, and Wheat.
Stone	Turquoise, Peridot, Pearl, Sapphire, and Moonstone.

ZEUS:

In Greek mythology Zeus was the Supreme Father God of Olympus. He was the Sky God and divine son of Rhea and Chronos. He was always involved in the land and His people, and that is why He was revered as the father of all Gods, and the Father of mankind. He was Father, King, God, and ruled with common sense and love, all institutions he oversaw and became a friend and protector of the people, patron of Princes, He was always available as a wise council, and prided Himself over the good welfare of his communities.

As King and Father of the Gods, He bestowed certain duties to all of the Olympian Gods, so that all Gods and Goddess performed their duties for the people, they punished mans misdeeds, settled all disputes, and became not only their Gods but also divine friends. Mortal were His children, so saw them as His foremost paternal responsibility and watched over them like a consumed father, where He rewarded his children, with charity, and offerings, but also gave out severed punishments for those that broke his laws against the Gods and Man. He created the first Social Order that the wealthy should always give a tithing of their wealth to the poor, usually about ten percent, more if they so desired.

CORRESPONDENCES:

Archetype:	Father, Ruler/King. Ruler of the Gods (not god of man), and Father of the Seasons.

Expression:	Ruler of the Sky, King of the Gods and Olympus.
Time:	Noon to midnight
Season:	Summer, Autumn and Winter
Object:	Thunderbolt, Scepter, Crown, and Dagger.
Number:	One
Colour:	Royal purple, dark blue, gold.
Animal:	Eagle, goat, cuckoo, elephant, Horse.
Tree:	Oak, Poplar, and Alder.
Plants:	Olive, Ambergris, Violets, Apple, Mistletoe, and Mastic.
Stones:	Blue Topaz, Carnelian.

ROMAN: DIANA AND BACCHUS/PAN

DIANA: (HEAVENLY OR DIVINE)
THE ROMAN GODDESS DIANA:

In Roman mythology it was Diana who was the Greatest Goddess of all Italy, She was Goddess of the hunt, the Moon, birthing, and the Protector of the forests and all wild and untamed life. She has the ability to communicate with every species of animal, tree and plant and could talk to all of them. She was immensely revered in all of the lands especially the Stregheria, which is Dianic Wiccecraft. Diana was revered by all women in particular those seeking fertility to have children. Although Diana is known as the Virgin Goddess of childbirth and women, She is one of three Maiden Goddesses who each swore never to marry; Diana, Vesta and Minerva.

Sacred Oak Groves were especially created for Diana, as they were sacred to Her. According to legend Diana (of the Moon) was a twin and Her sibling was Apollo (of the Sun), they were born on the Island of Delos, as the children of Jupiter and Latona. Diana as one of the twelves Olympian Gods and Goddesses was a supreme Goddess in Rome, as Goddess of the Moon, protectress of Children and of the Hunt. Diana was the Great seal of Chastity. She is always depicted standing by a Cypress Tree in a short toga with a drawn arrow, but it was not the hunt of animals She hunted for but the hunt for men's souls to guide them to the Underworld for rest and peace and rebirth. Next to her are always standing deer, rabbits, and gentle creatures of the woods. Diana is the traditional Goddess revered by Wicces and woman, and was always revered at Her festival in April called Nemoralia, the festival of Torches and lights which were placed by her worshippers surrounding Nemi, the Sacred lake of Diana also known as "Diana's Mirror". All these lights with the reflection of the Moon on the mystical lake showed that in darkness there is always light, this was a festival to also honour life, and it was forbidden to hunt or kill any animals on Nemoralia. Catholics later adopted this Festival as The Feast of Assumption.

THE ANCIENT TEMPLE OF DIANA

The original Temple of Diana, which stood where the Vatican now stands, after it was demolished and restored as the Temple of the Virgin Mary. Although Diana was the Goddess of the Hunt, woodlands and the Moon, She was always honoured more so as the Goddess of woman and childbirth.

Diana is still revered and worshipped at a Festival on August 13th, in dedication to her and Her mysteries. Of all the Goddesses that have been revered throughout the World Diana alongside Isis, Demeter and Freya were the greatest and most adored. They are all Goddesses of woman and of the Moon and of Nature.

BACCHUS:

The Great God of Wine, drama, sensuality and feasting was also known as "The beautiful God". He was the Blessings of Nature, and represented all Natural life and beauty. The 'Bacchanalia Festival' named after Him was the festival drunken orgiastic celebrations. Bacchus was the divine son of Jupiter and Semele. His name derives from the word "bacha" meaning berry. He is likened to the Dionysus and Pan. Being the God of the Vine, all wines were under His careful watch, he was Lord over fun, laughter, and freedom of sexual expression.

The Christians later saw His celebrations as debauched and spread the gossip that they were filled with deceptions and political conspiracies, where in 186 BC the Roman Senate issued a Decree stating that "Senatus consultum de Bacchanalibus" saying that is was now illegal and prohibited throughout the entire country. Through Christianity many ancient Festivals of the old gods were banned, under threat of imprisonment and torture, and also the stadium of lions. But His followers met in secret and worshipped Him as their Major God of the 'Dei Consentes', (the Council of the Gods). Bacchus is also described as having a beautiful masculine body, with a wreath on His head of grape vines, and He always held a bunch of grapes to show He alone was God of Grapes and the Vine. Bacchus had many female followers and they were given the title of Bacchantes, which later was shared with men as well.

He had many lovers until he met His great Love and married Her, Ariadne and He were the happiest of Gods and He beared many children; Charites, Hymenaios, Oenopion,

Peparethus, Priapus, Staphylos, and Thoas. In Bacchus Rites goats and pigs were sacrificed due to them being destructive to vegetation especially the grape vine. Bacchus did have another love and She was the Goddess Venus whom He also loved but never as much as his first love, Ariadne.

Goddess and God Questionnaire

NAME: _____

Research: _____

Time Questions took: _____ Date: _____

1. Who is Jehovah and where was he God? _____

2. What is the TAO? _____

3. Who was and is the last Goddess? _____

4. What is Heaven and Hell in your own words? _____

5. Explain the terms Patriarchal and Matriarchal, and which came first? _

6. What and when is the Golden Age? _____

7. What Goddess and God are you drawn to and why? _____

8. What is the name of Cerridwen's drought? _____

9. Who is Cerridwen's Consort? _____

10. What are the Egyptian names for Isis and Osiris? _____

11. How many pieces was Osiris cut into by Set? _____

12. What are some titles conferred upon Ishtar? _____

13. What was Ishtar's Consort and why? _____

14. What does the name Freya mean? _____

15. What is the name of Her Magickal Necklace? _____

16. What is Odin's steeds name? _____

17. What was Demeter Founder of? _____

18. What was the name of Her Festival Celebration? _____

19. What was Her husbands name and who was he? _____

20. Who were Zeus' parents? _____

SELF-DEDICATION
RITUALS AND
EXERCISES

DEDICATION RITUAL

All my life through my spiritual search for the Truth I have found that it is important to my progression spiritually on my Path that I always have some form of Dedication Ritual. Now this may be your first full ritual, and being our first ritual we get quite excited and nervous at the same time especially if we are going solo. Within Wicca always know that nothing can harm you if you are in a world of light and love, and am sure of the ritual that you are performing, this is why we always do the Lesser Banishing Ritual of the Pentagram (LBRP) which will be covered in-depth at a late date. Always remember the Wiccan Rede; "An it Harm None, Do What You Will". Every Ritual or ceremony that we perform as Wiccans and Wicces are firstly invoking the Goddess and God for protection and as we are a religion first, and Magick takes a secondary role, we are always surrounded by Light and Love, and protected by our Mother Goddess.

Our Dedication ritual not only involves the acknowledgement of the Goddess and God, but also dedicates our servitude to the Earth, the Shining Ones, The Elements and their Elementals, because whenever we do any form of Magick within the Magick Circle we know that we are connected and working on every level or Plane from the Physical, mental, Astral, Psychic and Spiritual. This assures us of Light, Love and Protection on all these Planes by the subsequent entities or deities.

THE RITUAL:

Because commencing with any ceremony you should over a few months or longer if that what it takes, as Magick is not a race. You will require special Tools and also a place to store them safely so they can never be touched by another, and also a Sacred Place, a shrine or Magick Circle which will act as your own personal Temple. You do not need much to start with except an open and true devout heart, and a willingness to listen and learn correctly. But some Tools will be needed, such as an Altar which can be anything you desire as long as it is not too high or too low, nor too deep, so you do not knock over items on your Altar when leaning across this is why I prefer sleeves on my Robes should not to be loose or long. These days you can even use a small card table, but only use it for your Magickal purposes. Have a virgin white linen Altar cloth; you can also have a green one representing Nature and Life.

On the Altar to the Far East of it place one white candle this will represent the Horned God. On the far right a black Natural candle, which represents the Goddess. A Thurible (Censer) is needed to burn your charcoal and incense, or if you do not wish something so elaborate select a small incense stick burner, which will do exactly the same thing. Obtain a container for your Consecrated Water such as a Goblet, or bowl that will not be used for anything else. If you wish to you can have a second vessel for Wine which is for your offering or toast at the end of your Rituals. Also you will need an Altar Pentacle, if you cannot find one, you can email me as we have hand made and carved in timber beautiful Pentacles for your Altar, or you can just get a plain dish and paint on it a Pentagram, and make it your Altar pentacle. It would also be advantageous to have Four Etheric candles for your Quarters (Watchtowers) they can be colored glass bowls with candles inside them, such as blue for the East, Red - South, Green - West, and Amber or Orange for the North.

The best time for doing your first Dedication Ritual would be anytime between a New Moon and a Full Moon. Make sure that you have written down exactly what you plan on doing for your ritual; write down everything in a numbered fashion so as to not forget the next step. This helps you to be "**PROPERLY PREPARED**". Next set up all your Tools and the Altar and make sure everything is clean and ready. Do not stress about your ritual, just relax and enjoy it openly, start with a ritual fast for about three hours prior to your Dedication Ritual. Be clean in yourself and either have a ritual bath or a shower with meaning. I always have a ritual shower just prior to donning myself with my Robes, and whilst showering I say the following:

"OH MY LORD AND LADY WHO HAS FORMED ME IN YOUR IMAGE, BLESS AND SACTIFY THIS FLOWING WATER FOR THE CLEANSING OF MY BODY AND MIND TO AWAKEN THE WICCE WITHIN. BLESS ME THAT NO DECEIT OR STUPIDITY BE HERE. MAY THEAE FLOWING WATERS WASH AWAY ALL NEGATIVITY AND BLESS ME WITH FOCUSSED WILL FOR MY ART. AND MAY THE GODDESS AND GOD BE WITH ME THIS NIGHT."

After this cleansing ritual, robe yourself, lock the doors, and turn off your phone. Turn the music on that you desire that is relaxing and gentle. Then you are ready to enter your sacred space, the Magick Circle.

1. Enter your sacred space, light your incense to make the atmosphere different from your everyday life and activities.
2. Then sit or kneel facing the Altar preparing for Meditation for at least 10 minutes leaving the day behind you, and entering the silence ready to accept the Goddess and God into your heart and welcome them to your Magick Circle in dedication to them.
3. When ready stand and do your "Self Blessing Ritual".
4. Light the Black Altar Candle and as you do so, say:

" I DO HEREBY LIGHT THIS CANDLE TO AWAKEN MY GODDESS TO THIS SACRED SPACE, I ASK THAT SHE BE PRESENT TO CLEANSE THIS MAGICK CIRCLE AND MAKE ALL NEGATIVITY AND DARKNESS BE GONE. WITH THE LIGHT OF THIS CANDLE DO I ILLUMINE THIS MAGICK CIRCLE MADE IN DEDICATION TO YOU. I OPEN MY HEART AND SOUL THAT YOU MAY GUIDE ME WITH YOUR WISDOM AND MAGICK."

5. Light the White Altar Candle and as you do so, say:

"I DO HEREBY LIGHT THIS CANDLE TO AWAKEN MY GOD TO THIS SACRED SPACE, I ASK THAT HE BE PRESENT TO CLEANSE THIS MAGICK CIRCLE AND MAKE ALL NEGATIVITY AND DARKNESS BE GONE. WITH THE LIGHT OF THIS CANDLE DO I ILLUMINE THIS MAGICK CIRCLE MADE IN DEDICATION TO YOU. I OPEN MY HEART AND SOUL THAT YOU MAY GUIDE ME WITH YOUR WISDOM AND MAGICK."

6. Take up your Pentacle that has some rock salt upon it, holding high in offering to the Goddess and God to the North and say:

"BLESSINGS BE UPON THIS PURE SALT OF THE EARTH, BE PURE AND TRUE ALWAYS IN HONOUR OF OUR LADY AND LORD."

7. Place the pentacle back on the Altar, now take up the Goblet/Chalice of Water and present it to the Goddess and God and say:

"I CONSECRATE AND BANISH THIS WATER OF THE EARTH AND OF LIFE GIVING POWERS. I ASK THE GODDESS AND GOD TO INFUSE INTO YOUR RAYS OF LIGHT TO MAKE IT SACRED AND TRUE."

8. Now approach the Altar and mix these two Elements together into your Chalice and say:

"SALT AND WATER OF THE EARTH, TOGETHER IN HARMONY,

CLEANSE THIS CIRCLE AND GIVE IT BIRTH.

PURIFY BOTH WITHIN AND WITHOUT, PURIFY AND
ILLUMINE THROUGHOUT AND ABOUT."

9. Now feel that your Sacred Space is Properly Prepared, stand in the centre of your Circle with arms upraised and your spirits high, knowing your Rite is true and pure and say your own dedicational words to the Goddess and God. Saying it in rhyme helps better.

10. After you have dedicated yourself sit and meditate on the answers you require for your chosen path and journey ahead.

11. Record your ritual and nights events and outcomes in your Book, including date.

May the Goddess hold you gently in the Palms of Her hands and always close to Her heart!

THE MIDDLE PILLAR EXERCISE

The Middle Pillar Exercise is a meditation of Hebrew cum Egyptian origin, the reference to the Middle Pillar, being of course to the Holy Kabala. We use it as a psychic door to enter our main microcosmic world. As a psychic cleaner it removes spiritual stains and tunes us in, to prepare us mentally for further and deeper work in a Magick Circle, alone or with our Coven.

Always wear clothing that is non-restrictive such as a robe if possible for any and all rituals. If possible be bare foot as we need to connect with the earth's energies, and footwear is restrictive. You should commence with a 4 x 4 breathing which is where you hold your breath for the count of four, then hold for the count of four, then release to the count of four, and then repeat until you are completely relaxed and focused, this breathing adds oxygen to your blood steam and helps the mind to tune out.

Visualize just above your head a sphere of soft, but brilliant white light… 4 inches in diameter… even though this light is so vividly bright… it does not dazzle or hurt your eyes… feel the light in your third eye… then explode the sphere so that a soft but brilliant white light fills your whole body… try to feel the light reaching out to all your extremities… then slowly bring the light back together and reform the sphere in your head…

Now move the sphere down into your throat… and at the same time change its colour to aqua blue… feel the sphere… then explode it as before… feel the blue light permeate your whole neck region with good health and love… Feel it push out any traces of negativity or ill feelings about anything at all… Feel it in your skin, bones, blood, and vessels and feel it cleansing out your system…

Now reform the Sphere and move it down to your Heart Chakra… and at this time change the colour to rose-pink… and repeat the explosion of light through every fiber of your chest and heart region… once more, the health and vitality should almost leave a taste in your mouth as your upper torso glows so… so… pink…

After you have basked in the pink ... reform the Sphere and move it down your torso to your genital region and lower abdomen region and change the Sphere to a russet reddish brown colour...repeat the exploding... permeating and reforming the Sphere...

After your genitalia region... move it down to your feet region where all the negativity has been forced by the previous explosions... Watch the dirty black colour slowly brighten as it absorbs your negative vibrations... Now rather than reforming the Sphere... push all your negative, black events to your feet... out o your life... drain it out of your body so there is no blackness left at all anywhere in your body... just a clean peaceful glow... Now spend a few minutes just feeling the Spiritually clean body... you may also choose to thank the Goddess and God, the Elementals of the Earth for helping...

WICCA AND THE
HORNED GODS

The Horned God is that Eternal "other half", the compliment of the Goddess, the male counterpart of the primal female creative force. He is all human, all-fertility, all-love. He is represented by the Sun, the giver of life and is directly responsible for the Seasons as the Suns warmth varies. Wiccans celebrate the changes of the Seasons with specific festivals. These are days of "power" and are the Sabbats that occur eight times a year. Though the Sun God viewed (symbolically) as the source of these days, both Deities are revered and honored at these times. The Horned God is also associated with the wilderness, the wild and undomesticated animals, in particular, the Horned varieties, such as the Stag, Ram, Goat and Bull. Horns were and still are obvious marks of masculinity, fertility and divinity; all ancient tribes bestowed upon their Gods – horns, that they too would be strong and virile. This has carried forward to today as the God of the Wicces, as is referred to as the Horned God or the Horned One, or simply Cernunnos (pronounced Kar-nay-na) which means "The Horned One".

The etymological origin of the word Wicca" is Anglo-Saxon and means "To shape and bend" (wisely). The word Wicce means Wise One. From here it is but a short debasement of the name to Wiccecraft, a name which has remained in use since its first recorded employment in 700 A.D., to the present day to denote the religion of the followers of the Old Religion in Pre-Christian Europe, and those that date from soon after the arrival of the Christian Missionaries and were made by Ecclesiastics, so that allowance must always be made for the religious bias of the writers of the time. The term Old Religion means the first religion of man as to the New Religion which is only 2,000 years old to denote the followers of Christ, Mohammed and Buddha, which all formulated around the same millennium.

As was mentioned above little is known of he early history of Wicca, except by the secret teachings that have been passed down by word of mouth of the initiated, that were originally told and passed down by mouth through family lines known as Hereditary or "Blood Wicces" of old, because the only public evidence of the time was recorded by Christian Missionaries on their arrival, with a lot of bias and twisted stories to suit their ideals and not the ideals of Pagans of the time.

In the Cave des Trois Frères' at Ariege in Southern France, was found a Paleolithic rock art painting depicting a man clothed in the skin of an animal and wearing on his head the antlers of a stag. The hide of the animal covers the whole of the mans body, and the hands and feet being drawn as though seen through a transparent material, thus conveying the information that the figure is a disguised human being and not an actual stag standing on its hind legs. Around him are also various representations of animals, which are placed where spectators can easily see them, whilst the figure of the Horned Man can only be viewed from part of the cavern, which is most difficult of access, and viewing from the gaze of outsiders. This fact suggests that a great degree of sanctity was attached to the representation and that it was purposely placed from the gaze of the profane. A like painting of the same period exists in Dordogne, the only difference being that instead of animals, 12 human figures surround the Horned God.

The end of the Paleolithic period saw the temporary interruption of the Cave paintings until the arrival of the Bronze Age. Now the Horned Man is found again all over the world especially in Egypt, Norway, Mesopotamia, Africa, North America, and Asia and in India. In the near East the figures were either male or female, and the horns were usually those of cattle, sheep, or goats, as the Stag antlers probably lacking, or possibly the Stag did not occur in those lands or else because it was so uncommon as a food animal.

Horned God's were in plentiful supply and were common in both Babylon and Assyria. The copper head found in one of the Tombs at Ur, is very early, possibly dating from before the time of the First Dynasty! In Egypt too, Horned Gods were in plentiful supply. The chief of these was Amon-Ra, originally the local deity of Thebes, later the supreme God of the whole country, and is usually represented in human form wearing the horns of a Theban Ram. But the greatest of all the Horned Gods of Egypt was Osiris (Usir), who appears to have been Pharaoh in this aspect of the incarnate God. The Crown of Osiris, of which the horns were an important part, was also the Crown of the Monarch, indicating to all who understood its symbologies, that King as God was the giver of all fertility.

The Indian figures of the Horned God found at Mohenjo-Daro, are of the earliest Bronze Age. There are many examples and in every case it is clear that a human was being represented either masked or horned. The most remarkable figure is that of a man with Bull's horns on his head, animals surround sitting cross-legged, and like the Ariege painting. This representation of a Shiva is called "Pasupati", meaning "The Lord of Animals".

Though it is not possible to give an exact date to the early legends of the Aegean, it is nevertheless evident that also there the Horned God flourished throughout the Bronze and Iron Ages. The best known on account of the dramatic legends attached to his cult, was the Minotaur - the offspring of a foreign bull and a Cretan Queen. Of the Horned God's on mainland of Greece, Pan is best known to the modern world, and in fact when a Wiccan wishes to use an image of the Horned God, it is usually either a representation of Pan, Osiris or Cernunnos that is used. That the legendary death and resurrection of the latter being very close to the Wiccans belief of the legendary beginning of the Wicca as a "Fertility Religion". Today there are many statues that are available for sale through online stores.

A few rock carvings in Scandinavia show that the Horned God was also known there at the time of the Bronze Age. It was only when Rome started on her conquest that any written records were made of the Horned Gods of old Europe, and these records show that a Horned God, whom the Romans simply called Cernunnos (Karnayna) was the supreme God of Gaul. The importance of this Horned God may be shown in reference to the Altar found under the Cathedral of Notre Dame in Paris. The date of the Altar is well within the Christian era. On three sides are figures of minor Gods represented as small beings, but on the fourth, is the head and like the Ariege painting, he wears Stag antlers, these being further decorated with rings of Withy and Mistletoe. Like His Paleolithic prototype, he is bearded, but in accordance with Roman artistic ideas, he is not masked, the horns and appendages are grown from his head.

This particular deity is the Horned God of the Wicces, since He conforms in every aspect to the picture of the Horned God worshipped by Wicces. The other possibility is that Pan, Dionysus or Bacchus, since all three Gods are Horned, and are all directly linked to Saturnalia and other rites connected with fertility. Of the old faith in pre-Christian Britain, there are as usual, few records, but as Dr. Margaret Murray says:

"It is contrary to all experience that a cult should die out and leave no trace, immediately on the introduction of a new religion. The so-called conversion of Britain meant the superficial conversion of the rulers only; the mass of the people continued to follow their ancient customs and beliefs with a very thin veneer of Christian rites."

In the case of the conversion of various tribes, the religion of the King was that of the tribe, and so when the king was bribed with treasures he so converted, when the King was converted to Christianity, the people generally followed its leaders example. However, these conversions were purely nominal in a majority of cases, and very often the Kings successor reverted to the Old Religion.

Whatever the religion of their ancestors the two religions existed side by side, (for awhile anyway), as was the case with King Redwald of the East Saxons, who "In the same temple had an Altar to sacrifice to Christ, and another one to offer up victims of the devil." This later reference is strange since Wiccans or more properly the worshippers of the Horned God, are only concerned with life and rebirth, and not death. And never in the course of our known history of our religion has any sacrifice of any living thing ever taken place. Indeed, was it not for the fact that the economy at the time was based primarily on hunting; Wicca might well have forbidden the killing of any living thing whatsoever.

The existence of the Old Religion is proved by reference to the Liber Potentialis of Theodore, Archbishop of Canterbury (668-690) that contains the earliest ecclesiastical laws of England, consisting of a list of offences, and the punishment due for each offence:

"If then anyone be found that shall henceforth practice heathenship, either by fyrt or by sacrifice, or in any way love Witchcraft, or worship idols. If he be a king's thane, let him pay X half marks to Christ and half to the King. For we are all to worship only one God and strictly hold one Christianity, and totally denounce all heathenship and other so-called beliefs."

The reference to idols here is very obscure, since there are no images of the Horned God as such. The best the followers of the Old Religion could do therefore, was to worship "Menhirs", a French word meaning "boulders", or more correctly (a pointed or phallic shaped rock). These as are tree's, are phallic symbols and symbols of fertility. The Priests of Elagabaal—a Syrian Deity, whose cult flourished under the Roman Emperor Varios Antonius, used to worship their deity under the guise of a pointed rock. The idea was that their actions which included masturbation upon the rock would give their God, symbolized by the Sun, the power to rise the next day again. Although strange in nature, Wiccans never worshipped their God's in this manner, but it is easy to comprehend the fact that phallic symbolism in worship has a huge following in those days. Even today old farmers of Europe still practice these same rites, in masturbation on their fields for fertility.

It is virtually impossible to understand Wiccecraft without first comprehending the position of the Horned Gods of the Wicca. The Horned God whose name is a closely guarded secret, but who has been called by others Satan (more correctly Shaitan), Lucifer—more correctly (Lucifuge meaning the Light Bringer), Beelzebub, or other names appropriate to the devil of the Christian scriptures, with whom they identified him. The reason for the mud slinging was two-fold. At first, not comprehending the situation, the Missionaries, not unnaturally mistook the Horned God for their own devil because of certain similarities, namely the horns and the animal likeness. On their realization of the true state of affairs, they also realized that Wicca was a firmly established pagan religion and constituted a grave threat to the survival of Christianity. So every means available had to be used to suppress this great rival, and it was the Wicca that provided the main excuse, in the appearance of the Horned God himself.

The Goddess whose name is also a closely guarded secret, is of greater significance to the Wiccans themselves, although She was hardly known to the outside world but very much known today. Wicca is Matriarchal in basis, and all prayers are usually directed to the Goddess. The legend of the Horned God of the Craft is very akin to that of Isis and Osiris in Egyptian mythology. In the latter, symbolically, Osiris gave over all His power to Isis, and in the same way, the Horned God was so enchanted by the youth and beauty of the Goddess, that He made over to Her all of His powers. In Wicca the Arch Priestess or Witch Queen is the Spiritual titular head, like the mother or grandmother, but the High Priestess is the head of her Temple/Circle/Coven and alongside with her High Priest run the individual covens and all the external affairs of the Wicca, and deal with its disciplines.

The worship of the Horned God continued well into properly documented historic times. In 1303, the Bishop of Coventry was accused before the Pope of doing homage to the devil in the form of a sheep. The fact that a man in so high a position as a Bishop could be accused of practicing the Old Religion shows that the worship of the Horned God was far from dead, and that it was probably still the main worship of the peoples. But the Bishops high position in the Christian hierarchy saved him from punishment, as was the case of Lady Alice Kyteler, in 1324 when she was tried before the Bishop of Ossory for heathen beliefs. Although Lady Kyteler escaped, her commoner co-religionists were hung, showing that there was ample evidence at hand. The most famous recorded example of the continuance of the Old Religion was the case of the Countess of Salisbury, in the reign of King Edward III.

She whilst dancing with the King dropped Her garter, and the King picked it up and fastened it upon his own leg with the words "HONI SOIT QUI MAL Y PENSE". It has always been assumed by the unenlightened that it was quite natural for a Lady to be so embarrassed by the loss of so personal an item of apparel. However the ladies of that period were so inured to rough talk and it took more than a dropped garter to shock them.

The truth of the matter is that the Garter is a badge of rank in the Wicca and it showed not only was she a worshipper of the Horned God, but also that she held a high position of a High Priestess. When the King attached the offending article on his own person he was in effect placing himself in the position of the Incarnate God in the eyes of his Pagan subjects. Not content with his action in saving his dancing partner, he then instituted the "Noble Order of the Garter", with twenty-six knights (two covens-one for the King and one for the Prince of Wales) It is equally remarkable that the Kings mantle as Chief of the Order, is powdered over with one hundred and sixty eight tiny garters, which with his own garter worn on his leg makes one hundred and sixty nine; (i.e. 13 x 13; = 13 Covens).

The last person to be appointed to the Order of the Garter, was Lady Margaret Thatcher who consequently is the seventh former Prime Minister appointed to the Order, and also the second Lady to be accepted. The first was Lavinia, Duchess of Norfolk in 1990. Appointments to the Garter are entirely the personal gift of the King or Queen of Britain, and are not made on the advice of anyone else. There are now not the traditional 28 members representing the days of the month, but there are twenty-four, and their emblem of the Order is a blue ribbon or garter worn by men below the left knee, and by women on the left arm. The Queen is the titular head of this order until she steps down or passes on her crown.

The underlying meaning of the sacrifice of the Divine Victim is that the Spirit of Horned God takes up its abode in a human being, usually the King, but it may be any other leader, who thereby becomes the giver of fertility to the people. Among other privileges his person becomes inviolate until his time has come. This is the origin of the Divine Right of Kings. After a set number of years, the King is put to death to ensure that the Spirit of the Horned God will not grow old like its human counterpart. The term of years was generally either 8, but it varied according to circumstances, this is in aligning with the Festivals of the year. The principle of the Divine Victim is very old and nearly every religion has practiced it at some stage in their history. Osiris was one, Jesus Christ was another; to name just two of the best known examples, while the two best known victims of the Wicca are William Rufus and Joan of Arc'.

William Rufus II reigned for precisely 13 years from 1087 to 1100 E.V. He was accidentally shot in the back with an arrow in the New Forest. An interesting fact about him is that Rufus means "Red", and is the true colour of the Wicces hair colour. Joan of Arc', the Maid of Orleans, was a Pucelle or High Priestess of the Wicca, and was condemned to death for what she was. One of the strongest accusations being that she wore men's clothing, a thing at the time only done by Wicces. The fact too, that a mere nobody, especially a child of 19 years of age, commanded an almost fanatical body of troops, showed them that she must have held an extremely important position in the Wicca, but as God Incarnate. It is also significant that she like other Divine Victims such as William Rufus, Thomas Beckitt, Giles de Rais, and Jesus Christ, made absolutely no attempt to save him or herself by word or deed, but rather willed their death.

This is the only time that the Wicca will draw blood, and the killing of the Divine Victim has always been scrupulously observed since the days of conception. Modern Wicces still worship the Horned God in the same way, as did our ancestors, but have changed it slightly to suit the needs of the people of today. The Four Great Sabbats in the Southern hemisphere are, Imbolg - August 1st; Lughnasadh - February 2nd; Samhain - May Eve; and Beltane – November Eve. These are still celebrated in honor of the Old Gods and Goddesses of the Earth. In the Northern Hemisphere these festivals are reversed due to the Seasonal Rounds being opposite to us in the Southern hemisphere. The four lesser Sabbats are the cross-quarter days of the year, the Equinoxes and the Solstices. They are Autumn Equinox - March 21st, Winter Solstice - June 22nd, Spring Equinox - September 21st, and Summer Solstice - 22nd December.

IN DEFENSE
OF THE
HORNED GOD

The medieval and post medieval trials gave perhaps undue prominence to the Wicces worship of the Horned God. The horns of the masculine animals, predominantly the Stag and the Bull, progressed from being a part of the direct representation of an animal form to being a symbol of Divinity, or of Divine inspiration. Thus the Horned God became the Archetype of the polarized God, who cannot exist or be conceived without his counterpart and compliment - the Goddess.

As part of the subjugation process, the Goddess and Horned God of the Old Religion became the devils of the New Religion. When the new Catholic church felt powerful enough to impose its monopoly of belief– the milestone being Pope Innocent VIII's Bull of 1484 A.D. condemning Wicces as heretics – it could no longer allow the Horned God to be an alternative visualisation of universal duality/divinity. And so, he was branded as Satan. In the process Satan's image was also transformed just as much as the Horned God. In the Old Testament, Satan appears as the "Adversary" not a rebel against the Christian Gods authority, but a sort of heavenly district attorney, drawing attention to the debit side of a souls record or testing a mans spiritual stamina. Not a very endearing function but certainly a valid and perfectly respectable task. The image of Satan as the Prince of darkness and evil at war with God is mainly a post biblical creation, and his horns once a symbol of divinity, an invention of the heretic hunting inquisition.

The process was simple, in light of the less than worldly life style prevalent with the masses. First put horns on Satan. Then point at the Horned God of the Wicces, for example Cernunnos, and say: "Look the devil, and he has horns to prove it". Later in time witch-trial records inaccurately and falsely promoted belief that Wicces worshipped Satan. The court reporter being employed by the Inquisitors would, when the defendant spoke of her own God, substitute the word 'devil'. Common falsehood, that Wiccans are devil worshippers in pronounced, vigorously by TV evangelists and individuals purporting to be exorcists on a holy mission. In a seemed attempt to drum up more business, even here in Perth they regularly put stories in the media telling people how they have saved yet another soul. The truth is, Wicca, the Goddess and the Horned God have absolutely nothing to do with, nor any association with the Christian devil. Satan is a creature of the Catholic Pantheon; and Wiccans take no credit for his infamous status in any way or form.

Whilst we are looking at misrepresentations of the Wiccan religion, apart from not worshipping the Devil;

- Wiccans are NOT Satanists.
- Wiccans are not ANTI-CHRISTIAN, anti– Islam, anti-Semitic, anti-anything.
- Wiccans are not crazy fundamentalist attacking other religions and faiths.

- Wiccans are not back-sliding Christians eager to worship their own concept of evil!
- Wiccans and our Horned God and Goddess do not need your money to build gaudy shrines!
- Wiccans do not run peoples lives by telling them what to believe in, do, think and feel.
- Wiccans do not prey on the vulnerable or virgin children!
- Wiccans do not sacrifice any living thing except our own time and dedication!
- Wiccans do not work to Harm any living thing!
- Wiccans are not black, white or gray, neither are Christians white or black?
- Wiccans are not ugly old freaks; they are beautiful children of the Goddess; and are Keepers and Guardians and Healers of the Earth and all life upon and within Her.

All Wiccans need is a clear night, with love and trust in their hearts, to share in freedom with likeminded sisters and brothers. And to worship openly and freely our Goddess and God and all that is to assist in creating a healthy ecological and environmentally sane planet and to be one with all. We also seek freedom of our religious rights, and wish to express it as we have for millennia.

"An it Harm None, Do What You Will"!

PENTAGRAM MEDITATION

Earth yourself, ground and hold within your hands your Altar pentacle focusing on the Magickal Sigils etched upon it… breathe deeply and in a relaxed and gentle manner… feel the Pentacle as a Talisman opening the Earth's energies drawing up from the Earth and magnifying through the Pentacle into your hands… place your Pentacle down and now become the Pentagram and stand in Pentagram Position… feel your limbs and full torso becoming the energized Pentacle… feel the energy flowing through your whole body the four limbs and your head… feel all fives senses being awakened by inner and outer… this making your fully aware of your own individual Earthly power in seeing, touching, feeling, smelling and tasting..

The feel that the Pentagram Position has awakened the Four Elements within your body… including the Fifth Element… The Spirit… you are now connected to the five stages of life as well as all that is known that you are now one with the earth and the divine Spirit of the Goddess.

1. BIRTH   the beginning, the time of coming into being and being fully aware…
2. INITIATION   adolescence, the time of individualization, knowing the power of being an individual…
3. LOVE   the time of Union with another, a full adulthood, sexuality and responsibility.
4. REPOSE   the time of Advancing Age, of reflection, integration, knowledge and wisdom.
5. DEATH   The time of ending, letting go, of moving on toward rebirth.

Get your Pentacle and label the 5 points around and experience each stage in turn… as it occurs in a life span and within the scene of each activity or relationship… Trace the interlocking lines and reflect their meanings… Love is linked to Initiation… here is the vowel system;

A - BIRTH - AILM - SHEOAK
O - INITIATION - ONN - BLACKBOY
U - LOVE - ERA - GOLDEN WATTLE.
E - REPOSE - EADHA - EUCALYPTUS
I - DEATH - IDHO – KARRI.

THE IRON PENTACLE

Earth yourself, ground and centre draw a Pentagram with interlocking lines and label at the points, in order around SEX, SELF, PASSION, PRIDE, POWER

SEX - is the manifestation of the primal driving force of the universe. It is polarity, the attraction of the Ultimate feminine (the Goddess) and the Ultimate masculine (the Horned God), and that individuality is highly valued in Wiccecraft

SELF-LOVE is the Foundation of all unconditional Divine Love. Celebrate yourself and you will see that Self is everywhere and in everything!

PASSION - Is the force and power of emotion, that gives colour and depth of vitality to anger, ecstasy, fear, life, joy, love and pain - the Goddess manifests in all human emotions. We cannot feel them in their full intensity unless we are willing to face them all, and understand and accept them all.

PRIDE - Encourages us to create, to do, to share, to grow and to enjoy the rightful fruits of our achievements. True Pride is not based on ignorance, comparisons or competition; it is an absolute sense of ones inner and higher worth. Pride carries with it the responsibility of acting in according with ones self respect and respect in others, ego means "SELF".

POWER - Is energy, force, and inner power, not power over others. When your five points are in balance; the life force within flows freely, filling us with vitality. Power is integrity, creativity, and courage. The mark of a Whole person who is at One with the Goddess.

Meditate on each of these points and especially the Top and explore the links and connections; form a Pentagram. Let your head and each of your limbs is a point of the Pentagram. When you are on the points they will all be in balance, if some points feel weak, work on developing those qualities. Absorb the strength of the Iron Pentagram.

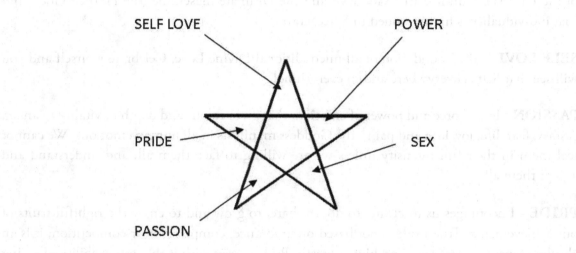

SELF LOVE

POWER

PRIDE

SEX

PASSION

THE HORNED GODS QUESTIONNAIRE

NAME: _____

Research used: _____

Time Taken in doing Questionnaire: _____ Date: _____

1. What is the Horned God and why do we revere Him? _____

2. What is the Middle Pillar and what was your result? _____

3. When was the word Wicce first recorded and by whom? _____

4. Where are the famous cave paintings of the Horned God? _____

5. What is under the Altar of the Cathedral of Notre Dame? _____

6. What is a Minotaur and how did it come into being? _____

7. What is Alchemy? _____

8. What is a Menhir, (explain)? _____

9. What do the words "Honi Soit Qui Mal Y Pense" Mean? _____

10. What is the Order of the Garter? _____

11. What does the Garter represent? _____

12. What do we mean by Divine Victim? _____

13. What is a Pucelle? _____

14. Why do we suggest that Jesus was a Wicce? _____

15. What are the Eight Sabbats and their dates? _____

16. What did the medical fraternity have to do with Wiccecraft? _____

17. Who is Satan, and how do we view him? _____

18. What is the difference between a Pentacle and a Pentagram? _____

19. What does Initiation mean to you? _____

20. Name as many Horned Gods as you can? _____

NATURAL
MAGICK OF
WICCA &
WICCECRAFT

Natural Magick is the ability to live naked to the whole world, showing everything and nothing to hide. It becomes the reality of releasing from the dark Abyss of illusion. It is about having the true ability to live in an ideal form of realism, which aids in truly dealing with the varied types of people and forces that really exist in our world, not with just who and what they appear to be. We have all become a creation of our own mind and created who we think we should be and not who we really are, it becomes an illusion and not a reality. When we think we know our situation, and ourselves in truth reality is quite the opposite where we cannot see our truth only the images projected by our own fantasy.

A true Natural Wicce knows and believes that everything is possible, for she is Magickally integrated with all of life to be able to visualize her desires in accordance with the Natural Laws, and not for her own selfish means. Connecting directly to the inner personal knowledge and senses for and have the inner and higher powers must be unshakeable. Make belief as firm as a rock, **NEVER** play Wicce and test the Natural Powers, know that they are absolute and real. True and real Magick transcends all time and space, it is the invisible within the visible, the gentle currents of life that transcends between each breath, the Magickal breeze that sustains and pollinates life, sustains petals on a flower, that holds the Sun and the Moon in the sky.

Natural Magick is the power of a leaf unfolding, and tree losing its Autumn leaves to make way for the new. It is the energy of a flowing river that carries life throughout the land. All these are Magickal and Mysterious forces of Nature and the Goddess. They are all the obvious and yet not-so obvious secret world of Magick.

To understand humility we must become humble, to understand patience we must become patience, to understand love, we must become love. We must take minute vacations and stop, enter the silence and look at the very beauty and life that surrounds us. We need to stop talking and learn to listen again, for Nature has much to say. Listen to the Elements and their varied sounds of harmony that echo throughout not only our world but also the whole universe. The Elemental voices are calling out to our very souls to awaken and listen before it is too late. We have stopped believing in magick as we have stopped believing in ourselves, due to the brainwashing and constant doubts and negatives that we are enforced with as children.

A true Wiccan or Wicce is in touch with all that is invisible within this visible world, and knows it to be the spirit and force of the Goddess and God. We must dissolve our delusions and wake up our inner Truth, once we have broken down our barriers and removed the hardened exterior that we created for years the freer and more in touch with the real world we can be.

True power exists when we are REAL, and not disconnected from Nature, we need to go back to Nature to remember where we came from and where we will eventually go. Everything in life has an eternal soul that runs like a spider web connecting everything together. Open your senses and FEEL the world knowing that everything is ALIVE and is connected, just waiting for you to reconnect as the ancient peoples of this Earth use to. The animal and plant kingdoms can teach more about life and love that we can teach ourselves. even the Crystals have a vibration that is calling out to us. Many countries especially Russia have been experimenting with plants scientifically, and they know with proof that plants feel pain and can communicate with us, we just need to listen.

The Delaware Laboratories in Oxford, England have been for the last 30 years been doing extensive scientific research into the reaction of plants and they have proved beyond any shadow of a doubt that if treated in a hostile or aggressive manner they really do wilt and then die more quickly.

To understand what it is to become a Natural Wicce one must not only study and understand Nature, but also learn to merge with Mother nature in all Her varied forms and life's, from the animal kingdom, plants and tree's, rocks and crystals. I have met many people over the years that were completely imprisoned in their own bodies and are complete takers and never give away anything. They just close themselves because of distrust and lack of faith. When mans ego becomes less important than our Natural world, then and only then will all of our doubts, fears and ego's fade away and then being replaced with a sense of **"PERFECT LOVE AND PERFECT TRUST"** will we find that peace that we each search for on a daily basis, not without ourselves, but deep within us. It is when we get to this stage we will know our TRUTH and let go of everything we thought we knew, wanted and needed, for the reality of just BEING in a state of absolute acceptance and harmony with the world.

There is no limitation, but a sense of perfect freedom and bliss, and this will be because we have forgiven ourselves and removed the restrictions set upon us by our forebears. When we eventually become One with the Divine and all of the Earth, we will no longer want for anything, we will not even need our Magickal Tools, as we have within us all that we will ever need.

I have over the past few decades watched as we have mined and taken from the earth constantly but never seem to give back. I look at even Crystals having a purpose in the preservation of the dying Earth. If they were a power source for us, then would it not be true that they are a power force for the Earth, which we are removing. It is like all the fossil fuels, ores, minerals, gases, oils, and trees. How long can we keep taking, without even stopping long enough to think; "That if we remove everything, then there will be nothing left for the generations to follow, except a global warming, with nothing left to take, no class room to learn from and in doing this Mother Earth will stop letting us take from Her, She will with a vengeance remove us from the destruction of this our ONLY world.

If you have to take from the Earth remember to give, back. We all have an exchange of trade such as money to buy things but what do we give to our Mother Earth. So from this day forward learn to give back, for each and everything you take possession of that is from the living Earth, give back a tithing of importance. If you have crystals, then listen to them truly, not to what you think they are saying but what they are really saying. Communication is the first step of learning to listen and becoming One with the bigger family of Nature. You are not separate from Her; you are just another piece in Her great puzzle.

Trees are much more soothing and healing than any aspirin or tranquillizer, and they are free. Trees and plants love to be acknowledged and communicated with and like humans they dislike being ignored. Each and every life form on the planet emits energy and a frequency that transmits and receives the Natural vibrations and sacred language of the living Universe. Trees and all plants are healers, and each species has their specified healing gifts that target certain ill-health problems. But always be careful of sick trees or dying trees, as these you should either stay clear, or instead of receiving from them, gift to them your healing energies instead. An untrained exorcist who truly does not understand will imprison a bad or evil spirit into a large strong tree, most trees can handle this form of negativity but some are not able to cope with excessive dangerous or malevolent spirits, and so they eventually become ill with a cancerous growth and die.

In ancient times all trees were believed to have spirits, either negative or positive. But many wizards, Druids and the like placed dislodged evil spirits into the trees as a prison, to hopefully in time learn of their errors and become a gentle spirit of light, when they would be released and freed into the Natural world.

The easiest way to find out whether a tree has a spirit of light and love or darkness and evil is to slowly, without actually touching it, walk Deosil around the tree with your palms facing towards it, opening your psychic senses and intuition and feeling what energy to tree is directing to you and the very world around it. Each tree gives of different energies, but usually within only a few moments you will know the truth of this tree and no whether to hug it, or heal it or just leave it be. But be sure in your feelings and feel the harmony or disharmony before making a decision. Learn to trust your Higher Self, the very Wicce within and her Natural instincts, we are all sensitive to everything in life if we just learn to open ourselves to its essence and step away from our own. Regular practice will aid you intensely, especially with different species of trees, as you will learn by instinct and Higher Awareness what the Magick is of each and every plant and tree. Within time you will be able to automatically sense and know the essence of every living thing, by learning to listen, feel and know just by the proximity when on your "Spiritual Nature Walks" of being in or near a certain tree. This will also work when just walking and holding your palms out to the Earth to all forms of life such as plants and flowers and even rocks and crystals. When you feel that you know the answers to their healing abilities and speak their Sacred Language write it all down in your Book of Shadows.

Listen to their voices, hear their songs that they have been singing for millennia, and know that they are a part of the great cosmic landscape of connected life on this Planet. Hear their music and the music of the Spheres, and listen to a symphony that will guide and teach you the ways of the invisible within the visible.

So do yourself a favor:

"LOOK, LISTEN, LEARN, LAUGH, AND LOVE.
AND HUG A TREE!"

SACRED POWERS
OF WICCA

Those of Wicca and the Craft know that by being in tune with Nature we learn to understand and work with certain vibrations that firstly affect the Astral Plane and then have a reaction on the Physical Plane. All of our thoughts, ideas, and even our fears are already formed there. For this is the plastic realm and everything that ever was, is and will be exist at the same time in the same place, therefore everything is duplicated. The Wicce when working in a Magick Circle which magnifies our Powers knows that when we send out an energy or thought form through Magick, it is magnified and charged especially in the use of Spells, Magick, Ritual, Ceremony and Enchantment. The Wicces of old could this very power moving through and within every living thing in waves of electro-magnetic rhythms of light and energy. By working with this energy and tapping into its very source of power, with training you can train yourself and make this power work for you in a powerful transformation on the Astral.

- SPELLS and Magickal Enchantments create vibrations, or energy wave-lengths, which cause reactions on the Astral. The reactions are what turn our thoughts and desires into MAGICKAL REALITY!

When a Wicce intends to create a thought-form such as a Familiar powerful enough to create an explosive vibration on the Astral, which causes a ripple effect on the Physical. This comes from much focus, visualization and knowledgeable will power. Do not think that you can just pick up a book of spells, read them and Magick will happen. That is not how it works; everything we do in this universe is done through constant training and learning. It must happen on all levels, for it to be **REAL** on the Physical it starts with the **MIND** being focused and unwavering, and then the **MENTAL** power is infused with your knowledge and the ability to believe unquestionably in Magick. Then it moves onto the **PSYCHIC** realm, then up to the **ASTRAL**, and then ascends to the **SPIRITUAL**. When all these are in **BALANCE** a marriage of the micro-macrocosmic worlds collide which creates true **MAGICK,** which is the true Art and science that causes changes to occur in accordance with one's Will.

Once the thought-form or Familiar is created on all Planes it works on the invisible levels by Magick and changes and effect to desired Will of the Wicce. If you truly want change in your world, then this is a long hard process of faith in the Natural and Magickal powers that dance within and around us. When this adventure starts the process has a rippling effect that grows stronger in time, to help you become the powerful Wicce that you already are, but just did not know until you were awakened.

Now this may sound all very hard to do this process, but it is well worth it in end. There is nothing like it in the Universe. It's like driving a car a bit scary with a lot to learn, but once you have learnt and feel comfortable with it, it is done almost automatically. Lots of rehearsals mean a perfect end result in your performance and the outcome. All Ritual and Ceremony is like the theatre, the Magick Circle becomes the stage with all your props, you put on special clothing to take your mind to a different place, and then the ritual is the play. It is how good your performance is that will make the play believable to the Energies, Elementals and Deities that will unfold your true gifts of Magick. With the right music to make the emotions swell as in the theatre, this elevates your consciousness and your Higher Wicce Self, which makes it become **REAL.**

If you have learned you parts, rehearsed them and are Properly Prepared, then true Magick has already started to take effect by opening the channels to the different dimensions of thinking, which brings all the worlds together in balance and harmony. This result ends in your desired effect coming into REALITY. Magick is real. Your possibilities are endless, as long as you remember the Wiccan Rede; "AN IT HARM NONE, DO WHAT YOU WILL".

- Successful Magick depends on the ability of the Wicce to focus their attention on a single objection; without letting their mind wander, then create the appropriate energy needed to produce the Familiar, which will affect their intended target and goal.

Magick is an Art, or Science, it is the Art of Wiccecraft, and offers an extensive library of study. Magick is the science of the future not just the past. And just like the Arts and Sciences, provides all Wicces with a variety of options. Remember that Wicca is fore mostly a religion and Magick is second place.

Some Wicces may be happy to just be at the level of being a Wiccan in connection with nature and the Goddess, but many others will aspire to reach for the stars and become highly trained and advanced in their studies and will become all out Magicians working with Ceremonial Magick. I have always believed that to learn and get the most out of Wicca you need to not be a solitary but work with in an organized and traditionally trained Coven that can help you with responsibility and the correct process of training as a whole. Wicca is not for everyone, but many have felt a feeling of coming home, and ascend through the Ranks to the Priesthood and deeper workings of Wicca. Many Seekers of Wiccecraft think that there is just one form of Magick, but there are many different styles and levels that are as different is as Dutch is to Spanish.

The first Principle of Magick is the **LAW OF SIMILARITY**. This sacred Law is the level of Intuitive Magick and Homeopathic side of Magick, where **"LIKE PRODUCES LIKE"**, or if something resembles or acts like something else it will have an equal effect on the other.

- The Two major Principles or Laws of Magick are; The **Law of Similarity and the Law of Contagion**.

The law of Similarity or an example of **SYMPATHETIC MAGICK** as it is also termed is the Fif-faths (Doll Magick), where the Wicce by using either a poppet, clay, wax or the like and fashions a doll as a representative image of the person they wish to influence. Depending on the skills and knowledge of the Wicce is whether this will happen or take some time. So always is Properly Prepared. Just in the preparation of the Fif-fath have many stages to perform. Firstly the creating of the Magick Circle, the LBRP, the Self Blessing Ritual, The Casting of the Magick Circle, the raising of Power, then the making of the doll as though giving birth to it, and Consecrating it, and sending it off to do your bidding or healing etc. Therefore all this Preparation for the Fif-fath will Magickally create a link between the two and with enough Will Power will take affect at the desired target, this Magickal partnership of the **LAW OF SIMILARITY.**

The **LAW OF CONTACT** usually referred to as **CONTAGIOUS MAGICK** states that objects or clothing that have been in a lot of constant contact with each other has absorbed energies and vibrations from the person, and will continue to act upon each other, even a great distances. The Magickal Astral connection can never be broken no matter what the distance. This is why when we make Fif-faths and we incorporate items that belong to the individual past or present whish are called **TAG-LOCKS** such as jewelry, hair, clothing, hand-writing, nails, skin, blood, urine, semen etc. They are all Magickally connected and will act accordingly, making your Spell more potent and effective.

- Tag-locks are items which once belonged to someone, and therefore carry their Astral and Auric essence and energy.

HOMEOPATHIC MAGICK AND CONTAGIOUS MAGICK can be ritually used individually and combined; when they are connected they act as a powerful affect. This is why Voodoo Magick has been so real and scary to many because of its powerful Magick.

Once you have been training for years and become proficient your Magick and Wiccecraft will just flow like a river, that your will power will be constant and things will just happen allowing

Magick and Karma to bring the Universal energies to you for balance. We will in time learn to be the true Wicce and bend time and space to our Will, not matter how simplistic or advanced your Ritual or Spell maybe. Your Universe will become alive and filled with Magick to work with. Let the Goddess and God always be your guiding light, and if ever you feel doubt, then do not proceed. Only continue with your Ritual when totally certain that it is for the right reasons and outcome. AN IT HARM NONE.

Work constantly with the Elements understands their energies and their life force as living entities. Know their Truth and connect with them, and they will connect with you and guide you constantly on your path of Magick and the Natural Laws of the Goddess. This will when you are ready make you a Doctor of Wiccecraft, helping others that need your help. Remember **HEAL THYSELF FIRST**, and then heal others.

Magick of Wiccecraft Questionnaire

NAME: _____

Research done? _____

Time taken: _____ Date: _____

1. What is Natural Magick? _____

2. Name something Magickal you have seen today? _____

3. What is the difference between positive and negative Magick? _____

4. What is your Element and why? _____

5. What tree are you drawn towards and why? _____

6. Have you done any Magick this week? _____

7. Have you healed a Tree this week? _____

8. When did you last walk with Nature? _____

9. Have you listened to Nature this week? _____

10. What is an Enchantment? _____

11. What is the difference between a Spell and a Prayer? _____

12. What is the Astral? _____

13. What form of Magick are you drawn towards and why? _____

14. What is the first Principle of Magick? _____

15. What is Contagion Magick? _____

16. What are Tag-locks? _____

17. What is the difference between a Wicce, Sorcerer, Warlock, Enchantress, and Wizard? _____

18. What is a Fif-fath? _____

19. What is Magick to you? _____

20. Who is the most Magickal person you have ever met and why? _____

BECOMING TRANSPARENT MEDITATION!

BECOMING TRANSPARENT... YOU ARE BEAUTIFUL... YOU ARE LIFE-FORCE ENERGY ITSELF... SEEKING TO EXPAND AND GROW... AND KNOW YOURSELF... BEGIN NOW BY SENDING YOURSELF A MOMENT OF LOVE... OF APPRECIATION... AND THANKS OF WHO YOU ARE RIGHT NOW... HOW FAR YOU HAVE COME... HOW HARD YOU ARE WORKING... HOW CLEAR YOUR INTENT IS... TO BECOME ALL THAT YOU CAN BECOME... AND BEGING NOW TO RELAX... RELAX DEEPER...

YOU MIGHT IMAGINE THAT YOU ARE AT A BEAUTIFUL MOUNTAIN LAKE... THE SUN IS CLEAR... THE LAKE IS CRYSTAL CLEAR... AND YOUR MIND IS LIKE THE MOUNTAIN LAKE... REFLECTING THE HIGHER PLANES OF REALITY... YOUR ATTENTION IS FOCUSED UPWARD RIGHT NOW... RECEIVING GUIDANCE AND ENERGY FROM THE HIGHER REALMS... AND TRANSMITTING THAT GUIDANCE CLEARLY... FOR YOU ARE LIKE A CRYSTAL... SO CLEAR... ALL THE COLOURS OF THE RAINBOW COMING THROUGH YOU... AS THE SUN IS SHINING... AND WITH YOUR INNER EYES IMAGINE THAT YOU CAN SEE YOURSELF AS ENERGY... PERHAPS YOU ARE A BALL OF LIGHT... PERHAPS YOU CAN IMAGINE LINES OF LIGHT... AS IF YOU HAD AN ILLUMINOUS CACOON OF ENERGY AROUND YOU... IT IS YOUR CONSCIOUSNESS YOU ARE SEEING... YOUR WEB OF YOUR CONSCIOUSNESS THAT WEAVES IN AND OUT OF EVERY CELL OF YOUR BODY... AROUND WHICH YOUR PHYSICAL BODY IS FORMED...

AND AS YOU SEE THIS ENERGY BODY WITH YOUR INNER EYES... AND YOU ARE AT A BEAUTIFUL MOUNTAIN LAKE... IMAGINE THAT ANOTHER BEING IS APPROACHING YOU... PERHAPS SOMEONE YOU KNOW... BUT INSTEAD OF SEEING THEM AS A PERSON... IMAGINE THAT YOU ARE ALSO SEEING THEM AS ILLUMINOIUS BEINGS OF LIGHT... LINBES OF LIGHT... AS THEY APPROACH YOU... NOTICE IN YOUR MINDS EYE THAT VARIOUS CENTRES WITHIN THEM ARE GLOWING MORE BRIGHTLY THAN OTHERS... OR PERHAPS VARIOUS

PARTS OF THEIR AURA'S ARE BRIGHTER THAN OTHERS... FOR INSTANCE FOR AN INTELLECTUAL PERSON THE AREA AROUND THEIR HEAD WILL BE QUITE LARGE... FOR A PERSON WHO IS QUITE EMOTIONAL AND STRONG WILLED THE ENERGY AROUND THEIR SOLAR PLEXUS WILL BE ENLARGED LIKE A TYRE AROUND THEM... ALSO NOTICE THAT AS THEY APPROACH YOU SOME OF THEIR ENERGY STARTS TO COME TOWARD YOU... AS IF IT WEREM MAGNETICALLY DRAWN AWAY FROM THEM... AND NOTICE THAT YOUR ENERGY IS RESPONDING... STAY WITH THIS FOR A MOMENT AND BRING YOUR ENERGY BACK INTO YOURSELF...

NOTICING THAT EVEN FINGERS OF ENERGY BEGINNING TO REACH OUT TO YOU AS YOU ARE BUILDING YOUR AURA IN SUCH A WAY THAT IS PASSES RIGHT THROUGH YOU... AND IF IT WERE AT A DIFFERENT FREQUENCY THAT THE TWO OF YOU CAN EXIST IN THE SAME SPACE... THEIR AURA'S ENERGY REACHING OUT TO YOU... BUT YOU ARE CHANGING THE FREQUENCY OF YOUR AURA SO THAT THEIR ENERGY PASSES RIGHT THROUGH... YOU ARE DOING THIS AT A PRETEND LEVEL RIGHT NOW... BUT YOU WILL FIND YOUR ABILITY TO SEE ENERGY... TO SENSE ENERGY... TO KNOW WHEN OTHER ENERGY IS AFFECTING YOU... CLEARER AND CLEARER... FOR AS PEOPLE IN YOUR DAILY LIFE APPROACH YOU PHYSICALLY YOU WILL BEGIN TO OBSERVE WITH YOUR INNER EYE ANY OF THEIR ENERGY THAT IS REACHING OUT... YOU WILL BEGIN FIRST OF ALL BY GENERATING A FIELD OF LIGHT AROUND YOURSELF... A BUBBLE OF LIGHT... SO IMAGINE NOW ONCE AGAIN... YOU ARE BACK AT THIS LAKE WITH YOUR FRIEND... THAT AS YOU'RE FIRNED APPROACHES YOU ARE BUILDING A BUBBLE OF LIGHT ALL AROUND YOU...

MAKE IT SHIMMER NOW... MAKE IT AS LARGE AS YOU WANT ABOVE YOUR HEAD AND BELOW YOUR FEET ALL THE WAY AROUND YOUR BODY... NOTICE THAT YOUR BREATHING CHANGES EVER SO LIGHTLY... AND RELAX YOUR BODY EVEN MORE... AS YOU GENERATE LIGHT ALL AROUND YOU AND RELAX YOUR BODY... YOU ARE BECOMING MORE AND MORE TRANSPARENT... FOR AS YOUR BODY IS RELAXED AND THE ENERGY IS FLOWING... ANY ENERGY FROM ANOTHER PASSES RIGHT THROUGH YOU... SO RIGHT NOW IMAGINE THAT YOUR ENERGY IS FLOWING... AND YOUR AURA IS BEAUTIFUL... THAT YOU HAVE PUT UP A BUBBLE OF LIGHT ALL AROUND YOU... THIS BUBBLE TRANSOFRMS ANY ENERGY THAT COMES THROUGH YOU... AND NOW

THIS BUBBLE OF LIGHT IS VERY CLOSE TO YOUR BODY… ABOUT 103 INCHES AWAY… UNTIL YOU'RE BODY IS OUTLINED… BY A SHIMMERING LIGHT… IMAGINE THAT WITHIN THIS LIGHT YOU ARE BEGINNING TO WITHDRAW YOUR ENERGY… PUTTING YOUR ENERGY INTO ANOTHER DIMENSION… OR FREQUENCY… ALL YOU NEED DO IS IMAGINE IT…TO MAKE IT SO… WE WOULD SUGGEST THAT YOU USE THIS EXERCISE WITH ANOTHER PERSON AS WELL… FOR YOU WILL FIND THAT THEY WILL SENSE A DIFFERENCE… BEGIN TO WITHDRAW YOUR ENERGY FROM WITHIN THIS BUBBLE AND PUT IT IN ANOTHER DIMENSION…

KEEP WITHDRAWING THIS ENERGY UNTIL THE BUBBLE OF LIGHT IS SURROUNDING A VOID… NOW SEE YOUR FIRNEDS ENERGY… PASSING RIGHT THROUGH… THERE IS NOTHING THAT IT CAN'T TOUCH… IT IS TRAVELLING RIGHT THROUGH THE SPACE THAT IS YOU… FOR YOUR CORE ENERGY…YOUR ESSENT SELF HAS CHANGED TO A SLIGHTLY DIFFERENT FREQUENCY…AND NOTICE THAT YOU CAN GENERATE LIGHT…AND ENERGY…YOU CAN MAKE YOUR BUBBLE GLOW EVEN MORE… WHAT IS HAPPENING TO YOUR FRIENDS AURA AS YOU BECOME MORE BEAUTIFUL IN YOUR FRIENDS ENERGY…

NOW LET THIS SCENE GO… IMAGINE A SCENE NOW IN YOUR DAILY LIFE… A PLACE WHERE YOU WOULD LIKE TO STAY IN YOUR CENTRE…TRANSMUTE ENERGY AROUND AND BE TRANSPARENT… IMAGINE A SCENE RIGHT NOW VERY VIVIDLY… MAKE IT SO REAL THAT YOU ARE IN IT… AS YOU ARE IN IT…IMAGINE THAT YOU CAN HEAR THE VOICES OF OTHER PEOPLE…THE SOUNDS IN THE ROOM…OR YOU CAN SEE WHAT IS GOING ON… NOW IMAGINE THAT SOMEONE IS COMING UP TO YOU…SOMEONE YOU DON'T KNOW…OR A SITUATION THAT WOULD TAKE YOU OUT OF YOUR CENTRE…

THIS TIME YOU ARE GOING TO REACT DIFFERENTLY…FIRST OF ALL YOU IMMEDIATELY RECOGNISE… WHEN ANOTHER PERSONS ENERGY IS COMING INTO YOU… WITH YOUR INNER EYES YOU ARE BEGINNING TO SENSE THEIR AURA REACHING OUT TO YOU…

THE VERY INSTANT IT DOES… YOU NOW KNOW IT… IT IS A DEEP KNOWINGNESS…IT COMES TO YOUR CONSCIOUSNESS IMMEDIATELY WHEN

ANOTHER PERSONS ENERGY IS BEGINNING TO TOCUH OR AFFECT YOURS... YOUR MIND WILL TELL YOU...YOUR INNER KNOWINGNESS WILL ALERT YOU...YOU WILL COME TO THE PRESENT MOMENT...AS YOU DO IMAGINE YOURSELF PUTTING UP A LIGHT... YOU NOW PUT UP A BUBBLE OF LIGHT... WHENEVER YOU THINK OF IT...UNTIL IT IS CONSTANTLY ABOUT YOU...ALL THE TIME...YOU PAY ATTENTION TO YOUR BREATHING AND INSTANTLY RELAX YOUR BODY...LETTING YOUR BREATHING BECOME VERY RELAXED... LETTING YOUR BREATHING BECOME YOUR BREATHING... FOR YOU MIGHT NOTICE THEIR BREATHING...THE SPEED OF THEIR VOICE...AND YOU SIMPLY LET IT GO AND STAY AT YOUR OWN SPEED AND PACE... BREATHING IN YOUR OWN CALM CENTRED WAY...

AS YOU PUT THE BUBBLE YOU BRING IT VERY CLOSE TO YOUR BODY UNTIL IT IOS TENSE AND BRIGHT...AND YOU BEGIN TO SWITCH THE FREQUENCY OF YOUR CONSCIOUSNESS...PULLING IT OUT FROM THE CENTRE OF THIS BUBBLE...STANDING SLIGHTLY ASIDE...SLIGHTLY DIFFERENT VIBRATIONS AND LETTING THE OTHER PERSONS ENERGY FALL RIGHT THROUGH YOU... FEELING RECHARGED AND REGENERATED AND WHEN THEY ARE NO LONGER REACHING OUT... OR TOUCHING YOUR ENERGY... YOU MAKE YOUR BUBBLE LARGE... THE SIZE OF THE ROOM...KEEPING IT ABOUT YOU ALL THE TIME...

YOU NOW KNOW WHEN YOU HAVE TAKEN ON ENERGY... IT COMES TO YOUR ATTENTION IMMEDIATELY... YOU GET VERY QUIET...YOU NOTICE INSTANTLY IF YOUR THOUGHTS ARE DIFFERENT... IF YOU'RE FEELINGS ARE DIFFERENT FROM YOUR NORMAL CLEAR CENTRE... YOUR OBSERVER SELF LETS YOU KNOW... AND AT THE SAME TIME PROVIDES YOU WITH A MODEL OF WHAT TO RETURN TO... YOU HAVE A FEELING A PICTURE A KNOWINGNESS... OF WHAT YOUR OWN ENERGIES LIKE... AND THE MINUTE YOU HAVE TAKEN ON ANY ENERGY...THE PICTURE OF YOUR OWN ENERGY BECOMES CLEAR... AND WITH THAT MODEL YOU BEGIN TO CREATE ONCE AGAIN... YOUR OWN CLEAR ENERGY... FOR A MOMENT NOW... JUST FOCUS ON YOUR OWN ENERGY... AT A DEEP KNOWINGNESS LEVEL... WHAT DOES YOUR ENERGY FEEL... DOES YOUR ENERGY HAVE A RHYTHM... HOW WOULD YOU EMOTIONALLY DESCRIBE YOUR ENERGY...

HOW WOULD YOU DESCRIBE THE NORMAL LEVEL OF YOUR THOUGHTS... HOW DO YOUR THOUGHTS FEEL...ARE THEY QUIET...ARE THEY FAST... ARE THEY RELAXED...

As you know yourself in higher and higher ways the centre that you return to will be more and more and more linked each time with the higher realm of the universe, and as you focus right now... on your energy... see if it has a vibration...if you are a ball of Light... how intense is the Light... how fast is it vibrating... how many colours are in it... how big it is... When you know... and you will know easily...if any of the energy you are feeling is not yours... you will come back to this model... where you are...you will instantly remind yourself of how you normally think, feel, and react... as you do that you will breath in such a way, you begin to restore a connection with yourself... you will focus on any part of your body that feels differently... for your body will always tell you where you have taken in the energy... you will notice immediately in your body, and you will begin to send Light ... YOU WILL NOW BEGING TO SEND LIGHT TO THAT PART OF YOUR BODY... WITH YOURE INNER EYES RIGHT NOW... GO THROUGH THE BODY... IS THERE ANY PLACE THAT YOU HAVE TAKEN ON ENERGY THAT YOU WOULD LIKE TO RELEASE...

BEGIN TO PUT YOUR OWN ENERGY IN THIS PLACE... FOR EVERY TIME YOU CHANGE THE PATTERN... TAKING OUT THE PATTERN THAT ANOTHER HAS PUT THERE... YOU WILL ALWAYS WANT TO FILL IT UP WITH YOUR OWN LIGHT... OTHER PEOPLES ENERGIES SIMPLY LOOK LIKE A PATTERN THAT IS NOT YOURS... SO IN YOUR MINDS EYE... IS THERE ANY PATTERN THAT IS NOT SURELY YOURS AND IF THERE IS SIMPLY IMAGINE THAT YOUR PATTERN IS STRONGER NOW UNTIL THE OTHER PATTERN IS COMPLETELY GONE... AND ALL YOUR ENERGY IS YOUR OWN BEAUTIFUL PATTERN... AND AS YOU COME BACK NOW INTO THE ROOM... YOU ARE GOING TO BE VERY AWARE OF YOUR OWN ENEEGY THROUGHOUT THE NIGHT AND DAY... HOW IT FEELS... WHAT IT IS... AND YOU WILL BE AWARE EASILY OF HOW TO BE TRANSPARENT... IF YOU WOULD LIKE TO STAY IN THIS SPACE AND WORK WITH THE ENERGY... DO SO NOW... AND IF YOU WOULD LIKE TO BRING YOURSELF BACK... DO SO SLOWLY AND GENTLY AND HAVE A WONDERFUL EVENING...

MAGICK IN
THEORY &
PRACTICE

With the study and practice of Magick, it is important that you adopt the proper mental attitude; the feeling that anything can be accomplished if one so desires and Wills that it be done. In other words you can bring forth whatever it is you wish to bring forth. In studying Magick you should for a while set aside the critical, "That can't happen because attitude". Which has been programmed inside all of us by our present technological society and by indoctrinated religions. For the time being except that Magick and all its principles are exactly what they claim to be, and in time you will see that the Magickal Arts do not contradict science but supplement it by filling in an area that science does not YET cover. Science is the Magick of the past, and Magick is the science of the future. Magick is as logically structured as modern physics and can give some reproducible results in exactly the same way. But it also requires an in-depth amount of study and training in order to get results that you need. Science and Magick overlap in one note-worthy area; this is in the field of Psychology, especially the works of Dr. Carl Jung, which will help you in your Magickal studies on the path of Wiccecraft.

The human being is the Universe in miniature, well psychically speaking, and the microcosm of the macrocosm. Man is influenced by the cosmos, and yet through us can influence the cosmos. This in harmony in the body manifests itself through sickness and anger, while harmony manifests itself through strength, health and beauty. The knowledge and understanding of the Four Elements in their proper aspects is important in keeping the body, mind and soul in its best condition. According to the most ancient Tradition of Hermes, The hermetic System, the body has four basic components:

Earth Element - feet, legs and genitalia.
Water Element - the abdomen and womb.
Fire Element - the chest, lungs and heart.
Air Element - the shoulders, neck and head.

These divisions we learn about and understand there importance in all levels of Magick, as the human body is our main Tool used in all forms of Magick. We have masculine energies that are Electric and feminine energies that are Magnetic, when these are concentrated on we can with time know how to repel or attract what we need and desire within the Physical world, this is Magick. Working with and knowledge of these forces especially with our Wiccan Tools such as a Sword, Wand, Athame. Pentacle or even a Word adds much power to the already Magickal energy, but know that these Tools only acts as a lens or a channel to focus and elevate the Wicce within. We like everything in the Universe has its own Natural Polarities, and Magick works through these. So if you are a right-handed person, you are active, masculine and electrical, whilst the left side is feminine, magnetic and passive. For a left-handed person it is the opposite.

THE POWER OF THE WILL:

For some Wicces their Will-Power needs to be worked with a lot, as you may have been programmed to not believe in certain things since being a child, but to others their Will is very strong and only needs to be fine tuned. PRACTICE. PRACTICE. PRACTICE. Make your belief as firm as a rock.

STRENGTH OF DESIRE:

Strength of Desire is always important, if you do something whole-heartedly and you know you will succeed then something triggers inside you and the process has already started, but if you doubt then you have already failed. The old saying; IF YOU WISH FOR SOMETHING HARD ENOUGH, BE CAREFUL, YOU MIGHT JUST GET IT." Whenever doing a Spell or Ritual always weigh up the balance, and ask yourself will this outcome be done naturally and in time, or does it really need a little help. You must always know when and when not to use Magick, as karma can be quite a bitch. She may not get you in this life, but get you she will!

Always understand your Elements and their Elementals, as this aids you in all your Spells and Rituals, as they are your guides both within and without. They give you a prod to move in the right positive direction (if you truly listen) or hold you back to stop you making a terrible mistake.

AIR ELEMENT - is of the east, the place of the rising sun, it is the realm of the Mind, and all things creative, it is the Astral World. The Elementals are the Sylphides, the Winged Creatures of Air. They teach you to listen and open your mind to the voices of Nature and aid you in seeing the Invisible within the Visible. When in your Circle sit a face the East and meditate on strengthening your mind and your will power. Increasing your mental ability to see clearer and awaken your creativity. Ask them to teach you also about the young masculine Power, of working with the God Force in Nature and your Magick Circle. Learn to meditate in your Circle facing the East and communing with this realm and asking for guidance, they will hear and teach you.

FIRE ELEMENT - is of the South, and the Heart, its Elementals are the **SALAMANDERS** which work within the fire of life. They work with deep emotions, such as love, hate, fear, faith etc. Salamanders are made up of the Dragon kingdom, and teach you also about masculine Power, of working with the God Force in Nature and your Magick Circle. Learn to meditate in your Circle facing the South and communing with this realm and asking for guidance, they will hear and teach you.

WATER ELEMENT - is of the West, and the Spirit, this realm is ruled the Elemental called Undines. They govern the watery realms of give and receive. They are the water maidens, Mermaids, all Magickal creatures of water. They will guide you in ways of your Psychic and Spiritual realms and guide you in learning to slow down and to take deep breaths, this realm teaches of relaxation and how to open up and receive, and also how to let go. This realm is the feminine realm of the Great Mother. Learn to meditate facing the West and communing with this realm and asking for guidance, they will hear and teach you.

EARTH ELEMENT - is of the North, where you place your shrine or Altar, here is the realm of the Physical, and the Elementals are the Gnomes, Satyrs, Picts, and the Elves. It is the feminine realm as well. And teach you also about feminine Power, of working with the Goddess Force in Nature and your Magick Circle. Learn to meditate in your Circle facing the North and communing with this realm and asking for guidance, they will hear and teach you.

1. The Astral Planes are not bound by Time or Space. Therefore two objects can exist in the same place at the same time.
2. The Astral Planes are "Plastic", and can be molded by Will and imagination.

The Hermetic Principle

The Tablets of Hermes Trismegistos (Thoth) state the maxim of Magick; "TRUE AND UTTERLY CERTAIN, THAT WHICH IS ABOVE IS LIKE THAT WHICH IS BELOW, BUT AFTER A DIFFERENT FORM, FOR THE REALISATION OF THE WHOLE." This can be interpreted that the Physical and Astral Planes are essentially the same, but only with slight differences to each other. These differences are in the plasticity of the Astral and their vibrations. The working of Magick comes under two different processes and generally both processes are used in any form of Magick and Wiccecraft. These are:

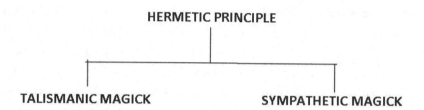

HERMETIC PRINCIPLE

TALISMANIC MAGICK   **SYMPATHETIC MAGICK**

Talismanic Magick: Since the beginning of man and Magick, we have realized that certain signs and symbols are keys or triggers to unlock the portals of Magick. These deep minded keys open a portal between the worlds so that Magick works at a high frequency, and sets its action in motion. It is similar as we have already as with the Law of Like unto like, where an abject acts in a similar way to its owner. So when we take an object that belonged to a family member or friend, even if that person has passed from this mortal world, its and his life force energies are still active and work in connecting to that person or object. That is why Psychometry is so powerful a Psychic medium in contacting parted spirits, but is it the actual spirit of the dead person or is it just the energy and vibrations of the person of when they were alive.

This is why Wicces and Magicians throughout history have connected certain colours, sigils and objects with esoteric and occult properties that associate with them in a Magickal way, such as silver of the Moon, Gold of the Sun, Lead of Saturn, etc. Talismans are therefore made of certain materials that are relevant to the need of the Spell or Ritual, and with certain symbols or sigils etched on them act as triggers and keys to open the Magick and act in accordance with what the Wicce desires. But always remember that the Will of the Wicce is of supreme importance in any operational Spell or Ritual.

As primitive humans developed their awareness, and their connections with the Universe physically and Magickally, we gradually over millennia developed ways to awaken and utilize this Magickal energy to shape to there will their environment. This concept birthed the first Religion of man, which we now called Wicca, but has always been known as Wiccecraft. Wicces have since the dawn of Man used what we term " **Folk Magick**" this was the Magick of Nature in its truest form. Although Christianity tried for not just a few years but for thousands of years to suppress our beliefs and our Ancient Religion, maybe the oldest religion known to man. Wicca has since the 1950's began a massive revival, an awakening of an ancient system of belief being needed for the 21ˢᵗ century.

When Wicca came out in the late 50's, it started a movement by slowly releasing its Craft, its set of knowledge to the world but under different labels. Magick was ancient and these ancient systems of Magick such as Channeling, Tarot, Crystals, Herbal Medicine, Meditation, Trance, Séance, Healing, Dreams, Charms, Talismans and more. Was all of Wicca, but now given to man under many new names? This was called the "Dawn of the New Age", where nothing was hidden anymore, everything was let out into the open for mankind to find and awaken within themselves their own truths. Without being told what to do, or believe under fear of retribution or pain of suffering in a Hell that was not of our creation.

This was the "Dawn of the New-Age". Which was created by Wiccans to welcome and open up magick and Wiccecraft slowly to the world. In Wicca, the application of Folk Magick is on the same level as a Wicces philosophy. It is pro-love, and pro-healing. It constitutes the bulk of ancient and modern Magickal practices performed by Wiccans and Wicces to improve their lives on all levels not just physically. Wicces carve their own future through timeless rituals and devout love of the Goddess and God.

THE SPELL:

The Spell as we have seen is the very heart of Folk Magick. By connecting with Nature on all Her levels, created Tools that can assist in the activation of Magick, a Wicces goal is to eventually be One with the Universe and all of Nature and to be in balance and Harmony both within and without. A Spell is our way of praying, but instead of asking God or Goddess to do it for us, we invoke our Higher Self and perform the Magickal Spell or prayer ourselves by utilizing what energies and knowledge we have learnt. In ancient times the Wicce knew emphatically that every Spell she did, would work, as she had absolutely no doubt. But today we have been that if we can't see it, then it is not real and tangible.

We have grown into skeptics that disbelieve everything until it hits us in the face. We have been programmed since birth to disbelieve in the kingdom of Magick. But I can tell you that you have removed this negative tarnish from your mind, the world will open up to the adventures of all that is real and reveal that Magick has always existed and always will, we just need to believe again.

Simply - Magick is the tapping into and the movement of Natural energies.

- **There is a Power in the Universe** - the Power of Life! (The Goddess) Everything in the Physical Plane is a manifestation of that Goddess Power. Magick by Wicces, is a method of releasing and/or directing that Divine Goddess Power. This personal divine power is combined with that of various objects such as herbs or crystals, which are seen as living energy sources.
- **This Power can be awakened and concentrated!** - Personal Power is awakened through music, chanting, dance, concentration or creative visualisation. Herbs or stones are alive and are roused with ritual. A Wicce will sense energy with the object, touch it in a metaphysical sense, and set it stirring.
- **Wicces are Natural beings of certain spectrums of different types of energy!** Only one type of energy exists, but the physical form in which it manifests determines its traits.
- **This Power can be fine-tuned to affect a specific Magickal result!** - The energies are narrowed down to the Spells purpose - money, love, healing, etc. This process has involved visualisation, creating images or using colour. Candles may be lit or symbols employed - Theban, Runic, Sigils.
- **This Power can be Directed or Moved; The attuned Power can be freed from its physical confines -**
- **This Power, once moved, will have an effect upon its target.** Because everything contains greater or lesser amounts of the same divine energy, everything can be affected by an introduction of similar energies.

CEREMONIAL MAGICK:

Ceremonial Magick is a contemporary system based upon ancient systems and traditions, usually more advanced and taken up not so much by Wicces but by Magicians. It is an amalgam of Sumerian, Egyptian, Indian, Judaic, and Semitic Magick. Freemasons and Theologians also contributed to its present structure (though they would not admit it). The prime goals of Ceremonial Magick are Union with Deity, or knowledge of and conversation with the Magician's Shining Ones.

A lofty Spiritual Goal, that points out the difference between Wiccan Fold and Ceremonial Magick. Some Ceremonial Magicians are organized into groups called Lodges or Orders, such as the famous Golden Dawn. Famous Magicians are Aleister Crowley, Dion Fortune, and Franz Bardon.

RELIGIOUS MAGICK:

Religious Magick and what Wiccans are famous for, as all our rites, rituals, ceremonies, spells and festivals are firstly performed in Invoking and welcoming the Goddess and God, to be present and open the Magick Circle. It is still performed today, as it was thousands of years ago in music, dance, prayer, meditation, ritual, and chants. The only difference is that we do Magick in the name of the Mother Goddess.

Wiccans use Magick to aid and assist, for personal needs not for gain. When we employ Folk Magick, we live by the Crede; "EIGHT WORDS THE WICCAN REDE FULFILL, AN IT HARM NONE, DO WHAT YOU WILL." Remember this always, and as our Lady would say;

"LOVE ART THE WAY, AND LOVE BE THE KEY,
IF THOU DOST HARM ANY, THEN THOU DOST HARM ME!"

Magickal Theory Questionnaire

NAME: _____

Research Done: _____

Time Taken: _____ Date: _____

1. What fluid is associated with the Fire Element and why? _____

2. What are the different names for Akasha? _____

3. What is Karma? _____

4. What are the Five Elements? _____

5. Where on the body does the Fire Element Govern? _____

6. What is the Astral Plane? _____

7. What are the Elementals and their Elements? _____

8. What is the Hermetic Principle? _____

9. Who is Hermes Trismegistos? _____

10. What is Talismanic Magick? _____

11. What is Sympathetic Magick? _____

12. What is a Sigil? _____

13. What is Folk Magick? _____

14. What is a Spell? _____

15. What is the Law of Contact? _____

16. Why is Will power important in Magick? _____

17. What's the difference between Ceremonial and Ritual Magick? _____

18. What kind of Magick draws you and why? _____

19. What is a Magick Kamea or Square? _____

20. What does the word Occult mean and why? _____

THE GREAT
MOTHER
GODDESS

Wiccecraft has been a word that frightens many people and is misunderstand by most. In the popular imagination, Wicces are ugly old hags riding broomsticks, or evil Satanists performing obscene rites. Modern Wicces are to be members of a kooky cult, primarily concerned with the cursing of their enemies and jabbing waxen images with pins, and lacking the depth, dignity and seriousness of the purpose of a true religion. But Wicca is a Religion a legally accepted religion, possibly the oldest religion in the world. Its origins go far back to the ancient awakenings of mankind at least 45,000 years ago. Prior to Christianity, Judaism, Buddhism, and Hinduism, which have only been in existence for 2,500 years of which has adopted, stolen and bastardized the ancient Pagan truths to create their own philosophies and mythologies. The Old Religion as we call it, takes its teachings from Mother Nature, and gains inspiration from the movements of Nature such as the Sun, Moon, Stars, Seasons, flights of birds, the slow growth of trees and the cycle of life itself.

According to Anthropologists who agree with our legends, Wiccecraft began more than 45,000 years ago, when the world was changing due to temperature drops where great sheets of ice crept slowly south of the continent. As it moved across the rich tundra life was booming and teamed with animal life, this is where small groups of hunters hunted the herds of deer and bison. They were excellent hunters with only the primitive of tools such as bow and arrows and spears. But within each clan, their was a gifted Seer, a Shaman, A Wicce a Wise woman or man who had the gift to call to the herds, where certain beasts would offer themselves up as willing sacrifices to the hunters. These Shamans were in tune with all of Nature and the very spirits that inhabited the Earth. They became the leaders and revealed to their tribes when was the right time to forage for food or when to hunt, by watching the Seasons and the Luna changes.

This Magickal insight eventually created images of a Great Mother Goddess as a birth-giver, and she who brings forth all life.

They never phrased this Magickal insight intellectually, but in sacred images of a Great Mother Goddess. She was the birth-giver, She who brings into existence all of life. These Shamans of old donned themselves with the Horn of the beasts to show their place in the clans and tribes as a powerful leader.

These great Shamans in certain parts of Europe and Britain were called the Wicce (pronounced weesh). They were always separate from the tribe, and lived apart. The women Wicces were seen as the embodiment of the Goddess. As they saw in Nature it was the female that brought forth all life. This was then formed into the veneration of female deities. In the caves of the Alps, great skulls of bears were mounted on niches, where they represented the Oracles that guided the hunters to the gaming herds.

The original Goddess of old Europe was called the "Lady of the Mammoths", which is about 45,000 years old. She was the oldest statue ever found of a Goddess figure, being carved out of ivory or stone as seen in the image below. She was revered throughout the Ukraine, Siberia, and Russia with her pregnant look to show She was the mother aspect of the Goddess. She was also honored in the West of Europe amongst the Scandinavians people, where She was pictured in ancient Rock Art in the great Caves. Famously Her image is seen all throughout Southern France, Italy, Greece and Spain. But all Her pictorials were deep in Caves away from prying eyes as if in a sacred space like a womb of the Earth.

Ancient records of the Goddess were etched in bone representing the lunar phases of the Moon and Her connection with women in particular. In many ancient cultures the Goddess is also seen embracing in Her hand either the tusks of a boar, the horns of a goat, bison, or ram, which represents the powers of the crescent Moon.

As the great Ice Age retreated many of the tribes became nomadic, as they followed the Seasons and the very food source that they needed to survive. All ancient cultures became Nomads and erected homes they could be easily taken down and moved when needed or when threatened. Some of these ancient nomadic tribes ventured across the north of Europe and crossed over Alaska to the America's, these became the Native American Indians of today. But there were some tribes and clans that remained where they made roots, traditionally by water where they turned to fishing and the gathering of shellfish and plants for food. These small camps eventually grew into large dwellings slowly over the generations they grew into large villages.

Whilst the men hunted, the women became the gatherers, and created their hearths and homes, they learn to eventually breed and keep livestock for their uses such as sheep, goats, pigs, cattle and even some birds were kept in cages for food. They realized that if they gathered at the right time of the year, they could also collect the seeds from edible grains and plants, and so began the first agricultural fields. The wild and untamed eventually became tame and from the fields came the first Agricultural Goddess of the grains and food of corn, rice, wheat, barley, and oats and much more in time. They Wicces and Shamans of the villages watched carefully the changing Seasons and taught them when to sow and when to harvest. Eventually other tribes and villages learned of these marvels and joined with them, slowly the clans turned into tribes, then into villages, then small towns into large cities.

Man saw in these gifts the promise from the Great Mother Goddess and She became so revered throughout all the lands as the Bestower and giver of life because of Her bounties from the wild Earth. Shrines were created in dedication and thanks to the Great Mother, in grottos and caves, which grew in the most elaborate of Temples the world has never seen. The Goddess was so varied and was pictured in all stages of feminine life, especially as the Mother, full and bold. She eventually gave birth to a Divine child, the Light of the World as a protector and guardian for Her human children.

These ancient Shamans and Wicces would venture out from their villages and travel far and wide teaching and learning from each other. As they walked to each other the Wicces had discovered that the Earth was covered with power lines where energy flowed throughout the Earth giving power in certain places where these grids crossed over. The Wicces traced out these power lines, these "Ley-Lines" and where these great lines crossed, they built and erected shrines and Temples, for all to come and worship.

The great Stones Circles were their handiwork these were the first physical Magick Circles that were places of time and space. They resonated with the Earthly Ley Lines and the electro-magnetic power energies that they created. Many people took pilgrimages to these sacred places to witness and be closer to the changes and sacred times of the Seasons and allotted to them were 8 yearly Sabbats. That showed and taught man the Magick of change and how it was in everything, and revered as the greatest lesson in life. These Seasonal rounds were times of great power and varied to the Season.

These ancient Stone Circles became places of great power and at certain times of the year also became Magickal Portals or Gateways to other worlds both visible and invisible. Ancient Wicces and bare foot Priestesses of the first religion could open all their senses and delve deeper into the Mysteries of the Earth Mother. From these sacred spaces of learned and knowledgeable Wicces came the first schools of Religion, Nature, Mathematics, Astronomy, Poetry, Music, Medicine, and the deeper understanding of Magick of the Cosmos.

These beautiful sacred places were Matriarchal and honoring the feminine in all life, especially the many diverse aspects of the Great Goddess.

But elsewhere in our world Patriarchal communities had started developing that devoted their time and energy to possessions and the knowledge is that strength is power, and so began the long line of wars, to take what others had, and to conquer everything they came in contact with. Invasions grew from just small bands of warriors fighting each other to the greatest wars known to man. War became away to get whatever you wanted, the weaker always lost and the more powerful and trained in the Arts of War, the better the win and the greater the treasures that were taken.

From these small communities of Patriarchy, large cities grew with a new line of deity, this time they were Gods of War and Conquest. These Gods became powerful and as they reached the far expanses of the world, the gentler Matriarchal races were conquered or destroyed. These warring peoples changed the history of the world from a world of love and compassion to a world of might is right. They drove the people of the Goddess from their lands, and they escaped far and wide to remote places where they could hide and stay alive. These were known as the Fae, the Faery Folk of the Goddess. The Picts or Pixies, these were the Sacred people of Elphane (Elfland). But history tells us that they were called the Samethoi, the first people of the Blessed Isles.

The Old Religion, which existed for over 50,000, was nearly extinct but in some places to conquer the people, they married the Goddesses of the Old Matriarchal Religion to the Gods and their Pantheons of the New Patriarchal Religion. Even the Celts and Druids followed by incorporating their ways into their beliefs as well. The Fae of Elphane lived their lives away from the new societies and kept secret as long as they could. They used their Magick to shield them and hide them from sight. They continued to grow their crops and fields, breed their livestock and live simply by staying in touch with the rounds of the Earth. Gradually over time laughter and singing returned and they lived as though they were free, but always in the back of their minds they knew that one day danger would find them, so they had to be prepared and preserve their ancient Mysteries. From here the first Covens were formed to teach the young and all who asked of the ways of Magick. The lead Wicce was their Clan Mother, Wicce Queen, and the Queen of Elphane.

There was much intermingling and even intermarriage between some invaders and the Faerie Folk, so even today some out there may have the ancient blood of the Fae running through their veins. This is what we believe to the bloodline of the Fae, and now many royal families of the Earth have this ancient bloodline coursing through their very bodies.

Through times belief has changed and with it its Magick, we who have reassembled the Old Religion of the Mother Goddess still hold the basic idea of the knowledge and truth of the ancient past, but have incorporated this truth with the changes and knowledge of the 21st century. We need the Goddess and what She brings more today than we ever have, we need to feel the same with Her tolerance, understanding, acceptance, compassion, true communication, gentleness, kindness and love filled with courage to take mankind from the brink of war to the brink of entering a new Golden Age of the balance and harmony, with the Goddess as the principle aspect of all Faith, it is the Mother we need now, not the Father. But we must have both for balance to truly exist in harmony.

THE GREAT MOTHER GODDESS QUESTIONNAIRE

Name: _____

Research Used: _____

Time taken: _____ Date: _____

1. Who is the Goddess? _____

2. What is the Goddess? _____

3. What is the oldest known statue of the Goddess discovered? _____

4. Name as many Goddesses as you can? _____

5. What is the Charge of the Goddess? _____

6. Is the Church of Wicca Matriarchal or Patriarchal? _____

7. Who is the Queen of the Wicces and why? _____

8. Who is the representative of the Goddess? _____

9. Who is the Lady of the Unconscious? _____

10. When is the Descent of the Goddess enacted and why? _____

11. What id Annwyn? _____

12. What is the name of the Light? _____

13. What's the difference between Wiccecraft and Sorcery? _____

14. Who is the Dread Lord of Shadows? _____

15. What is the Necklace of Stars? _____

16. What is the Triune of the Goddess? _____

17. What are the three phases of the Moon? _____

18. What is the difference between an Esbat and a Sabbat? _____

19. What is Wicce money called? _____

20. Which Goddess draws you and why? _____

MAGICK OF
COLOUR

Colour has an intense energy that radiates powerful influences on humans, especially our psyche and emotions. Are emotions are sometimes triggered by certain colours, and becomes and integral part of our own innate creativity and self-expression. Colours gives life to our homes, our hearts, and when we wear certain colours it elevates our feelings and emotions so that we either feel more attractive, sexy, business like, or strong. In Magick Colour also takes on a very important role as it also triggers not only our inner emotions and Psyche but also raises and elevates the Psychic energies on an Astral level in Magick. So in connecting deeper to these Magickal colours we must understand their deeper meaning and what vibrations they relay to our psyche.

The Sun and emitted source of solar light is the source of all colour. As white Light has within its spectrum all of all the colours, but is not actually a colour within itself but a carrier of colour. By the power of the source and its certain energy, it also activates the energy frequency of all colours, which vibrate at certain frequencies to omit the Magickal vibration, which we use in our Rituals and Spells.

Red - The most powerful colour is of energy, power, strength and expansion, it resonates a high sexual vibration as well, is a creative force that gives life to its colour. But on the flip side in its negative mode it represents anger, destruction, pain, war, and hate. It is the colour of survival, self-pleasure and very much lust. It associated with the Fire Element and the ancient Primordial Earth, Pachamama - the first Earth Mother followed by Gaia.

Pink - When you mix the power of red with the softness of white it reflects the gentler side of red. It softens sexual and survival instincts to more a sensitive and sensuous nature to protect and care. It resonates Love more than Sex or Lust; it is about sensuality and the desire to give to others emotionally. It is the Heart Chakra. All relationships that are built on the foundation of Pink are far superior and last more than those built of Red.

Orange - Again we use Red and combine its power with Yellow to create this colour of Fertility and Change. Yellow is mental where Red is physical. This colour radiates rationale and assertiveness, self worth when in a positive mode, but when in its negative mode it is about survival and logic. But foremost about Fertility is the creation of something new.

Gold - Resonates with yellow but is of a Higher Vibration, it resonates Joy, happiness, laughter, and good Cheer. Gold is a gentle masculine force that is about Communication of truth and love to others. It is the higher essence of creativity sharing its beauty, colour and artistry with warmth and unconditional love to the world. It is the colour of Perfection combined with the vibration of Wisdom. This colour is attuned to the Yellow of the Chakra the Solar Plexus.

Yellow - Is of the high intellect of the mind, very analytical, full of knowledge and a must to learn, quite logical and must always have a sense of learning or boredom will set in. Yellow is of the outer Sun and the Internal Sun, the Solar Plexus; the colour Yellow encourages rational thinking and logic. Yellow is magnetic and attracts and sends out vibrations of desire. It is associated with the magnetic ability to receive, and also to send out telepathic responses. This is the colour of the true teacher, the Mentor, as they are always the student first, then the teacher.

Green - The beautiful colour of life and Nature, it is the power of being restful, and regenerative, but also is about calmness and the ability to take your time and replenish your energy reserves. It is a soft, and cool colour that is associated with the feminine aspect of life, and teaches trust and love, knowing that as you give so shall you also be given. This means not only with others but also more importantly with self-love. Too much Green creates vanity and conceit and lack of consideration towards others. But Green is the radiance of life and love combine and is the bridge between the two. It like Red are associated with the Heart Chakra but on a higher frequency and represents Spiritual and Divine Love.

Brown - Where represents the surface and energy of the life of the Earth, Brown is the deeper vibration of the Earth, the very Soul, it is the primordial Nature and the need for continued life. All life starts in Green and at the end of life ends in Brown, the cycle is complete with its re-absorption. Brown is about stability of home life and material wealth. Too much Brown and you are filled with greed, to little, and you lose the zest for life. It is at the Base of your Chakras and is the Root or base Chakra.

THE PERSONALITY OF COLOUR

Colour as we have seen is an integral part of not only our lives, but we need colour to show individuality and know what its vibrations portray. In Wiccecraft Colours enhances our Rituals and Spells and make it less hard and simpler. If everything is in sync with each other they will act on their own just with a little Magickal intervention from us. Let your Ritual or Spell speak for itself, as each will act upon each other making the vibration clearer and more Powerful.

Each colour vibration also has a numerical vibration, which is in balance with each other. Numerology is a science of Magick and like Colour can determine your life and actions and events. By adding and using your alphabet, in sync with the numbers sets off a colour rainbow vibration that we can use in every day life and in Magick. Here is a Personality Chart that will give you your Magickal Personality number and colour, which is your *"Soul Number"* or *"Wicce Number"*.

LETTERS	NUMBERS	COLOURS
AJS	1	RED
BKT	2	ORANGE
CLU	3	YELLOW
DMV	4	GREEN
ENW	5	BLUE
FOX	6	INDIGO
GPY	7	VIOLET
HQZ	8	PINK
IR	9	GOLD

EXAMPLE: TAMARA

NAME:	T		A	M	A	R	A
NUMBER:	2		1	4	1	9	1

COLOUR: Orange   Red   Green   Red   Gold   Red

Total Number 18 – when broken down to a single digit is 9. 1 + 8 = 9

THE COLOUR OF PERSONAL EXPRESSION

Red: The Leader. With power, creative, leader, sexual and master of they're destiny. Stand securely and firmly on the ground full of ambition and creativity. Red people hate to follow; they need to be leaders, as they get frustrated and confused easily. Red people live their lives to the fullest with aggression, sometimes to the detriment of their own lives.

Orange: The Listener, gentle natured, peacemaker, with plenty of energy and interest to be challenging, they love to organize and always persuasive. They love the quiet and calm, and seek peace and harmony. Balance is their key tendency of searching their Truth. But can be demanding.

Yellow: The Dreamer, who is thoughtful, creative, and intelligent and loves to move forward, Yellows truth is in the future; they live little in the past or present and usually miss opportunities. They constantly are building castles in the sky, and need to be grounded often. Although they are Intellectual and love to be the centre of attention with a large array of friends, they at many times prefer to be alone.

Green: The Nature Lover. A Lover of Life, Earthy, understanding, tolerant, peaceful, and accepting, seeking truth for their own well-being. They love to create and achieve in a positive way, through honesty. But sometimes get caught up in their personal ideas and views. They need to nurture, reflect, connect and nourish.

Blue: The Psychic. A spiritual person, reliable and dependable, but has a free spirit. They seek Truth on all levels and build their lives based on devotion, trust, loyalty and a deep connection with the Environment. Blue can be an activist for the preservation of species, planet, and seeks knowledge and skills to help the Natural Earth.

Indigo: The Philosopher, The Priest or Priestess who is a Spiritual leader, and lover. Indigo sees beauty in all things, always strong in their positivity to understand and accept others. Indigo believes in unconditional love, for without this emotion there is no purpose in their life. Good at solving problems but sometimes loses concentration and gets off track. Needs to be away from turbulence and negative people. As they absorb this negative energy and can lose sight.

Violet: The Spiritual Teacher. Has deep perception and understand of Spirit. Violet needs to know WHY in everything, and in everything do they question. They are the true Occultist to searches the closed off areas restricted from lay people. They yearn for tranquility in their Environment. They are the Lucifuge, The Light Bearer who brings the gift of Spirit and the Goddess to man. Violet does need to be grounded so they do not become too Heavenly and ignore their own physicality. If this happens they have flights of fantasy and will not find their Truth.

Pink: The Lover. Pink is the true friend, and is usually friends to everyone; they connect with reality especially in Nature and have few illusions, as they always understand material life. Pink are able to judge fairly and be arbitrator between people, as they can always see both sides truthfully. Pink loves to succeed and achieve their dreams especially for their family, as they are the Provider.

Gold: The Hope of the World. This masculine colour denotes intellect, gentle energy, god force, especially Universal hope and love to the world. They love to be the centre of positive attention, always spreading laughter and joy and are a ray of sunshine. Gold find it hard to live up to others ideals, and sometime needs to aware of depression, as they become disappointed within themselves if they fail their families.

COLOUR IN
CANDLE
MAGICK

Working With Candles

The first step in Candle Magick is to choose a candle by selecting a colour and shape, which represents your Magickal purpose and desire. Next you will have to anoint the candle this is done by wiping the entire candle with specific Magickal Consecration Oil. The oil is usually made of some plant or flower, which also represents your desire. Place some oil on your fingertips. As you concentrate on your desire, rub the oil into your candle, starting from the centre and rubbing upward. Then rub the oil from the centre downward. Be sure to cover the entire candle with the oil, even the wick, as doing this infuses it with your desire, or rhyming spell.

When you are planning a Magick Candle Spell, try to keep all your symbolism or vibrations the same. For example: if you were doing a love Spell, you would want to use a green candle and love drawing oil, like rose, lavender or Venus Oil. For a peaceful home, use blue candle and Tranquility oil, I would even burn matching incense. The whole idea is to keep your colours, objects, and thoughts similar in meaning and symbology. By doing this, your energy is focused for a maximum positive end result.

- *REMEMBER CANDLE MAGICK IS SIMPLE, IT IS ONE OF THE EASIEST AND SIMPLEST MAGICKAL RITUALS YOU CAN DO. ALWAYS REMEMBER MAGICK IS LIKE A DOUBLE EDGED SWORD; AS IN ALL MAGICK USED, IF IT IS USED FOR THE WRONG REASON, IT COULD AND WILL REBOUND THREEFOLD! SO ALWAYS DO YOUR SPELL WITH A FULL HONEST HEART AND NOT FOR WRONG REASONS.*

COLOUR DAY	DAY	ZODIAC	ANGEL	PLANET	TIME	MEANING
Red	Tuesday	Aries	Samael	Mars	1 hour	Power, strength, lust, courage, action, protects from Fire
Pink	Friday	Libra	Anael	Venus	1 hour	Love, calming, friendship, heart opener, beauty, peace, the Arts.
Orange	Sunday	Leo	Michael	Sun	2 hours	Career, action, sales finance, healing, attraction, results
Yellow	Wednesday	Gemini	Raphael	Mercury	3 hours	Intellect, healing, communication, selling oneself, writing, persuasion.
Green	Friday	Taurus	Anael	Venus	4 hours	Love, fertility, luck, health, money, Art and music, creativity, goals.
Blue	Friday	Libra	Anael	Venus	3 hours	Creativity perception, beauty, peace, tranquillity, harmony, the Arts.
Indigo	Thursday	Sagittarius	Sachiel	Jupiter	2 hours	Psychic powers, **self-awareness, Wisdom, prestige, awareness, truth.**

Violet	Tuesday	Pisces	Asariel	Neptune	1 hour	Ambition, **spiritual development**, Ocean connection, power, secret life.
Silver	Monday	Cancer	Gabriel	Moon	3 hours	One with the Moon Goddess, love, Magick, female empowerment, Insight, clairvoyance
Gold	Sunday	Scorpio	Azrael	Pluto	1 hour	One with he Horned God, nature, Wealth, prosperity, mining, death.
White	All Days	Aquarius	Gabriel	Saturn	1 hour	Protection, secrets, karma, occult knowledge, dissolve negativity, property.
Brown	Monday	Virgo	Raphael	Mercury	4 hours	Stability, Earth energy, indecision, Grounding, healing the Earth.

CANDLE MAGICK HINTS

- If you can make your own candles. While the wax is in a liquid form add a corresponding oil, herb or flower, even colour. For example, if you are doing a money spell you could add Heliotrope Oil and mint leaves, green dye.
- When anointing a candle, close your eyes and concentrate, visualize, see in your minds eye, what the candle represents. Anoint with your fingers from the centre of the candle upwards and downwards, removing all negative energies, and then from the outside of the candle to the centre, bringing in positivity.
- Always allow the burning time of the candle to complete its time as shown in the graph.
- Read and know your Spell or Ritual, rehearsal makes perfect. Know your Spell.
- Don't forget to make your ritual check list "PROPERLY PREPARED YOU SHOULD ALWAYS BE."
- But remember the law of threefold return! Only do the ritual or Spell if you are 100% sure!

DEVELOPING:

1. Make sure to always keep records in your book, write down the preparation, the tools, the time and date, your emotions, phase of the Moon, even the successes or failures, as this is how you learn.
2. You must always be comfortable, with loose clothing or robe and a relaxed meditative body. Know your Spell, this will make you more sure and comfortable.
3. Have a total fast at least 3 hours prior to your ritual or Spell.
4. Meditation first prior to your ritual and Spell.
5. You are now ready to enter your Magick Circle, so acknowledge the Goddess always, and call to the Elements and the Elements to guide you and assist when necessary.

Magick of Colour Questionnaire

Name: _____

Research used: _____

Time taken: _____ Date: _____

1. Give as many meanings of the colour of red as you can? _____

2. What are the colours of the rainbow from bottom to top in order? _____

3. Explain the colours black and white? _____

4. What is your favourite colour and why? _____

5. What is the main colour in your home and why? _____

6. Which of the colours is the carrier of all other colours and why? _____

7. What are the cool feminine colours and why? _____

8. What are the warm masculine colours and why? _____

9. What colours match up to what Chakra's? _____

10. What is your personality number and colour? _____

11. What is the main colour of your underwear? _____

12. What colour cars attract you and why? _____

13. What is the first important thing to do in Candle Magick and why? _____

14. What is the colour of stability and grounding and why? _____

15. Have you done a Candle Spell? Explain _____

16. What do you do with leftover wax etc.? _____

17. What are the colours for Altars Candles and why? _____

18. What colour did you notice in nature the most this week? _____

19. What is Magick and why is colour important? _____

20. What colour do you dislike more than the others and why? _____

THE 21
FESTIVALS
OF WICCA

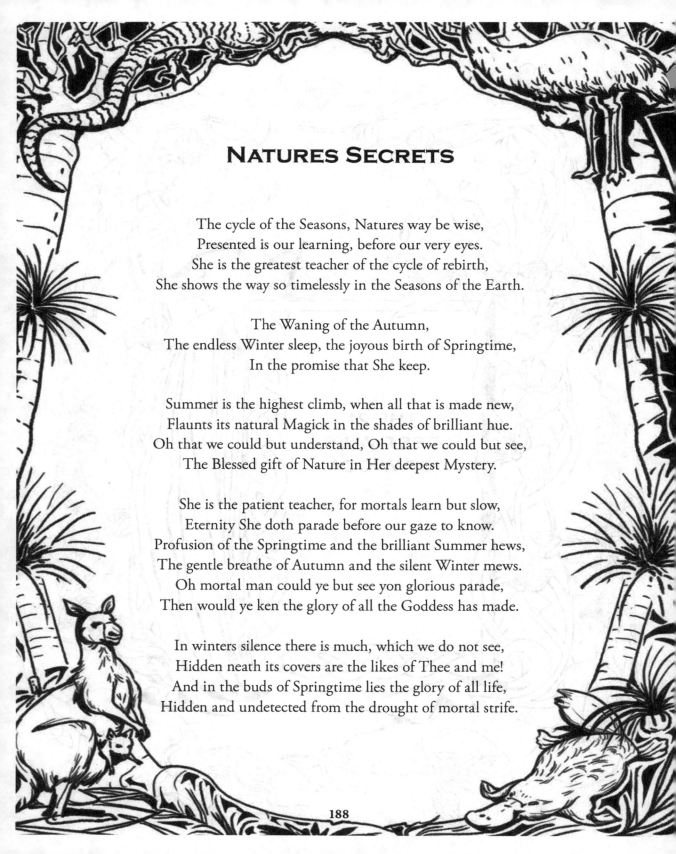

NATURES SECRETS

The cycle of the Seasons, Natures way be wise,
Presented is our learning, before our very eyes.
She is the greatest teacher of the cycle of rebirth,
She shows the way so timelessly in the Seasons of the Earth.

The Waning of the Autumn,
The endless Winter sleep, the joyous birth of Springtime,
In the promise that She keep.

Summer is the highest climb, when all that is made new,
Flaunts its natural Magick in the shades of brilliant hue.
Oh that we could but understand, Oh that we could but see,
The Blessed gift of Nature in Her deepest Mystery.

She is the patient teacher, for mortals learn but slow,
Eternity She doth parade before our gaze to know.
Profusion of the Springtime and the brilliant Summer hews,
The gentle breathe of Autumn and the silent Winter mews.
Oh mortal man could ye but see yon glorious parade,
Then would ye ken the glory of all the Goddess has made.

In winters silence there is much, which we do not see,
Hidden neath its covers are the likes of Thee and me!
And in the buds of Springtime lies the glory of all life,
Hidden and undetected from the drought of mortal strife.

In Summer do we show ourselves before the eyes of man?
But mortal men beware! beware! Ye do not understand!
For we are Natures Creatures, of us ye doth no naught,
　　Elusive as the Shadows that forever is not caught.

Canst thou see oh mortal man ye be the cause of grief,
For Nature is our Mother, and mortal man Her thief.
Destruction rendered by thy hand, oh man ye dost not know,
Thy ignorance is splendid and grandly doth it show.
For we yet be the Faerie Folk, we be beyond thy ken,
And ere ye walk thy wisdom, ye must first walk the world of men!

THE 21 FESTIVALS

"Let them that know look to the skies and to the Earth, for they are the measure of a man and a woman. Let them that know the changing Seasons, be wise in the Mysteries of their own True Being, for that which is without and can be seen, is also that which is within and is invisible."
From t he Emerald Tablets of Thoth

It is strange to think that sensible people still dance naked under the stars at these festivals as they did thousands of years ago, to have the same mentality means that we are either completely off our rockers, or something deep within is calling us back to that very essence that connected our ancestors. Mans barriers have removed us from Nature, as Nature has removed Herself from us. But Nature and all She has to offer is our divine right and our heritage to awaken and share with all other species of our planet. Ignorance, fear, and greed have removed us from our Earth and its very Nature. We now live in concrete jungles with false light, false heat, and trinkets and possessions that we would die for.

The more advanced and technological that we become the less we make time for Nature and what is offers us. We would rather sit at home watching TV, playing games, and being on our phones than connecting with the real world, Nature. Man use to survive only by being connected to Nature and its Seasons, and we have forgotten to know is really out there. We are in the midst of a world revolution, where we are taking over the world with our parasitic hunger, by destroying everything that is in our way, even if it is good for us, we don't seem to care. We seem to think all is ok, but in truth we are destroying our home, the only one we have. Our lives use to depend on Nature, and guess what they still do.

We need to reconnect with the very Earth itself, and get out into our gardens and get dirty, feel the Earth between our fingers, and feel what it is like to take care of the Earth as She has cared for us. We need to reconnect NOW.

As Sir Robert Graves says in "The White Goddess", there are vast numbers of people whose only awareness of the Seasons is by the weight of their underwear, and the size of their electricity bills'. Inside all of us we must realise that something is WRONG; and it is our fault, our ignorance, we cannot escape from our ancient origins, and most people admit to a yearning to return to a more Natural way of life, however vague their ideas are on how this can be done. As Wordsworth said: "One impulse from a Vernal wood, may teach you more of man, of moral evil and of good, than all the Sages can."

I find it hard to believe that we can ever return back to Nature having the simple life of being truly One with the earth like our ancestors did. But I do believe we should make a bloody good try, by maintaining our lives and our small world like our gardens, then our streets, then towns. We can start small and with like-minded people advance to care for this our world before it is too late. The Wicces Festivals celebrate the different times of how we connect and work with Nature to make this a better world. All our festivals stem from our ancient calendars revolving around the times of the Seasons and their mid way cycles. But just as importantly is that the Moon and its very lunation's measure our times, years, months and days, and even our hours. All a Wicces power ceremonies are either on or before each and every New Moon and Full Moon.

Each lunation of the Moon is called a Month, or 28 days, which are still called "Common Law Months". If you look at the 28-day month, and seven-day week (4 x 7 = 28) is just a unit of the Common law Month. If we go a step further we can see that 28 is exactly dividable into the 364 daily year.

Robin Hood, who lived in the time of Edward III, exclaimed in a ballad celebrating May day, where he sang; "How many merry months there be in a year, there be thirteen, say I."

Throughout the ancient world man was aware that most of their Goddesses and God were personifications of Nature. E.g. the Corn Goddess Ceres still lends Her name to our breakfast " Cere-als". Eostre, the Teutonic Goddess of Spring and Birth lends her name to the female hormone "Eostre-gen", and then later being bastardized by the Christian faith into Easter. Man always watched and learned from Nature and it was understandable that they would deify certain important aspects of Nature giving it a Goddess or God aspect. All of ancient life and even our agricultural life of today is closely associated with the Seasons and their very important phases of the times to plant the seed, (impregnate) fertilize the crops (birth), Grow the seed into plants and trees for food (life), know when to harvest the crops (death), take from the first of harvest new seed (rebirth). This is the very cycle that Wicces are guided by and learn by. It is the very foundation of all our belief system.

If we were to lie, in the very centre of our Magick Circle (representing the 360 degree's of the Magick Circle) when lying in Pentagram position (we add 5 extra points). This then symbolically makes us One with Nature and the Circle of Life, the 365 days of the year. This is known as the Secrets of the Wicce and called The Epagomenes, The true secret of Immortality.

If we go a little further with our mathematics, the human body has 21 extended parts of the body, (10 toes and 10 fingers and the head) this totals and represents also our 21 Power days or festivals of the Wicces year. 8 are Patrifocal and are the Festivals of Nature, the Seasons and the cross-quarter days called Sabbats, which honor the masculine side of Nature - The Horned God, and 13 Full Moons called the Esbats, honoring the female side of Nature - The Goddess.

The **Esbats**, being of more importance to the Wicce, where a ritual of dedication and power are just prior to the peak of the Full Moon when our Goddess is at the strongest and most powerful phase. This is where the High priestess as the Representative of the Goddess on the Earth stands within the Magick Circle as the Clan Mother of Her people. At this time all main rituals and Spells are performed where the energies of Moon are invoked and used in the Magick Circle. But we must not forget that the New Moon is the first stage of the growing Full Moon, which is approximately 2 weeks before, is just as important. It is where we can start all our Ritual that is to be completed at the Full Moon.

The 8 Sabbats of Solar Festivals are celebration more than working power nights of the Full Moon. The Sabbats are to take time to thank that time of the year and our Horned God for all that He has bestowed upon us, and to celebrate the joyous times of giving and receiving from the Earth. We light great Balefires in the centre of our Magick Circle to representing the return of Light and Light and usually call back the rebirth of all life that has passed.

The two most powerful and important Sabbats Beltane (bel-tana) which is held November Eve, in the Southern hemisphere (May Eve in the Northern hemisphere). Beltane celebrates the birth of Summer and the time when the Earth gives up Her bounty, this is why we have great fires called Balefires, to Magickally bring back the Sun. Wiccans watch for the rising Sun the next morning to witness the Birth of the Sun, and the beginning of a new Season.

In the Southern hemisphere we celebrate November Day instead of May Day, and bring out the Maypole for fertility dances and sing with the whole family being involved.

May Eve – Samhain: (sow-ween) the Samethoi Lord of Death and Lost Spirits were called "Saman, Samana, Shamhain or Samhain. From this word we also take the name Shaman. His holiday was called "The Vigil of Saman" or "Samhain" This ancient God was shown as a ghostly skeleton holding a sickle in His hand, remind you of anyone else? He later came to be known as "The Grim Reaper" or "Death".

The Samethoi considered May/November 1st as being the Day of Death, who's Festival, fell on May 1st, May Day. Because the days are getting shorter, and the nights longer, the cold air takes hold and the beginning of Winter slowly creeps in. On this sacred night our Wicces New Years Eve, we invite all those that have passed in the previous year to come and join with us and make merry once more.

Samethoi Priests and Priestesses led the people in huge processional ceremonies with hundreds of people joining in celebration of a good year for harvest and to see our families and friends once more in revelry. To This day some "All Hallows Day" also calls it. "Hallowe'en" "Hallows Eve" and later it was adopted by the Christians (as all our Celebrations were) and called "All Saints Day". Jack-O-Lanterns were named for a man called Jack, who could not enter Heaven or Hell. As a result he was doomed to wander in darkness with his lantern until Judgment Day. He acted on behalf of the God Samhain. If you had lighted Jack-O-Lanterns in your window, Death would pass you by.

So May Eve is the opposite of Beltane as it is celebrating the Dying Sun seeking the Gateway to the Otherworld (Annwyn), to some it is a time of sadness, but to those of the Wicca, Samhain is the time when the doors of Annwyn, the Underworld are open for Wiccans and they can communicate with their ancestors for whom they look for guidance. Samhain is symbolically of the Death of God, and recognizes the inevitable outcome of life.

To these two Major Sabbats, two more are added, which are also the Cross-Quarter days; Lughnasadh (loo-na-sah) on February 1st in the Southern Hemisphere (August 1st Northern Hemisphere) Lughnasadh is our Thanksgiving and gives thanks for the Bounty of the Earth of the Summer that has been shared with us. It is the ancient Gaelic Fire Festival of the Horned God Lugh, and being at the beginning of the harvest where the Horned God is weakened by age when the first grains and fruits are cut. He is ritually sacrificed and scattered throughout the fields and orchards so that He and the new crops will be more bountiful than before. The first grains are made in a "Bread Dolly" which represents the Horned God, and sacrificed and broken into many pieces which all shares and the remainder given to the fields.

Imbolg: (eem-bolc), which means Lambs Milk. Is the other Major Festival and celebrated on the 1st August in the Southern Hemisphere (February 1st in the Northern Hemisphere). This is the sacred Feast of Conception, when the first signs of Winter warming with the energies of the birthing Sun, shows man that it is nearly time to prepare for tilling the Earth and the planting of seed and grain for the next seasonal crops. Time to feed the livestock and take them out into the pastures for exercise and feeding. Imbolg is the Festival of post-natal recovery, especially the recovery of the Earth Mother, our Goddess. Balefires are lit to welcome back the return of the Sun and its warmth to the cold wet Earth.

These Four major Sabbats are the Four Major power days of the Wiccan calendar, but there are four more which are called the Lesser Sabbats, they are the Seasonal Festivals and point out the very height of their Season, where the Major festivals are Gateways between the Seasons, where they change from one to another.

The first is **Mid-Winter Solstice (Yule),** also called Yule which is held on June 22nd in the Southern Hemisphere (December 22nd in the Northern hemisphere) which is the shortest day of the year and the longest and darkest night. It is at this time when the promise of the Mabon calling the birth of the Sun God comes again through the Love of the Mother Goddess. It is the very height of Winter and the coldest time of the year.

The Spring Equinox - (Equinox-meaning equal hours of day and night). September 21st in the Southern Hemisphere, (21st March in the Northern Hemisphere). Ostara or Eostre day marks the first day of Spring when the beautiful warrior God reaches His prime. It is the rebirth of life in nature, the Awakening of the Earth and all life bringing the gifts of the Great Mother in its Fertility. Wiccans absolutely love this time when the earth smiles with her colorful flowers, and the birth of animals frolicking in the fields. It is where we decorate the Sacred Symbol of Spring - The Eostre Egg (which has also been adopted by the Christians) and we hide them to give the finder fertility and a fruitful year ahead.

The Summer Solstice - Celebrated December 22nd—the 25th in the Southern Hemisphere, (June 22nd - 25th in the Northern Hemisphere). Solstice means (standing still or Sun Still), it is the longest day of the year and the shortest night. Summer Solstice is when all Solar and Earth Natural Powers are at their peak. It is a time when some may wish to dance under the stars skyclad (being dressed by the stars). It supposes to be the hottest time of the year but here in Australia our hottest time is a couple of months later, usually around February.

The Autumn Equinox - is the Mabon celebrated on the 21st March in the Southern Hemisphere (September 21st in the Northern hemisphere). Again Equinox - equal days and nights. This is where the young Horned God offers up his life for His people and His children, he prepares to be returned back to the Earth so that he may be born again in a younger and more virile body.

The Wiccan Year calls this our Eight Spoked Wheel of Death, Birth, Life, Initiation, Love, Fertility, then Death and Rebirth. In Wicca, the Initiated Wicce see that there are two types of Death - The Death of the body is the lesser as it frees the Spirit, and the Death of Initiation binds it. When Wicces are Initiated they are bound by cords to Bind them, they are the Bonds that keep us tied to the World of Man and keep our Spirit in Annwyn (the Underworld) until such a time (when knowledge and wisdom permits), they will sever the Bonds with the Magickal Sword of Endeavour (TRUTH) and correct their Light. They will ascend from the Annwyn and victoriously emerge back into the world of Abred (world of man).

In our Mysteries we see that the Goddess each year lives thirteenfold and the Horned God eightfold. The Goddess is Alive and Magick is all around us.

As you enter my home above the door is a sign that says:

"IF I AM INDEED WISE I DO NOT BID YOU ENTER THE HOUSE OF MY WISDOM, BUT RATHER LEAD YOU TO THE THRESHOLD OF YOUR OWN MIND".

Listen to your own inner Truth, and awaken your Soul, your Wicce within. Kill off the outdated conceptions that have been bred and brainwashed into all of your life if it is truly Wisdom you seek. Know that you cannot understand a Masculine God without a Feminine Goddess as total balance and harmony. You cannot understand Death without Life; or man without woman: light without dark, negative without positive. He who denies this is a Fool.

In Scotland interestingly, most of the Midsummer Fires have vanished, but there is one place where the custom persisted until the middle of the 20th century and may not be gone forever even yet. This is Durris in Kincardineshire, where in the 18th Century, Alexander Hogg tended cattle in his youth and every year helped to prepare the Midsummer Balefire for his Lord. When he died in England, a wealthy merchant, he left his money for the continuance of the Bale Festival in his old parish stipulating that there should be a great fire on Cairnshee, the material for which had to be a collected by the herd-boys of the nearby farms. Each boy received a silver sixpence and in the latter years of the custom, the youngest "among" him had the privilege of lighting the fire. While it burnt, the people danced around it, to the music of pipes. This ceremony has not been held since 1945 and no one knows when or if it will be revived. Due to the running out of funds, this annual ceremony has ceased, but hopefully the locals and more can restart this ancient tradition and bring back the sacred Bale Fires of the Summer Solstice.

AUSTRALIAN NYUNGAR SEASONAL RESOURCE WHEEL

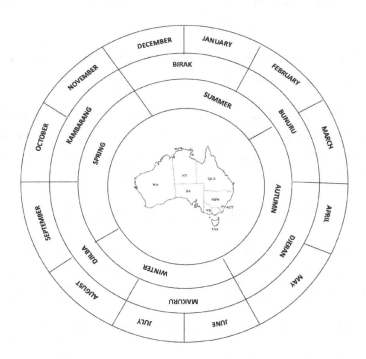

Australia is a massive island, classed as the biggest island in the world; it changes its weather patterns very quickly. We have all the Seasons that the rest of the world has, but we are situated on the globe in an area that covers far more than most, as we have the Tropics, one of the largest deserts in the world, snow, torrential rains and severe flooding, drought, and even cyclones.

When we have our Seasons, Nature truly reveals these amazing changes, with the fullness of each Season. We too can break our Seasons down to Four Seasons, but to many indigenous Aboriginals we actually have six Seasons. But for this chapter will be covering the main Four Seasons.

Djilba: Starts to become warmer from August through to September, our end of Winter to the middle of Spring.

Kambarang: The rain is decreasing from October through to November. From the middle of spring through to the end of spring.

Burak: Very hot and dry with dry easterly winds during the day and Southwest sea breezes in the late afternoon (called the Fremantle Doctor) (I was actually given the nick-name by the Nyungar people "The Fremantle Witch-Doctor") from December through to January which is the middle of summer.

Bunuru: Hot Easterly and Northern winds from February through to March. From

Halfway through to summer to about a third of the way through autumn.

Djeran: Becoming cooler with the cooling winds from the Southwest from April

Through to march, a third of the way through autumn to the end of autumn.

Makuru: Cold and wet with strong Westerly gales from June through to July. This is

The start of Winter, through to the half way point of Winter.

TREE COMMUNION MEDITATIONS
CENTERING

Work with a healthy Natural Tree. It should be taller than you and well rooted, a large Jarrah or Eucalyptus Tree works well for this meditation. Greet and Honor the tree, then sit at the base of the tree... with your back against the trunk... connect with the tree... and let it teach you about being grounded... and centered... with each in-breath draw up healing power from Mother Earth throughout your being... and with each out-breath... let stress and problems dissolve, being cleansed away from the Air around you... feel nurtured and supported by the tree... be with the tree in this way for at least 10 minutes... when you feel very grounded... centered and balanced... stand up and turn around... face the tree... touch the trunk with the palms of your hands... offer it a prayer... and thank it for the knowledge it bestowed upon you...

Always leave an offering and always give thanks.

SHE-OAK OF STRENGTH

Find a large healthy and friendly She-Oak Tree to work with... as you look at the She-Oak Tree Friend that you selected... hold the palms of your hands on its trunk... and then feel its strength... it durability and power... silently ask the tree to help you to learn about patience... and your own strengths within... then, when it feels right... hug the tree... and feel yourself become one with the tree... then ask the tree to help you receive Inner Guidance in response to these questions:

· *In what way am I Strong?*
· *How can I better connect with my Inner Strength in daily life?*
Then give an offering and give thanks.

WILLOW OF TRANSFORMATION

Find an old Willow Tree... greet and honor it... and silently ask it to help you get a better understanding of the Power of the Crone... that of ending... release... and transformation... ask the Willow to teach you about the cycle of Death and Rebirth... ask it to teach you about being tolerant and understanding; ask the Willow to aid you in getting Inner Guidance to these questions:

> · *What do I need to end in my life?*
> · *How do I go about this transformation?*
> Leave an offering and always give thanks.

When you feel complete in receiving guidance from the Willow... face it and feel yourself releasing and transforming... finish... touch the Willow, send love and thanks... and give an offering.

EUCALYPTUS OF BEGINNINGS

Work with a vibrant Eucalypt Tree... greet and honor the Eucalypt... silently ask it to aid you in understanding Inner Birthing's and Beginnings... Commune with the tree feeling at One with it... physically Make contact with the Eucalypt in a way that feels comfortable to you and the tree... touch it with your hands...hug it...nestle in it... or position yourself in some other way... feel the energy of the Eucalypt flowing through your body healing you and focus on this for awhile... notice how the energy of the Eucalypt is different from the other types of trees...now focus on the sacred power of the Eucalypt to aid you in receiving Inner Guidance in answer to these questions:

> · What new way of being do I need to Birth at this point in my life?
> · How should I begin this and bring it into manifestation?

When you feel complete with receiving guidance... separate from the tree... and face it and feel yourself radiating vitality and the power to Birth new Beginnings in your own life... when you feel complete with this... touch the Eucalypt and send it love and thanks and leave an offering.

Natures Secrets The 21 Festivals

Name: _____

Research Done: _____

Time Taken: _____ Date: _____

1. What does the word Vernal mean and why? _____

2. What is the Life Cycle of the Horned God? _____

3. What are all the dates and names of each Festival in order? _____

4. What do we mean when we invoke or evoke? _____

5. When is the beginning and end of the year? _____

6. When is the Fertility Festival? _____

7. How many Full Moons in the year? _____

8. What is a Maypole and when is it used? _____

9. What are the 13 Zodiac Signs? _____

10. What is the Modern name for Betrothal Day? _____

11. What does Deosil and Widdershins mean? _____

12. When does a Blue Moon appear? _____

13. What does the words matriarchal and patriarchal mean? _____

14. When is Harvest Time in Australia? _____

15. Where does the word Easter come from? _____

16. When is Mabon? _____

17. Where originally do Easter Eggs come from? _____

18. Why do we place horns on our God? _____

19. What is Nature showing you this week? _____

20. When did you last get your hands into the Earth? _____

THE BURNING
TIMES

All throughout history there have been atrocities performed by evil, greedy, ignorant and incredibly vague stupid people. These people were so hungry for power and success that they would gain their power at any means, even if it meant the destruction of one life, or millions. We hear so much about the Inquisition and the persecution of accused Witches in Salem, U.S.A. where only a handful of people were tortured and murdered. But what of the widespread Inquisition by the Roman Catholic Church and the millions of tortures and barbaric mutilations and murders that were undertaken in the name of the Catholic Church and the Inquisition. Whole towns and villages were wiped out by order of the Pope.

It saddens me to know that many of these people actually never believed in Wicces, but they believed in freedom from torture for themselves and their family, and the amazing amount of money that was being offered and what they had to do to get it. The Inquisition quickly became good business where everyone got paid for something associated with the accusations; from accuser, to guards to collect the accused, jailers, cooks, court room clerks to write everything down, priests, torturers, speakers of the court, judges, then came the writers of the tortures that were needed to extract confessions from the accused. Anyone could be accused such as that of a neighbour, or someone they didn't like; ugly people; women who lived alone; midwives; town beauties who rejected advances from men of stature or priests; herbalists; female children of accused women; (as the seed of Satan was passed from mother to female child), prostitutes, homosexuals, sluts, deformed or people with defects or loss of limbs. The honest truth that any and all could be accused for any reason, after which they were taken by town guards, imprisoned and tortured until they said they were Wicces and then they had to give a quota of a full coven, which was usually 13 members, this they did to either save their soul or for the mercy of a quick death. To save their families from this torture and death many scared people just randomly gave names of neighbours and people they did not like, just to save their family.

Europe's medieval period lasted from the 5th to the 16th Century, the longest war in history. During this time and over a period of 1000 years, torture was often used to extract confessions, or obtain the names of accomplices or for any information at all about any offences and crimes against the Church and god. Laws and local customs did not impose limits of the treatment and tortures of prisoners to which torture could be inflicted. In fact, confessions were not considered genuine or sincere when so-called "light torture" was used such as drowning, toe wedging and strappado.

Different types of torture were used depending on the accused crime, gender, and social status. Skilled and fully trained torturers would use methods, devices, and instruments to prolong life as long as possible whilst inflicting agonising pain. Many prisoners were tortured prior to execution in order to obtain additional information; in many of these cases, the execution method was part of the torture endured by prisoners. There were hundreds of different torture techniques and devices. I recently visited the Museum of Medieval Torture Instruments in Prague where I viewed some the instruments used. Here are some of the barbaric torture devices they created and used to extract information.

THE JUDAS CRADLE

Also called the Judas Chair, was particularly a cruel invention by the Italians. Using ropes, the prisoner was lowered onto the pyramid-shaped seat with the point inserted into the anus or vagina. Victims would be slowly tortured by intense pressure and stretching of the orifice, resulting in permanent damage and sometimes death. In most cases, the victim would succumb to tears in the muscle tissue that would later become fatally infected. Heavy weights would also be added and tied to the legs to assist the affect, often resulting in death by impalement. A similar device, called the Spanish Donkey (or wooden horse), achieved the same effect. Victims straddled the triangular "horse" were forced to place their full body weight on their orifice, which rested on the point of the angle.

EAT RAT DEVICE

This was device was strapped onto the chest or stomach of the accused with several hungry rats inside the metal cage, and then a fire was placed upon it to heat up and for the rats to escape they had to gnaw, scratch and chew their way through the accused prisoner, killing them slowly and very painfully.

THE SPLITTING SAW

The method used, was to hang the victim upside down, so that their blood rushed to their heads, which kept them conscious during the long horrifying torture. The torturer would then saw through the victims' bodies until they were completely sawed in half, but most were cut up only through their abdomen to prolong their agony, with all their entrails hanging out.

THE PEAR OF ANGUISH

This <u>revolting and painful contraption</u> was used during the Middle Ages as a way to torture women, sometimes men who were accused of anything especially self-abortions. It was also used to punish liars, blasphemers, and homosexuals. The Pear of Anguish was inserted into the victim's orifices usually the vagina for women, the anus for homosexuals, and the mouth for liars and blasphemers (which is why it's also known as the Choke Pear). The device featured four metal leaves that slowly separated from each other as the torturer turned the screw at the top. The torturer could use it to tear the skin, or expand and stretch it to its maximal size to mutilate the victim. It rarely caused death, but was usually followed by other torture methods. As they felt this was a good starting point to make them repent, if they could.

BREAKING WHEEL

Also known as the Catherine wheel, this torture device was used to torture and kill victims in public executions. The device was typically a large wagon wheel with radial spokes. Offenders were bound to the wheel and their limbs beaten with a club or iron cudgel. The more the victim screamed the better the show. The gaps in the wheel allowed the limbs to give way and break. Disturbingly, the survival time after their bones being "broken" could be extensive, with some accounts of victims living for several days prior to succumbing to their horrendous injuries and infection. Having one broken bone is painful enough but having dozens of broken bones is a horrifying thought.

THE IRON CHAIR

This torture device was used extensively during the Middle Ages. Victims would be placed and strapped onto the chair — which featured hundreds of sharpened spikes usually between 500 and 1500 spikes on every surface. — Followed by the gradual tightening of iron or leather restraints, forcing the spikes deeper into the flesh. It also sometimes had a special compartment underneath for heating the spikes. This could go on for hours, sometimes days. The spikes did not penetrate any vital organs as they were not long enough so that blood loss was minimized — at least until the person was released from the chair. Death always followed. The Iron Chair was often used as a psychological instrument of torture; victims would often confess after being forced to watch other victims being tortured on the Iron Chair.

HEAD CRUSHER

It's pretty self-explanatory. The device, which is basically a vice for the head, slowly crushes the skull and all facial -bones. Even if the torturer stops before death, permanent damage to the facial muscles and pressure on the brain would occur. The head crusher was widely used during most of the Middle Ages, especially in the Inquisition. With the chin placed over the bottom bar and the head under the upper cap, the torturer slowly turned the screw pressing the bar down against the cap. This resulted in the head being slowly compressed. First the teeth were shattered into the jaw, then the jaw smashed and broken, not to mention what happens to the skullcap. The victim slowly dies with agonizing pain, but not before his eyes were popped out from their sockets.

COFFIN TORTURE

In nearly every town this torture device was out in full display as a warning. This was one of the most dreaded forms of torture during the Medieval Period. The accused was placed inside this caged coffin, rendering them completely immobile. The time frame varied according to the crime, it could anything from 3 days up till the person actually died. With some court orders, like blasphemy was punishable by death. Victims were often put on public display, with a sign above their head speaking of their crime, where they would be mocked and abused by angry locals.

It was the most preferred due to the low cost and that it could hang out in the village square for all to see and fear as a warning that they are watching. The torturers also forced obese victims into smaller cages to heighten their suffering. They were usually left there until the crows came to feed on their carcasses, usually whilst they were still alive and screaming for help, which never came due to fear of the establishment.

THE BREAST RIPPER

This one's particularly horrendous — not that the other forms of torture aren't, but some just make your eyes water thinking of them. Also known as the Iron Spider, it was mainly used on women who were accused of adultery, self-abortion, heresy, blasphemy, or accused of being Wicces. It was also used for interrogations. The device, which was often heated during torture, contained four "claws" which were used to slowly and painfully rip off the breasts, one at a time. The instrument would be latched onto a single breast of the woman. Blood sometimes splattered onto her children, who were made to watch. If the woman did not die, she would be disfigured for the rest of her life. Image credit: Flominator. Other variations of this torture also existed.

NECK TORTURE

Humiliatingly painful, this punishment was something of an endurance test where the victim would be hooked into a neck device, and walked through the town for all to witness; it was either made of metal or wood, which prevented the victim from adjusting into a comfortable position. The cruelties of this punishment lie within the fact that they were unable to lie down, eat, or lower their head at all. When they eventually did they were pierced!

KNEE SPLITTER

Popular during the Inquisition, this device consisted of two spiked wooden blocks, which were placed in front of and behind the knee. The blocks, which were connected by two large screws, would be slowly turned and made to close towards each other, destroying the knee underneath completely, making them cripple. The number of spikes on the blocks varied from three to twenty, often depending on the offence and the status of the victim. The Knee Splitter even though the name implies it was for the knee's was also used for other body parts, especially arms.

SITTING IN THE TUB

The victim would be placed in a wooden tub with only their head sticking out. After that, the executioner would paint their faces with milk and honey; and soon, flies and ants would begin to feed on there flesh. The victim was also fed regularly and would end up swimming in their excrement. After a few days, maggots and worms would devour their body as they decayed alive.

THE BRAZEN BULL

Also known as the "Sicilian Bull", it was designed in ancient Greece. A solid piece of brass or steel was cast with a door on the side that could be opened and latched. The victim or sometimes victims would be placed inside the bull and a fire set and lit underneath it until the metal became literally yellow as it was heated. The victim would then slowly be roasted alive all while screaming in agonizing pain. The bull was purposely designed to amplify these screams and make them sound like the bellowing of a bull.

IMPALEMENT

Given its name, it should come as no surprise that this was the most favoured method of execution by Vlad the Impaler. In 15th century Romanian, who inflicted this form of torture on thousands of victims just for his amusement, where the victim was forced to sit on a sharp and thick pole? When the pole was then raised upright, the victim was left to slide down the pole with his or her own weight. It could take the victim 3 days to die using this method and it has been said that Vlad once did this to 20,000 people in one day all while enjoying a meal, listening to the screaming sounds of thousands of those suffering.

HERETICS FORK

This device consisted of a metal piece with two opposed bi-pronged forks attached to a belt or strap. One end of the device was pushed under the chin into the upper throat, whilst the other down into the sternum, and the leather strap was used to secure the victim's neck to the fork while the victim hung from the ceiling or was somehow suspended so that they could not sleep. If their head dropped, the prongs would pierce their throat and chest. This was not an instrument that would puncture or damage any vital points so it avoided death but prolonging pain.

It also kept the person in pain so they would eventually give in and tell the torturer what they wanted to hear.

CRUCIFIXION

Principally practiced in antiquity, though it remains practiced in some countries today; it is one of the most well-known execution methods due to the crucifixion of Jesus Christ. It is a deliberately slow and painful execution where the condemned person is tied or nailed to a large wooden cross and left to hang until they die, which usually takes days.

THE LEAD SPRINKLER

This torture tool was filled with molten lead, tar, boiling water or boiling oil, it was used to torture victims by dripping the contents onto their stomach or other body parts like the eyes and face, sometime their genitalia. Using this device the torturer would proceed to pour molten silver on the victim's eyes, which resulted in agonizing pain and eventual death.

THE IRON MAIDEN

Also known as the Virgin of Nuremberg, the Maiden as depicted shows the caged door where the victims were placed inside one of the two doors, with great sharp spikes that penetrated the victim's flesh and body, the spikes being carefully placed so as to not puncture any vital organs. The interrogator would scream questions at the victim while poking them with jagged edges. When completely closed, the screams from the victim could not be heard outside, nor could the victim see any light or hear anything. This increased the psychological pain. Additionally, the spikes blocked the wounds so it took many hours - or even days - for death to occur.

THUMBSCREW

Though there are many variations of this small yet ingenious torture device, the thumbscrew or 'Pilli winks' all function the same. They were designed to slowly crush not only the fingers and toes, but larger devices were also used to crush knees and elbows. Its primary intention was to extract confessions from victims and it was first used in medieval times, but later adopted and loved by the Inquisition.

ROPE TORTURE

A rope is the easiest to use of all the torture devices since it is easy to find and can easily be fashioned to inflict a number of terrible methods of torture depending how and where it is tied. For example, it could be used to tie the victim to a tree leaving the victim exposed with no way of defending himself from animals or other humans; it could tie victims down on an ants nest; or scorpions, it could be used to hang victims at the gallows for entertainment purposes while ultimately inflicting death; and it could be fashioned to restrain the victim's limbs while attaching the other end to horses who would then be made to run, consequently severing the limbs. This was called drawn and quartered.

GUILLOTINE

One of the most notorious and famous forms of executions, especially in France, the guillotine was made of a razor sharp blade attached to a rope. The victim's head was placed in the middle of the frame as the blade dropped, severing the victim's head from the body. This was all very quick and there was no torture associated with it as it was fast and clean, more for the trill of the spectator, it was often considered the most humane method of execution.

TONGUE TEARER

An oversized pair of scissors, it effortlessly cut the victim's tongue. Their mouth would be forced opened with a device called a mouth opener, and then the iron tongue tearer would slice or cut off the tongue with its rough grippers. Some just had a flat grip for tearing the tongue out of the head.

CEMENT SHOES

The American Mafia introduced the cement shoes when they executed enemies, traitors and spies by placing their feet inside cinder blocks and then filling them up with wet cement. Once it dried, the victim would be thrown alive into a river or other deep body of water. This was a well-loved form of execution.

CROCODILE SHEARS

Often used to mutilate those who would attempt to assassinate the king, this iron pincer was heated red-hot before being used to clamp down on the victim's appendages and tearing them from their bodies.

REPUBLICAN MARRIAGE:

Besides the guillotine and burning at the stake, Jean-Baptiste Carrier employed this act of torture during the French Revolution. It involved binding a naked male and female together, back-to-back and then throwing them into icy waters to drown. When water was unavailable, they would just be run through with swords or bayonets. It was the preferred method used to execute nuns and priests during that time, as he was not religious at all.

HANGED, DRAWN, AND QUARTERED:

During medieval times, the penalty for high treason particularly in England was to be hanged, drawn and quartered in public, although it was abolished in 1814, it was responsible for the death of thousands of victims. In this torture technique, the victim is dragged in a wooden frame called a hurdle to the place of execution. The neck would then hang them for a short period of time until they are near-death (hanged), followed by disembowelment and castration where the entrails and genitalia are burned in front of the victim (drawn). The victim would then be divided into four separate parts and beheaded (quartered).

THE TORTURE RACK:

Turning the handle the torturer slowly causes the ropes to pull the victim's arms and legs apart. This was done slowly day by day causing the victim to suffer for a longer period of time. Eventually, the victim's bones were dislocated with a loud crack. If the torturer kept turning the handles, some of the limbs were torn apart, usually the arms first.

SPANISH DONKEY:

This is one of the many torture devices during the Spanish Inquisition. The victim is put astride, naked, on a donkey-like apparatus, which is actually a vertical wooden board with a sharp V-wedge on top of it, sometimes with nails or spikes on the top. After that, the torturer would add varying weights to the victim's feet until finally the wedge sliced through the victim's body.

SCOLDS BRIDLE:

Primarily on women, the device was an iron muzzle in an iron framework that enclosed the head. A bridle-bit or curb-plate, about 2-3 inches long and 1 inch broad, projected into the mouth and pressed down on top of the tongue. The curb-plate was frequently studded with small spikes, so that if the victim moved her tongue, it inflicted pain and made speaking impossible. Wives who were seen as witches, naggers and liars, were forced to wear them, locked onto their head.

THE SPANISH TICKLER:

Sounds like a kinky sex toy right? Wrong? This horrific device was used in most of Europe during the Middle Ages. This instrument was used to tear a victim's skin apart. Due to its shape, bones and muscles were not spared. The victim was naked and bound, making him or her completely defenceless. Then the torturers began the sometimes-public act of mutilating the victim. They often began with the limbs and slowly moved into the chest, back, neck and eventually the face. After which the victim died.

THE GARROTTE TORTURE:

The victim was tied to the instrument and his or her neck forced inside the iron collar. With the handle that can be seen in the picture, the executioner slowly crushed the victim's neck causing death from asphyxia, this was done very slowly to make it last.

PILLORY TORTURE:

The pillory was used to publicly humiliate a victim usually prior to being made guilty. Even though it was meant as a mild form of punishment, the crowd usually made it Lethal. The pillory often served as a post for Flagellation and humiliation. When The victim was restrained; they were subject to the crowd and their spiteful reactions.

SHREWS' FIDDLE/NECK VIOLIN:

Is a form of rigid fiddle where the wrists are locked in front of the bound neck of the victim by a hinged board or steel bar? It was originally used in the 18th century as a way of punishing women who were caught bickering or fighting in public.

There were so many more hundreds of torture devices that were dreamed up by the sadistic torturers of the time, as it was big money, and by dreaming up new way of torture could mean selling the device in their hundreds to other torturers. In the end it became nothing more than a money making and fear-mongering scheme for people to come back to the church, but most importantly to always fear the power that the church had gained over the centuries. Remember the Roman Catholic Church started out as an army then had a great idea that to conquer with weapons was not necessary as they could conquer by religion and the power that it brought, and the fear that it created.

THE WICCAN
HAND FASTING

THE HANDFASTING

Most of the symbols and rituals that are found and used in mainstream weddings have their roots in ancient Pagan Ceremonies and Rites. I would also like to note here that Paganism has many facets of its religious beliefs and in fact is probably the most eclectic and diverse religion in the world. But the main Pagan religion that we are concerned about is Wicca, and is the oldest religion on our planet. During the past 60 years of coming out of the "Broom Closet" from being the most secretive and hidden religion in the world to being recorded as the fastest growing religion in the world's history.

One on my greatest achievements and enjoyments is being a legally Registered Minister of Religion for the Church of Wicca and the ATC, and their official Celebrant performing weddings and funerals all over Australia.

The joining of two souls under the watchful eyes of the Goddess and God is so exciting, and to assist the passing spirit into the Summerlands is also uplifting. But alas this chapter is on weddings, and a wedding is a celebration, for two people who have come together and found a connected heart with mutual dreams. They have shared reality and decided to create a Covenant of devotion between themselves. A Wiccan Wedding is then a letting go of the past, and a welcoming of the future.

THE HANDFASTING

How many of you have heard of the term "Handfasting", and what do you think it means?

The fact is that hundreds of years ago when the lands and peoples were ruled by, Lords and Barons and the like, etc. The King for services gave these titles in payment to the Kingdom, usually in battle or wedlock. They were also given Law over there lands, which meant that the people were under their jurisdiction, and that they could take and do whatever they wished, without resistance from the locals, also the Lord of the land was given a small army to defend and protect it and its people.

Their was also a legal entitlement called "The Right of the Lord", and it is through this title that the Lords were allowed to take any bride they wanted on the wedding night before the groom. He would take her innocence, and usually returned her to the groom the next day. So to avoid this, the couples were married in secret, this was called "The Handfasting", and lasted for a period of year and a day. After this time of secrecy where no one knew, in a year and a day's time they organized a public celebration and wedding for the public.

In doing this they avoided being taken away, as the Lord rarely took a bride who was not chaste and virtuous, this sadly led to promiscuity and was later abolished.

Due to the rise of the conquering Christianity the common folk adhered to the ways of the ancestors, but like so many they struggled with two religions existing side by side, and the New Religion was adopting the ways of the Old Religion, which made it easier for many. But their were still quite a few that remained loyal to the Old Ways, and when it came to love and commitment, they still followed the practices of the traditional Handfasting, which was done in secret. As the outer world did not see their marriage at all, but in the cycle of one year and day, they would then come forward and ask the blessing of the local priest to marry them according to Christian law. Because this was a public event, all the people gathered for this great celebration, and even the Lord of the realm knew of this wedding. He then with guards rode down to the festivities to take his prize. The bride was to be his on her wedding night before the husband. This was the "Right of the Lord". In modern times we still remember this as a time when maidens were taken against their will, and forced to bed with the local authorities, as his Right, we also remember that many maidens committed suicide, rather than being taken by another man. This is the real meaning of the Handfasting, nothing more. It was meant to protect and keep sacred the love of two people, even if for only a year and a day. That is why during the Handfasting they were bound by a red ribbon or cord, binding their souls together for as long as they desired sometimes for a year and a day, sometimes eternally.

THE OPENING CEREMONY

As Wiccans do not usually have gourdy elaborate shrines and stone temples, all we need are a clear day or night and a special place to create and cast our Magick Circle, which is the Temple of the

Wicces. The Earth is the floor of our Temple, the stars are our ceilings, and all of surrounding Nature is our walls and witnesses. We always when possible have the guests seated or standing forming a ring around the Circle area, creating a sense of theatre, as all ritual is theatre. Guests should have been asked prior to the ceremony to each bring a bell no matter what type or size. The Altar is in the North, set up with the appropriate Tools; the red Cord or Ribbon, a basket of rose petals, the "Wedding Candle", 2 Altar candles, The Pentacle with cake on it, Chalice of Water and Chalice of Wine, and Flowers are placed around the Circle perimeter.

Once all are seated or readied and the bridal party is near, I sound the ceremonial Conch Horn, all then stand as the Bards lead the bridal procession into the Magick Circle. The Maidens sprinkling flower petals for the Bride to walk on. She is usually escorted by the father or elder brother, and sometimes even her mother. They join the groom who waits patiently for his bride. The Procession is a very ancient one, and has its roots way back in ancient times when it represented the long journey of the two souls finding each other after much searching. This is the last journey that the bride as a Maiden will take. In fact whilst she is walking down the aisle she is suppose to be reflecting on her long path of life that leads up to this very day. Together their burdens will be shared, therefore halved. They together at the end of the procession stand under a Rainbow Archway, which represents the seven blessings:

Purple - to bless their spirits:
Dark Blue - to bless and awaken their dreams;
Sky Blue - to bless them with peace and harmony"
Pink - To bless them with compassion and love.
Yellow - to bless them with light, strength and courage.
Orange - to bless them with fertility and sensuality.
Red - to bless them with passion and commitment.

In Wicca we always invoke firstly the Goddess and God, as we are religion foremost. The Altar is symbolic of the Earth on all its levels. On the Altar each side are two Altar candles each representing the Goddess and God, we light the first one being the one on the left and saying:

"We are all Children of Light, and I bring to flame these Sacred Candles.
One to represent the Moon and our Great Mother Goddess,
The other for the Sun and our Great Father God.
Goddess and God of the Bride and Groom watch over
them that they may grow in joy and love."

Whilst the couple is still standing in front of the Altar, everyone is formally welcomed and greeted on their behalf and their parents. In the introduction I address the couple saying:

"For N. _____ and N. _____ are in love and wish to make their vows the way of the Old Religion of Wicca, they wish not to be treated as two separate people but as one loving unity.

The intent is more permanent than ' till death us do part', as it involves the concept of soul mates, which is a continuing relationship through all incarnations. The soul mate concept is a very ancient and serious in Wiccan life as it is reflected in the legend of the Goddess and God, where it is written: "That to fulfill true love, you must return again at the same time and place as your loved one, and you must meet and know and remember and love them again."

The "Giving Away of the Bride" ceremony, then takes place followed by the legal declaration.

Cord Binding Ceremony

Among the more ancient Wiccan traditions is that which calls for the couple to have their wrists bound together with a red ribbon or cord, for they will be working hand in hand from this moment on. It is like an umbilicus between the couple. The colour traditionally red is symbolic of love and passion, and is one of emotion incarnate of the Magick, which is evoked to manifest as Mundane Pleasure. Yet red does not deny the presence of the spiritual, for when used as a ritual colour, it represents a commitment on the Earth or Physical Plane.

"AS THIS KNOT IS TIED, SO ARE YOUR LIVES NOW BOUND,
BODY TO BODY, MIND TO MIND, HEART TO HEART AND SOUL TO SOUL."

"This betrothal Cord is woven with all the hopes and dreams from your family and friends to you both on this amazing journey of Love and Adventure together as husband and wife. When we tie the Magick Knot we will bind all of your desires, your dreams, hopes, joys, love, sensuality, fertility, commitment, loyalty, sensuality, strength and courage. In this sacred binding of your hands know that this knot shall remain as long as love remains. May it keep your heart true and guide you both together in loyalty, honesty and commitment of love. Never allow this Binding Cord be used in anger, for it is the Bond of Love. Two true lovers learning and discovering together entwined and balanced by their love through good and bad, remember with anger there should be reconciliation, all of which will enlighten your love but strengthen the bonds between you. May the sacred Winds of the east gently bless you with their breeze? May the Fires of the South increase your desires and excite you kindling the flames within. May the Waters of the West bless you with fertility and heal all past wounds. And may the Winds of the North make you firm and strong that your feet will always be firm of the Earth together.

As you breathe in the sacred breath of the Air may your own sacred breath be truthful and loving each to the other. May you always listen to each other and deeply hear what the other is saying, let your hearts beat as one, remembering that Love is Your Law, and Love is Your Bond."

THE OATH

"_____Do you take_____your lover?
And your friend, to be your sword partner? Will you keep your love and trust,
Caring for and cherishing your lover and will you keep the promise of this rite?"

Answer is given

"_____Do you take_____your lover?
And your friend, to be your sworn partner? Will you keep your love and trust,
Caring for and cherishing your lover and will you keep the promise of this rite?"

Answer is given
HPs. then raises arms in the air and says:

"Above you in the heavens are the radiant stars, and below you is the Earth of stones.

As time passes remember that like a star should your love be constant,

And like a stone should your love be firm. Be close. But not too close not.

Give each other space to be an individual, knowing that
when you come together it will be more intense.

Be understanding and have patience each with the other,

Knowing that storms will come, but they will subside very quickly.

Be always free in giving affection and warmth to each
other, and always be sensuous to one another.

Have no fear, and do not let the words or ways of the unenlightened give you unease,

For the Goddess and God have blessed you this day, now and forever.

Know that it is the decree of your own fate and your hearts that you are united again,

As you were in the past, never to be divided."

"Let the Sun and the Moon, and the Trees and the Stars, and those who are
assembled here bear witness that N._____And N._____Have been
joined together in the sight of the Goddess and God, and whom they bless.

While forms are divided may the souls always cling together,

Sorrow with sorrow, joy with joy, and love with love."

BLESSING OF THE CARDINAL DIRECTIONS

All within the circle now face the East as East Warden says:

"_____And_____,
Today your journey begins of a shared life, bound together by the vows of this rite.
You commence your life as husband and wife, love and dedication through day and night.
Many years you will share, and countless the moons to watch.
If your vows of sacred trust you keep, happiest will be many of your days.
The Lords and Ladies of the sacred winds of the East whisper joy unto your lives.
For all your loving times together may you delight in each other's smiles and eyes?
Sharing together rainbows, dreams and life fulfilling of desire.
Let your inner Love surface and be free and wild as Faeries in flight."

Fire Warden then faces the South and says:

"_____And_____,
Today your journey begins of a shared life, bound together by the vows of this rite.
As husband and wife you will share many paths and roads of individuality.
Knowing that all your days will be filled with warmth and love for each when as a couple.
If your vows of sacred trust you keep, happiest will be most of your days.
For the flames of life have ignited and joined the flames of love within you both
The Lords and Ladies of the South rekindle and spark your passion for each other always.
Let your love awaken anew an eternal twin flame to light and illumine your days together."

Water Warden then faces the West and says:

"_____And_____,
Today your journey begins of a shared life, bound together by the vows of this rite.
As Wife and Husband you will have many dreams that will be shared in the tides of life.

The ebb and flow of the cosmic ocean will take you on all paths of emotion.
If your vows of sacred trust you keep, joyous will be many of your days.
Like the oceans of the sea your emotions are constantly moving,
Guide them with love and you will always share the reflection of love in one another's soul."

Traditions and Superstitions

Jumping the Broom:

During the hundreds of years of slavery, African slave couples who were not allowed to get legally married. But they made a public statement of their love and commitment with their own, with drums and rattles beating in the background to the rhythms of heartbeats. The betrothed couple together jumped over the broom together, sweeping behind all past worries and troubles. The Broom symbolized the art of home making for the newly weds, where it was decorated by the loving family and friends. Pagans and Wiccans the world over, as a sweeping away of their problems and evils, adopted this custom. In Africa smooth Cowry shells were also given to the Bride to encourage fertility, these shells were once used as currency in all of Africa, and were more valuable and previous than gold.

Fire:

The parents of both Bride and Groom traditionally carried a flaming torch from their Hearths to light a new co-joined Fire in the newlyweds Hearth in their new home. It was the joining of two families as one.

Bride's handkerchief:

This is an age-old custom from Belgium. The Brides family takes a handkerchief embroidered with the Brides name to the corner. After the wedding it is displayed proudly and through the generations handed down to each daughter on her wedding day traditionally with her name added.

Surnames:

It was considered unlucky for a woman to marry a man whose sir name began with the same letter as hers.

Honeymoon:

The term "Honeymoon" means "Lust under the Moon" is an ancient custom of sensuality between the Bride and Groom, to make love in the fields under the Moon for fertility, and to bring down light into their lives.

Something Old-Something New:

Something borrowed, something blue and a silver sixpence in your shoe'. The rhyme originally started in Victorian times, but actually stemmed from the ancient Celts where:
Something Old - kept us in connection with our ancestry and heritage
Something New - helped them to focus on their future as husband and wife.
Something borrowed - Reminded us of our friends and to bring them into your new married lives.

Something Blue:

Was to signify that not all times will be blissful, that there was going to be many difficult times ahead, but to remember their love as they will pass quickly.

Brides Dress:

White has been the colour only since Queen Victoria made her children wear white for purity, usually it was a green dress or the prettiest dress that they owned at the time.

Bridesmaids:

Were traditionally dressed the same as the Bride, to confuse the evil spirits; it is the same for the Veil.

Shoes:

It was customary for the Bride's father to place a gold coin in the left shoe, for prosperity and the mother to place a silver coin in the right shoe for harmony.

Crossing the Threshold:

The Bride would be carried to bring prosperity into the household. If she walks in, they would traditionally struggle through their life.

The Mirror:

When the Bride is ready to leave the house for the wedding, a last look in the mirror will bring her good luck. However if she returns to the mirror once she has begun her journey, it will result in bad luck. This is why she has maids to assist and to keep away all bad luck and evil.

The First Purchase:

The first partner to buy an item after the wedding is considered to be the dominant one in the marriage.

Confetti:

Traditionally in Rome, it was sweets that were dosed over the couple to bring good fortune.

The Best Man:

His duty was to guard and protect the Groom from bad luck and to offer up his life if needed.

Pinching the Bride:

In ancient Egypt maidens pinched the Bride on her wedding day for good luck to help bring them a man for marriage.

Spider:

In old Britain finding a spider on the wedding gown brings exceedingly good luck, as long as you do not harm it.

The Coup De Marriage:

The Wedding Cup, this special cup is passed from generation to generation, in many Aristocratic French families.

Keeping in Line:

At the ceremony as they kneel for the Blessing, the groom may put his knee on the hem of the brides dress as a sign he plans to keep her in line. The Bride in turn may step on his foot as she rises, as a sign that she is reasserting herself.

Day of the Week:

Although most weddings are on weekends, usually a Saturday it was considered unlucky in the past. A famous old saying advises a wedding in the first half of the week:

> MONDAY FOR WEALTH, TUESDAY FOR HEALTH,
> WEDNESDAY THE BEST DAY OF ALL.
> THURSDAY FOR LOSSES, FRIDAYS FOR CROSSES,
> AND SATURDAYS FOR NO LUCK AT ALL.

The Month:

Advice of which month to marry was given by the following medieval rhyme:

"MARRIED WHEN A YEAR IS NEW,
HE'LL BE LOVING, KIND AND TRUE.
WHEN FEBRUARY BIDS NO MATTER,
YOU WED NOR DREADS YOUR FATE.
IF YOU WED WHEN MARCH WINDS BLOW,
JOY & SORROW BOTH YOU WILL KNOW.

MARRY IN APRIL WHEN YOU CAN,
JOY FOR MAIDEN AND FOR MAN.
MARRY IN THE MONTH OF MAY,
AND YOU WILL SURELY RUE THE DAY".

MARRY WHEN ROSES IN JUNE GROW,
OVER LAND AND SEA YOU'LL GO.
THOSE WHO IN JULY WED,
MUST LABOUR FOR THEIR DAILY BREAD.

WHOEVER WED IN AUGUST BE,
MANY CHANGES ARE SURE TO SEE.
MARRY IN SEPTEMBERS SHINE,
YOUR LIVING WILL IS RICH AND FINE.
IF IN OCTOBER YOU DO MARRY,
LOVE WILL COME BUT RICHES TARRY.
IF YOU WED IN BLEAK NOVEMBER UNTO JOYS WILL COME AND CARRY.
REMEMBER WHEN DECEMBER SNOWS FALL FAST,
MARRY & TRUE LOVE WILL LAST.

MARRIED IN WHITE YOU HAVE CHOSEN RIGHT,
MARRIED IN BLUE YOUR LOVE WILL BE TRUE.
MARRIED IN PEARL YOUR LIVES WILL BE A WHIRL.
MARRIED IN BROWN YOU WILL ALWAYS FEEL DOWN.
MARRIED IN RED YOU LIFE EVOLVES AROUND THE BED.

MARRIED IN YELLOW UNSURE OF YOUR FELLOW.
MARRIED IN GREEN NATURE TO BE SEEN.
MARRIED IN PINK YOUR SPIRIT WILL SINK.
MARRIED IN GREY YOU WILL TRAVEL AND GO FAR AWAY.
MARRIED IN BLACK YOU WILL WISH YOURSELF BACK."

A green dress is thought to be extremely lucky for Pagans and Wiccans and the Irish. But another expression is that a woman has a green gown to imply promiscuity staining being due to rolling in the green fields.

Handfasting Questionnaire

Name: _____

Research Used: _____

Time Taken: _____ Date: _____

1. What is a Handfasting? _____

2. What is the Handfasting really? _____

3. Why do we bind the wrists? _____

4. Why do we wear wedding rings? _____

5. What does the word bride and word groom mean? _____

6. Who was the Founding Goddess of Wedding Ceremonies? _____

7. What is the 50th anniversary gift and why? _____

8. Explain Broom jumping? _____

9. What are the worst day, month and colour to get married? _____

10. Why do we have the guest in a circle? _____

11. Why do we have a giving away of the bride ceremony? _____

12. What does a Veil represent and why? _____

13. Who started brides wearing white and why? _____

14. Can same sex couples be legally married in Australia? _____

15. Can we have legal Wiccan weddings in Australia? _____

16. What is the Rose Ceremony? _____

17. What is a Coup de Marriage? _____

18. Why do we honor the Four Quarters? _____

19. What are your views on marriage? _____

20. Who is the only legal Wiccan marriage Celebrant in Australia? _____

DEATH-THE
RITE OF
PASSAGE

Death should exist with the same levels of joy and reality as does birth, for our body when it dies, sets the soul free from Earthly toils and fear and pain. Death is the end of mortality but the spreading and awakening of our wings as an Angel with the ability to merge into the Dreaming State of rest and peace, before we again enter the tomb/womb of the Great Mother. For many people who experience that which Buddhists call the *"Right Dying"*, Death is a Gateway to the Astral Temple called heaven filled with their creations of their faith. But to those who die with fear and guilt of a sinful life (Christian views) by what they believe and have been taught will enter Purgatory, the Gateway to the Astral temple they call Hell. Glad I am not a Christian, believing feeling that Death is evil and feared as a punishing realm filled with torture, pain and eternal damnation.

This ignorant Western belief system makes billions of people cling to this reality as a balm against the fear of dying. It is the culmination of all their worst fears that their God the father condemns His children to an eternity of suffering. What a horrible way to end our beautiful mortality.

We also look at modern medicine that devotes immeasurable costs to prolonging life unrealistically for what end result. I prefer the Faith of the Inuit Indians of North America, where when they know the time is right, they go out say their farewells. Then sit on an iceberg and are pushed out to sea where they contemplate the Universe and life and death and rebirth. Listening in the silence waiting for the sound of footsteps, as the Crone nears to take her on her next stage of bliss. This is beautiful and respectful; we need to let our people leave this world respectfully and with total dignity.

I have no desire for present medical chemicals and treatments to keep me alive with no beneficial outcome except at great expenses to my family that is left behind. The machines that make us cling to life for the wrong reasons. My grandmother was an incredible and busy lady all of her life, and ended up with dementia. She existed in a hospital for many years as an object with no idea of anything, no thoughts, no feelings, no life, and I knew her well and know that she would just say let me go. But modern man and medicine encourages us to hang on at all costs. We need to show love and compassion, accompanied with dignity and respect, we have to be gracious for them, not for ourselves, we should welcome Death, with the same joys as we welcome life.

Our stress and anxiety about Death is born only from the terror instilled by the Christian culture. In honesty how many Christians truly believe that they will die without sin? They have been taught that they will be judged, not knowing truly what to expect? We see in our world of today so many devout and faithful who live a life of humility, truth and give, give, and give more unconditionally, and they remain still terrified at the consequences of suffering in Hell. Is this truly the gift of the same all-loving father - God? Yet we see millions who have no faith, do not even care about death and they live lives filled with lavish lifestyles, wealth, and endless desires and happiness. (Heaven on Earth). Is this why there is confusion in our world, why many turn away from solicited faith?

I believe that the Goddess is everywhere and in everything, whether you believe it or not. She watches over us and guides us when needed. If this is true and the Goddess is in everything, then how can we ever truly die, end, and finish with life. I believe we just go to sleep and awaken in another reality another existence called Reincarnation. Life is about learning our lessons and moving forward whether in this life or the next. There are many Wicces, Shamans, and Magicians who believe we choose to consciously reincarnate. So we then become a student of the Wheel of Birth, Life, Love, Initiation, Death and Rebirth.

I know that I am not ready for death yet, as there is still so much more for me to do, oceans to swim, mountains to climb, forests to explore, and much more. But when the times comes I know I will just bow my head graciously, say my farewells to all those I love, and enter the Silence, and dream of my return, holding high my Athame and reclaiming the word Wicce again this time with more balance, harmony and love.

Many Wiccans and Wicces believe that reincarnation is a desirable choice. We believe our work is unlikely to be done in just one lifetime, and no matter how many painful lessons, which wait in the next life, one carnation is insufficient to fulfill a Wicce. I welcome my return. I know it will take me many lifetimes to evolve train and myself and attain my personal goals before I feel that my part in the "Great Work" is complete. Far more time is needed to finish weaving the lessons of Karma with those who share in my Magick Circle's, before I take my leave of this beautiful world.

If death is a reality, Should we not transform it into a time of Spiritual Growth, as Spiritual growth comes when we learn that the lessons of life and spirit are actually the same! We look at many other faiths and traditions and they have role models, we also as Wiccans have many role models, many World Elders who have helped bring the knowledge of our Craft to the world.

My Wiccan role models are Thoth, Jean de Arc, Gerald Gardner, Raymond Buckland, Starhawk, Stuart Farrar, Pete Pathfinder, Jubabe and my loving mother Valma.

I am of the Wicca. The idea of returning, according to the sacred Lore of Wiccecraft, of holding anew my Athame, of reclaiming my Book of Shadows of Elphane in a disciplined, loving manner, is exciting. I always hear the term, *"I wish I could do that again."* Well guess what folks, you will, in your next life.

The problem is that if we devote all our time to spirituality, we become flighty and cannot be grounded with reality; our minds waiver and we do not know the difference between real and imaginary with the opposite that if we focus too much on the physical we lose that spiritual connection with the divine and the invisible within the visible. *"As Above, So Below, As Within, So Without".* This is what we should live by all the time, not just when we feel like it. If you continually work upon improvement and learn from your mistakes, your next life will be inevitably better. One of the most useful ways to *"Keep Pure your Highest Ideals"* is to be mindful of your next incarnation. For those who work within a Tradition like Wicca, the images and symbols of that religion ought to be as ingrained as any desire. For the Wiccan Priest/ess, religion is life, lived daily. I am reminded of a phrase I heard from one of my mentors David the 5th; where he said: That when he was asked why was he a Wicce, he simply replied, *"Because I can be nothing else".*

The Ritual for the Dead should be conducted by a Wicce and is influenced by the Bardo Thodol of Tibet. This Ritual has been established so that it is easily adapted for any person of any belief system. A Wiccan may for example choose to have this Ritual performed for a family member, assisting that relative in moving into the Realm of Bardo. When performed as a single Ritual, this form is of use for anyone who wishes Spiritual assistance. For members and Initiates of our Covens, preparation for this Rite includes not only a legal Will, but also the compilation of what we call a Spiritual Will. A spiritual Will is essential in determining the disposition of one's Ritual Tools and Regalia. The acquisition of Magickal possessions implies a responsibility for all Priests and Priestesses to determine the disposition of one's sacred Tools. I have over my lifetime collected so many rare artifacts and created many more, all my tools, writings and regalia will be left to a spiritual body *"Raymond Backland's Museum".*

It is my belief that Death is a time of Spiritual wonderment, an opportunity to seek Union with the Goddess and God. Death is an Initiation into a State of Being which is similar to that of Dreaming; the mind continues to experience, to imagine, and to create; yet there is no substance, NO EARTH; for this is the Astral (or place of the Stars) World of Being.

RITE OF RESTORATION!

Come to your house, Come to your house, beautiful Being!
Return to your house, your body waits, renewed and ready!
Come occupy your form for your travels beyond,
Swift and sharp is your mind, strong and mighty are your limbs,
Your beautiful limbs, Moving without limit, your beautiful limbs!
Clear and bright are your eyes, your beautiful eyes.
Seeing without limit, your beautiful eyes.
Full and pink are your lips, your beautiful lips.
Red and moist is your tongue, your beautiful tongue.
Tasting without limit, your beautiful tongue.
Clear and soft is your skin, your beautiful skin,
Protecting without limit, your beautiful skin!
Strong and steady is your heart, your beautiful heart.
Deep and full is your breath, your beautiful breath.
Breathing without limit, your beautiful breath.
All things are perfect within you; all functions are restored within you.
Wholly perfect. Wholly Restored!
Awaken into this Body of Light justified Spirit, your trials are passed.
The Measure is made, the weight is balanced.
As a new Being you go forth in the daytime, you go forth in the Light.
As a new Being you go forth in the Night. Go forth-Beloved one,
Isis is before you! Anubis guides you! Osiris welcomes you!
Until rebirth you shall remain an honored guest at His table, at the
Table of Osiris you take your seat. Whole and perfect, among the
Blessed, you take your seat".

A WICCE SAYS FAREWELL

No Church bells for me shall toll, as for some ancestors did ring!
Nor choir shall add my name to toll and those with whom the Angels sing!
Let no one drone a doleful prayer, nor mourner wet his sad faced eyes.
For my true Self will still be there, although in Earth my body lies.
I'm free from Earth's dark coiling mess, foes that did not understand,
I've broken free, O Joy O Joy! I bless the day that freed me from
their hand. I'm Light as Air, I move quite free,
No longer cased in leaded shell, I've friends to meet and things to see,
Now in a fairer land I dwell.
From here I am in all parts whole, my body matched as before,
But healthy Temple of my Soul, as long foresaid in ancient Lore.
Long Centuries in ancient past, in evidence Stone Circle stand,
We knew to what we came at last, ere later Priest this wisdom banned.
In these long days of peace and skill, the bridge was crossed in death and life,
And ere there are those who cross it still, in spite of Cord and Flame and Knife.
False accusation was our lot, but still preserved our knowledge stand,
Defiant of the hostile plot!
Safe in each Covens careful hands, in life, in death, tis all the same,
In warm body, we love and mate, we all knew this before they came.
And spreads their dirge of fear and hate.
Uncluttered by Earths mask of clay, we meet again, our loved ones dear,
Be just a visit for the day, or at the end of life's long drear!
And there and here are much the same, except its better there,
As taught by Priest and Lord and Dame, so dance and sing without a care!

Death Questionnaire

Name: _____

Research Used: _____

Time Taken: _____ Date: _____

1. What is Death in your own words and how does it make you feel? _____

2. Where does the word Death come from? _____

3. Explain Reincarnation in your own words? _____

4. What is Bardo? _____

5. What is a Requiem? _____

6. What do you believe happens at Death? _____

7. Name as many Gods of Death and the Underworld? _____

8. Name as many Goddesses of Death and the Underworld? _____

9. What are other terms used instead of Underworld? _____

10. Who are the Guardians of the Underworld? _____

11. How Rites of Passage are there? _____

12. Why do we not say goodbye? _____

13. What shape is sacred to Life Eternal and why? _____

14. What do you prefer cremation or death? _____

15. What is the cycle of the Seasons, and which is associated with Death? _____

16. Who Is the Dread Lord of Shadows? _____

17. Upon Death we talk about the Light, what is it? _____

18. Have you been here before and if so explain? _____

19. Have you ever met anyone from your past life? _____

20. Have you been a Wicce in a past life? _____

THE SACRED
BOOK OF
SHADOWS

Book of Shadows

Every faith or religion that has ever existed on our planet has a sacred or Holy Book, a Bible as such that teaches about life and a set of rules and stories to help guide their followers on their Spiritual journey. The Book of Shadows (BoS), as such was never an ancient written truth of our ways as it has always been an oral tradition, passed from Sage or parent to child but is our ever growing and ever changing bible, and more than that it is more of a Spiritual Diary a Sacred book that holds all of your thoughts and spiritual rituals. Whenever you come across a book that has information that you feel is beneficial to you and your journey then write it in your BoS. When you do this always put the date, as your journey changes so too will your BoS, and new truths will reveal themselves to, the deeper you go and become aware of your Wiccan journey. The term Shadows is quite important as shadows change and grow too.

When you have a Full Moon or New Moon or just celebrate life and Nature in general writes it down in your BoS. But always put the date to keep everything in order so as to know where you were at that stage in your journey, and mostly to know if you are moving forward or going backwards. Start your BoS as an introduction to your belief system, and sayings that can keep you firm in your belief. Add important data about what you follow or believe in such as Meditations, Dreams, Trance States, Spells, Rituals, Luna and Festival Celebrations, also initiatory processes as you grow and feel wiser and more Magickal, especially being more connected to Nature and the Great Mother Goddess. Write into your BoS a set of self-disciplines, a set of instructions that you must know and learn by heart. As you must know your BoS completely so as to never go off track. Always go by your inner gut feelings, as your soul knows what is right and what is important, more than others tell you. Know your own Truth, and don't let anyone sway you or lesson your ability to be who you really are and put a pause on your Spiritual Quest for that inner reality of what Wiccecraft is!

I myself over 5 decades have had dozens of BoS's and have kept my original one's but have also re-written them and added much to my personal BoS. I now would have in excess of 25 different BoS. My last one (maybe) is a huge hand made BoS with over a thousand recycled pages that I am slowly adding to and making complete of all that I have known and learnt. Not only from this life but also what has been awoken in my previous incarnations. Enjoy your journey, as your BoS will become so important and sacred that it will be your greatest Magickal Treasure, and maybe by handing it down to your children can become all that it is meant to be.

Making Your Own Book of Shadows

- Buy yourself a blank journal and make sure it has many pages, as this will fill up very quickly if you're serious. Add decorations such as pictures, drawings, and leaves from nature, and feathers.
- Start with a Prayer blessing your writings and your journey that it is true and that the Goddess is with your always guiding you on your journey. Write your own dedication or Self Blessing Ritual and like everything in your Shadows learn it, know it, and believe it.
- Then write in an Index of all the pages to follow so that you may find them quicker. Keep this next part as an Important Message to yourself stating that "Properly Prepared I Must Always Be". Then write a Consecration or Blessing ritual to bless your paper pages, pen and Book, so they are dedicated only to the Magick of your sacred BoS.
- Add in the Wicces Rune, a chant that you must say and perform every-time to enter your Magick Circle, this is used to raise and build power for your purpose. Next pages write your own Consecration of Water and Blessing of Salt. We Consecrate Water as it is impure, and we Bless Salt as it is pure.
- Next write about the Elements and their Elemental Beings, these you work with on a daily basis, these help you to keep in balance so that your Magick is in balance.
- Next write about Candle Magick, as this is the easiest and simplest form of Magick that you can start using and doing with great success until you gain more confidence.
- Then write your own Magick Circle Preparation and how to cleanse and banish negative energies, and invoke Positive natural energies.
- Now its time to write down how to form and cast your Wicces Temple or better known as the Magick Circle.
- Write your own New Moon and Full Moon ceremony include the invoking of the Goddess and God and call in energies to assist you with your Magickal Spells or Rituals.
- Write and prepare your own Rite of Dedication, which we call a Wiccaning, this is where the Goddess and God bless your soul and you dedicate your spirit to Wicca and the Goddess and God.

- Prepare and create your own Initiation Ceremony, which will take you eventually from being a Wiccan Neophyte to an Initiated Wicce, take your time and do not rush elevation to this level.

- Write about Spells and how they should always be in rhyme as being in rhyme speaks for itself.

- Learn to raise energy and Do the Witches Rune as a Spiral Dance within your Magick Circle to aid in raising Power.

- Collect and learn about each of your Magickal Tools that will be used in your Magickal studies such as; Thurible (incense burner), Altar, Altar pentacle (To bless and Consecrate things on), your Athame (the Wicces dagger), Chalice for Water, container for Salt, Incense container, charcoal blocks for the incense, 2 Altar candles representing the Goddess and God, Statues of the Goddess and God, robes to wear only for ceremonies and Magickal work.

- Learn and write about the Eightfold Paths of Wicca and what the Wicce must learn and follow.

- Know the symbolism and meaning behind the Wicces Pyramid and the Magick Circle.

- Write your Seasonal and Sabbatic Festivals; Blessing of the Animals 4th January; Lughnasadh 1-2nd February; Betrothal Day (Valentines Day) 14th February; Autumn Equinox 21-23 March; Samhain (Halloween) May Eve; May Pole Day 1st may; Winter Solstice 21-23 June; Imbolg August Eve; Spring Equinox 21-23 September; Beltane November Eve; Summer Solstice 21-23 December.

- Learn the Laws of Nature and of Magick so as to not go wrong "An it Harm None, Do What you Will".

- In the back of your BoS write all your poetry, prayers, songs, Invocations and Evocations.

- Also add all the books that you have read, loved and recommend.

This then makes it complete; keep a second BoS for all the rituals and ceremonies that you do including meditations and their outcomes. Good luck and Goddess Speed.

WICCANING REQUIREMENTS

In Wicca there are 7 Traditional Rites of Passage, although there are 3 Degree's, these are for the formal training, which occurs with each of our Covens, and they are:

1. **The Seeker:** The Student like yourselves who seeks to know of the Wicca, and therefore studies the Outer Court Lessons, this takes around 6-12 months before asking to be Wiccaned.
2. **The Cowen/Wiccan:** (my affectionate term is Blessed Bunnee) this is someone who has been Baptized/Wiccaned into the Wiccan Faith. It is where they choose to dedicate their lives to the Goddess and God. If they wish they then commence in the study and practice as a Cowen in the Advanced Wiccan Studies in preparation for Initiation if they so desire to enter the Priesthood, this study is for approximately another 6 - 12 months.
3. **The Wicce/Initiation:** This is the formal Initiation of the Wicce into the Study of Wiccecraft, and where the deeper meanings are taught. They also copy out their Book of Shadows from my Book. This training is in-depth and takes about 2 more years to learn and know by heart!
4. **The Priest/ess/Ordination:** After Elevation as a Priest/ess you are now a Legally Ordained Minister of a religion, and have more formal in-depth training, and select a chosen field into which to specialize, such as Chaplain, Celebrant, Funerals, Prisons or Hospitals, Teaching, Psychologist, or any specialized field to help our Faith in outer acceptance of the world. This usually takes minimum of another 2 years prior to maybe starting their Circle/Church/Coven.
5. **The High Priest/ess Elders:** Usually after several more years, if you decide to form your own Circle/Church/ Coven, here you need a working partner to be your own Clan Mother/Father. A person should only become a High Priest of High Priestess if they wish to have their own coven and not for any other reason.
6. **Magi or Crone:** Only after running your own Coven for many years, and deciding to retire, do they officially claim the title Crone or Magi, and become a respected Elder of the Wiccan Community for always.
7. **Death-Final Rite of Passage:** Death and Transition into Annwyn in readiness to either come back or attain to be one of the Shining Ones/Ancient Ones.

THE WICCANING

Our Baptism is called a Wiccaning, and is done to enact a Rite of Dedication to the Goddess and God, and our Magick Circles, and to enact an oath of allegiance and secrecy from a prospective Wicce; also to introduce a prospective Wicce to Ritual. It is also denouncing any other rites of dedication or oaths that they may have entered into and accepting our Faith and way as theirs.

REQUIREMENTS: The Seeker must be studying Metaphysics and Mediation. They must have expressed to learn more of the Wicca. After the Wiccaning the Cowen is considered to be under the protection of the Coven/Church and if the Fellowship are in complete agreement, the Cowen may attend all the Sabbats and other Coven events. Their place in the Order is to help keep all Sacred Tools and Equipment clean and Properly Prepared! During the Wiccaning the High Priest/ess purifies and Blesses the Seeker; firstly the High Priest/ess takes away all the impurities from their body and mind, by the laying on of hands saying;

"I TAKE FROM YOU YOUR SIGHT,
FOR IT IS DIMMED AND SEE'S ONLY UGLINESS;
I TAKE FROM YOU YOUR BREATH OF LIFE,
WHICH IS MANIFESTED ONLY UNTRUTHS;
I TAKE FROM YOU THE BEAT OF YOUR HEART
FOR IT BEATS WITHOUT LOVE;
I TAKE FROM YOU I TAKE THE SACRED SEEDS OF LIFE
FROM WHICH ONLY GROWS LUST;
AND FROM YOUR FEET I TAKE THE LIVING EARTH
FOR YOUR FEET HAVE LEAD YOU ON A PATH TO NOWHERE."

After a slight pause with presuming that the Seeker lives no more and is no longer tormented by the evils of life. They are now reborn into a life of love and beauty with a Blessing from the High Priest/ess saying:

"BLESSED BE YOUR FEET THAT HAVE BROUGHT YOU IN THESE WAYS,
ALONG THE PATH THAT YOU HAVE CHOSEN. TO YOU DO I GIVE
THE LIVING EARTH THAT YOU MAY KNOW HER AS MOTHER;

*BLESSED BE YOUR KNEES THAT SHALL KNEEL AT OUR SACRED
ALTARS AND THAT SHALL KNEEL IN HUMILITY TO ALL LIFE,
KNOWING THAT ALL IS SACRED AND WORTH A BENDED KNEE;*

*BLESSED BE YOUR PHALLUS/WOMB WITHOUT WHICH WE WOULD NOT
BE, TO YOU DO I GIVE THE SACRED SEEDS OF LIFE. FOR THIS IS THE
GATEWAY OF LIFE AND DEATH, AND YOU WILL FEAR NEITHER.*

*BLESSED BE YOUR BREASTS/CHEST FORMED IN BEAUTY AND STRENGTH
AND HEALTH, TO YOU DO I GIVE YOUR TRUE HEARTBEAT THAT YOU WILL
LOVE ALL THINGS, FOR ALL THINGS ARE OF THE GODDESS AND GOD;*

*BLESSED BE YOUR LIPS THAT SHALL SPEAK THE SACRED NAMES,
TO YOU DO I GIVE THE BREATH OF LIFE SO THAT YOU MAY SPEAK
OF THE GODDESS AND ALL BEAUTIFUL THINGS IN NATURE;*

*BLESSED BE YOUR INNER SIGHT, THAT YOU MAY SEE
TRUE BEAUTY IN ALL THINGS AND IN ALL THINGS SHALL
YOU SEE THE FACE OF THE GODDESS AND GOD:*

(Then anointing the brow with oil saying)

*AND TO THE BODY DO I GIVE THE SACRED TOUCH OF THE GODDESS
TO ILLUMINE AND AWAKEN YOUR SOUL, THAT YOU MAY BE A TRUE
BEACON OF HER DIVINE LIGHT, WHILST WALKING ON HER PATH."*

NEEDED

1. Acquire a forest green or brown robe with hood.
2. Acquire a 9-foot cord (Singulum) green.
3. Purchase a bottle of red wine/port for the Circle as an offering.
4. Wear or have a Pentagram Necklace.

5. Make and bring your own anointing oil.
6. Make Sabbat cakes for the Circle.
7. Be Properly Prepared and Ready!
8. Be at the Covenstead (or designated place) on time NOT EARLY AND NOT LATE.

THE INITIATION
OF A WICCE

Initiation comes in many forms, whether it is self-Initiation or the Traditional Initiation into a genuine Coven. In reality it is hard to put ourselves through the tests that are required in Initiation, so I believe that we need to put our lives and souls in the care of a Mentor who can truthfully take us through this immense journey, probably the greatest step you will ever take as a human and as a Wiccan, and soon to be Wicce. Being in a Coven also means many to learn from and share. Initiation is yours for the asking when you have proven that it is definitely your path, and the High Priestess accepts you into her Spiritual family. Initiation is also about true preparation for Immortality, as humans are only partly immortal until their Higher Self is awakened and Initiated to the next level. It is where we learn, devote and become attuned with The Goddess and God and all of Nature. It is about being one with Creation, and the ageless, deathless, sexless soul of the Wicce.

It is the absolute Spiritual Bond with the Goddess that we owe our allegiance and practical Magickal work. Initiation means *"To Begin"*, a birthing, a new start. It is about dedication to a set of different rules and principles away from our mortal lives. The sad thing is that man is moving further and further away from nature and the Spirit of the Universe and seeking the new God of the 21st century, Science. I believe it is only time before robots and computers will be invented to aid in the freedom of the daily drudgery of man. Science is moving forward with Artificial Intelligence. We are already becoming a world of lazy people who spend more time watching TV and being on their mobile phones than interacting with real life and real people physically. Most of man will continue to fish, hunt, and travel in recreational vehicles, drink beer and grow fat, and watch TV and become fat, lazy and feeling sorry for themselves on all levels.

If there are to be excursions into outer space, with the view of setting new colonies outside of the Earth. Then what will become of these new homes is they destined for the same as our Earth? Many years ago when I had the Spirit Earth Magazine in 1994 I wrote an article titled *"Save the Moon"*. This was what was in the article.

Save the Moon from Humans!

Here we are again, the great-civilized people of Mother Earth, on the hunt again. On the hunt for a new car, because the old one is past its prime? No! For a new house because the old one is falling down around you? NO! Maybe a new relationship because the old one is no longer satisfying you, NO! Then what is it that we are so hungrily trying to claim as ours alone? We the human parasites of our beloved Mother Earth, find it not only exciting at the prospects of destroying our own planet over the last 200 hundred years, we now have to look to the skies for something else to abuse, use, and eventually destroy through greed, ignorance and power. We have been smothering and poisoning our Earth, and now man is looking at reaching to the heavens, (well, the Moon anyway) and contaminating it also.

That beautiful shining orb that shines in the blackest night to give us hope in all darkness. The Moon a sacred symbol of our Blessed Lady, is what rules the waxing and waning of all the oceans on the Earth. The Moon flows through you also in your body, which is made up of 70% water, and gently moving the human tides within us. The flow and the ebb, for as we are one with the Moon, especially the female of our species. We are Lunar ruled, the only creatures entrusted to the care of our planet, and to revere the Moon. And now man is looking at invading the Moon and eventually doing the same thing their as we have done to the Earth.

The International Hotel chain *"The Hilton"*, wants to build a 5000 bed-dome-shaped hotel on the Moon. The 325 meter high hotel would be supplied with solar power and would have its own beaches and farm. Hilton International has already asked a British architect to design the complex, in close co-operation with NASA experts. The Hilton chain has so far spent more than $260,000 on the project, whilst the Japanese competitors have set aside roughly the equivalent of up to $65 million for similar ventures to the Moon. The Shimizu Company, for example: has plans to set up inflatable buildings, while the construction form Nishimoto wants to build a holiday centre in the shape of a snail shell. What the fuck is happening? For the Goddesses sake, and for the sake of the Moon, we need to stop these Utopian thoughts and clean up our act. We need to heal what is sick, mend what has been broken and love that which we already have before setting off on a Star Trek adventure, in the fight and race to always be the first. Especially as these people are only interested in the end result, and that is to not only be the first, but also to add to their empire, with the wealth that they have already accumulated through greed.

The Moon has so much effect on our planet and our lives, which knows what will exactly happen when they start to mess around with the Moon. Maybe we will cause problems in her magnetic energies, or set her off balance. Even if we slow down her continued revolutional spirals, we could destroy not only the Moon by setting her off balance, but when this happens we will inevitably lose our beloved Earth and everything upon it. We do not need a war to end our planet; all we need is stupidity, ignorance and the greed of more power.

REQUIREMENTS OF A WICCE

The Degree of Wicce is the **LEVEL OF POWER** - The Initiate must have been Wiccaned into the Wicca. Although this is not a prerequisite, but preferred. They should have a good background of the history of and meaning of Wicca. They must have attained the age of 18, unless special circumstances exist which allow this rule to be varied. They must have studied with and done a 12 month "Nature Diary" (in my next book) it must be completed in full. They also want to devote themselves to Wicca as a Wicce of the community.

After doing all this these are the other requirements that are needed for Initiation:

1. They must write a formal letter requesting Initiation to the High Priest/ess.
2. They must know and understand the Holy Ordains and believe in them.
3. They must attain a black hilted knife with a double-edged blade.
4. They must be proficient in Meditation.
5. They must know the Self Blessing Ritual and the LBRP.
6. They must sacrifice one bad habit prior to Initiation.
7. They must make or acquire a White robe for Initiation.
8. They must purchase a 9' white cord as their Singulum.
9. They must acquire 3,9' cords each being red, white and blue, for healing.
10. They must help and make their own Pentacle.
11. They must have a chosen Magickal name.
12. They must make their own anointing oil.

      13. They must purchase a bottle of red wine/port for the Circle.
           14. They must make Sabbat cakes.
   15. Thy must dedicate themselves for a further 1-2 years of training in the Wicca.

The Degree of Wicce is where the Mystical Training begins in earnest. Upon Initiation the Wicce will be advised of those skills and studies to be learned and Awakened prior to the acceptance of Ordination into the Priesthood. They must learn self-confidence; self-reliance; self-responsibility; and self-discipline; remember the motto: *"TO KNOW, TO WILL, TO DARE, AND TO KEEP SILENT"*.

Are they rebellious and seek sensation? Do they just live in a fantasy world and wish to escape from reality? Do they seek Magick and Power? Or do they truly seek Earth Centered Spirituality and its progression? The answer is that people come for all these reasons, plus more. Neither one of the reasons matter as one gets out of Wicca exactly what one puts into it. In the days of old, in the greatest of Temples of Greece, Rome, Egypt and Assyria, the Mysteries of the Goddess were so powerful that the High Priestesses could send away the aspirants to sell everything they owned, and to return with the money in exchange for Initiation. This likened to corruption, so that when the Christian religion appeared and was free to all, the people of the ways of the Old God's and Goddesses readily took them up.

Today, we who have been reawakened and reassembled the ancient wisdom, realise that ones does not have to pay through the nose for knowledge, neither should the public be press claimed into a creed that they owe only partial allegiance. Modern Initiates are told in their oaths, that they are free to come and go and they're conscious dictates, and so it is. Initiation, awareness, enlightenment, consciousness, begins when the Wiccan finds that the established forms of religion, fail to give them what they desire, and does not answer to their present needs, especially the needs of women, spiritually.

The Seekers, who come to Wicca, usually do so by hearsay, word of mouth, the media, etc.! Upon the meeting of the Seeker, the High Priestess usually knows instinctively whether the Neophyte belongs in the mind of her Circle, that is why we have a 6 month Outer Court training so we can get to know and they us. It is my belief that a Wicce returns back to the spiritual family they knew in a previous life. The Initiate will when the time is right be told their date for their Initiation; they must obtain their tools and robe. They will be told to bring these things on the night of the meeting set aside for their Initiation. The Man in Black or the

Maiden who then gives them the Abjuration; and abjures them to walk away if they have come with falseness in their heart, or if there is fear then approaches the Wiccan.

If the Wiccan still wishes to proceed, they are then blindfolded, bound and stripped of all physical possessions are brought to the boundary of the Magick Circle, and the Dwelling place of the High Priestess, the Coveners and the Goddess and God.

The Initiate now standing at the Portals, the sacred entrance to the Magick Circle: blindfolded, skyclad and bound, and stripped of all physical possessions.

The Wiccans hands tied behind his/her back, and other Cords appropriately placed. They are attended by one of the devotee's of the Coven, usually the Maiden. The Charge of the Goddess is then read out to them, this in fact is the instructions that the Goddess gives to Her children to "Keep pure their highest ideals". To come between these Portals from the Dreaded World of Men into the Sacred Realms of the Goddess and the Horned God, with true intent and divine love and trust. You must come with the password to enter the Magick Circle:

"I COME WITH PERFECT LOVE AND PERFECT TRUST".

The Initiate is then Challenged with the Sword, the naked blade against the naked flesh. In other words they are asked again if they still wish to proceed further into the Mystery School of Wicca. If they give the assay, they are then taken into the second stage of the ritual, and they are asked if they are willing to suffer an Ordeal and be purified and he or she are then Ceremonially Scourged (lightly). After this is performed they then proceed into the third stage, where their Measure is taken, they are then asked to swear an oath of secrecy and an allegiance to the High priestess, the Coven and its members, even though it should cost them their life. Progression into the fourth stage, they are now Anointed and Consecrated a Wicce. The Magick Cords and the Blindfold are now removed and the fifth and final stage of the ritual proceeds.

They are now presented with the Working Tools of the Wicce. At the conclusion of their first performance of the Sacred Mystery all their new sisters and brothers under their new spiritual name welcome them, and then plans are made for their training within that degree, up to the Priesthood and Ordination, if they so desire. Remember Perfect Love and Perfect Trust are our key words.

Wicce – The First Degree, The level of Power and of the Moon.

The Tools for this level are the Thurible - which represents Purification: The Athame - representing Illumination. The Pentacle - representing Perfection; The Book of Shadows - representing Hidden Knowledge; This is the level of Matrifocal training and is the level of the Goddess and all Her Sacred Mysteries!

Priest/ess – The Second Degree, The level of Knowledge and of the Sun.

The Priesthood training begins and is Patrifocal, that of the masculine, the Horned God. The Tools are The Boline - representing Divine Love and Healing through the plant kingdom: The Magick Wand - representing Will Power. As a Priest/ess you are committed for three years to give service to the Wiccan community as a whole; dedicated in a field e.g. Chaplain at schools, hospitals, prisons, celebrant or healer, etc.

High Priest/ess – The Third Degree, Level of Divine Love – The Stellar Combination of it all.

It is the degree of Divine Love, the Marriage of Heaven and Earth becoming One, this unification of Androgyny as the Goddess and God as One. The Tools here are the Scourge - which represents Time; The 3 Magick Cords - which represent Sacred Space; and the Ceremonial Sword - which represents Infinity thus Eternity.

The Macrocosmic Stellar Three Degree's have much to do with the Mysteries that deal with the Magick Circle. The Scourge is the symbol of Time. Traditionally this Tool has 8 thongs, each with 5 knots, being a total of 40 knots in all. 8 is the seasonal time cycle of the year, thus being 8 Sabbats. Five is the life-time cycle of the Horned God, the 5 points of life, the 5 elements, the 5 points of man; the 5 Planes; and the 5 points of the Pentagram.

The cycle of the Horned God, he is born, Initiated, Married, Sacrificed and Dies, in order to be Reborn again. The total of 8+5 = 13, which equals the number of the Lunar Months of the same year. 40 are the number of days between the Spring Equinox and the Birth Festival of Beltane. 40 are also the number of weeks for the gestation of the human embryo. 40x7 equals 280 days, which equals 9 months. Therefore the Scourge contains divisions of micro-macrocosmic time.

PERFECT LOVE AND PERFECT TRUST!

Most Wicces are aware that the Age of Aquarius began in 1829, and will last 2000 years. Many Seers have predicted great changes and upheavals that will take place in the history of mankind. In fact, if we are to believe recent translations, Nostradamus predicted almost total destruction. The ancient Egyptians of almost 4,000 years ago predicted that during the Age of Aquarius, when the Planets have lined up, there would be a great explosion of psychic power - some good and some evil.

As R. Lewis said in his book, "The Thirteenth Stone", "The planets follow the Sun in a great cycle which as I have said takes 25,920 years to complete. During this time the Sun appears to be in a particular part of the zodiac for a period of 2,160 years. Roughly speaking, from 4,000 to 2,000 B.C.E. The Earth was in Taurus; when the Shamanic and Horned God's were around. It then moved on to Aries for Another 2,000 years, when the major wars started, and at the time of the Spreading of the Christian Gospel, it had moved into Pisces, the fishes which is the true symbol for Christianity."

According to our Astronomer Priests, Pisces was going to be an Age of Iron, and a time when the Sun would dominate the Moon. It would be an Age of masculine material science rather than a balanced era; the coming world would turn its back on the Priest and all this hard won wisdom. The tree would be cut down. All this was to happen within a Great Month, a twelfth part of the 25,920 years in which day and night, light and dark, good and evil alternate. Pisces is to be followed by Aquarius, which is governed by Saturn. This according to our Astronomer Priests would be the beginning of yet another Golden Age. In this Age the tree would again bear fruit, and mankind would come to live in peace, harmony and justice.

The main concern of the ancient Priests was that their Spiritual heirs should not have to start from scratch, as they once did. With them in mind, a vehicle was prepared which would carry all that they had learned through the stormy seas of the Piscean Age. The Christian Bible was built as a Trojan horse, which would meet the religious needs of the people of Pisces. Wicca was and is prepared for to take people through the Age of Aquarius and to suit the religious needs of the people of Aquarius. And so it was that the SCRIPTURES WERE WRITTEN, giving the materialistic, male-dominated people of Pisces a Material God to worship. At the end of that dark time, God/dess would send an Interpreter of the Law, who would reveal to the Children of Aquarius all that hard-won wisdom. In John 4-22; Jesus in the role of teacher is heard to say; "Ye worship, ye know not what!"

This could cause destruction and then a new beginning. This prediction is in the sacred care of the Inner Temple of Isis in London. It is my personal opinion that there was a slight miscalculation, as twenty year here or there are infinitesimal, when you are dealing in thousands of years. I felt it was a little premature and more likely to commence at the turn of the last century, also one must bear in mind that our calendar dates from the birth of Jesus, and may or may not be worth consideration.

The prediction which is written on a clay tablet in the script of the ancient Temple, states that there will be a Universal use of Arcane Sciences, the discovery of resources available but not yet identified and finally Chaos, followed by rebirth.

If one studies the headlines in the newspapers of this day, one could easily believe that this psychic Chaos is well under way. Man is becoming more selfish, cruel, greedy, radical, and indifferent. In America there was 9/11, in Indonesia the constant bombings. In the USA many years ago a young man from a rural Australia, whilst on a visit to LA was mugged twice, stripped naked and chased to his death on an electric railway line in the subway, by a jeering crowd who stood and watched and did nothing whilst he died. In Melbourne, a young girl staggered from a train into a crowd of people her nose was broken and bleeding, she had been assaulted. She pleaded for help, but not a person slowed down to help her. They all through fear looked the other way and did not want to get involved.

This is a description of the obvious, but the more ghastly and insidious attacks are the psychic attacks being inflicted by EVERYONE!!!!! Yes everyone, as we do this without even realizing what we are doing. Know and remember; that everything starts from a thought, and if infused by intense emotion, becomes more realistic, and is created on the Astral counterpart into the physical; so we do well to remember, do not wish ill on anyone or anything; never boast and never threaten; and the Goddess will smile upon us. Remember the Karmic Law; "Whatever you do good or bad, will come back to you, threefold!"

We of the Wicca all have one thing in common - love and concern for the Mother Earth, and ALL life upon and within Her. Our aim is to free our people from the fear and promote Love and Trust. In Wicca we have what we call the "Wicces Rune", and a couple of the lines are "Queen of Heaven, Queen of Hell". For me these words mark the knell of fear, separation, and illusion. Wicca is not puritanical sweetness or a hellish diabolism.

It is the essence of life, encompassing all Nature; by the wisdom of our Goddess we are made into the creation by a design, and not a chance. The design, our very being must have a purpose, what is it? From day one we become magnets that surround us with situations that bring us experiences s placed into good and bad. Surely the purpose of our very existence is to ensure that we gain as many life experiences by finding both good/bad; pleasure/pain; success/failure. Surely we should strive always to live our Highest Ideals and live by the words; "An it harm none." We are aware that we will have our failings; most of us know upon awakening, that we will meet failure and success to varying degrees.

Our Goddess and God rule a Holistic Nature through all aspects. When we stumble through lack of Inner Strength, immaturity, ignorance or stupidity, we are not condemned or judged by our Gods, we merely learn from our mistakes, and must learn to be all the stronger and wiser for that experience. Good/Pleasure and Bad/Pain are hidden teachers; but they are not the real lesson. The true lesson is in which we react, adhere and grow. Our Goddess abides in every extreme of our consciousness, always ready to give the gifts of the Cauldron of Cerridwen to Her needy Children. So when we fail, we are not cut off from Her, as She allows us to make our mistakes so that we can hopefully learn from them.

We all need to go through light and dark cycles, as everything in nature does, even in Christian mythology Jesus descended into the Underworld. The great strength of our Goddess is in that we are inspired, and loved and always uplifted that we may grow and understand our total individuality. In this awareness we learn to harmonise with Nature in all Her deepest Mysteries. So once we have learned this, we become a true child of the Goddess and God and know that we have arrived home. With each Rank or Degree in the Wicca, we have many in-depth Mysteries that can only be taught and passed on from Traditional Covens, but with each solid and devout step we get a lot closer to the Oneness we seek with Deity.

The Goddess is the Soul of the Living Earth, and a Divine link with all things primordial, dark, still, and warm as if in the Tomb or Womb of Eternal Time. The Goddess has many thousands of names; She is the Inner Reality, manifested in all Life. The Goddess is not separate from the world; She is the world, and all things in and on it. She is the very essence of everything, the very breath we take is of her, and every heartbeat is by her loving grace. She illumines our souls and awakens us to the Mysteries of Nature and of ourselves.

After a millennium of Herstory, the Goddess is reawakening, not to conquer or master the masculine forces, but to affirm, the two great life principles, the electrical-male and the feminine-magnetic polarities, which are active in the Universe and to affirm that together they form a Unity, a Unity that affords us a vision of harmony and balance of the Human Spirit. By reconnecting the opposing yet connected forces of the Universe, the forces of Light and Dark, Night and Day, Masculine and Feminine, Yin and Yang, Consciousness and Unconsciousness, Birth and Death, Form and Energy. The continual Spiral Dance of life eternal, always giving and in return always receiving.

To truly understand the Goddess, and gain a deep insight into an Initiation of the Mysteries, you need to go back, back to the time thousands of years ago, when all of mankind's survival depended upon an intimate knowledge of aligning their intuitiveness with the forces and cycles of Nature. A transformation of personality was implied in every Initiation, from the Mundane Plane to the Fool Stool of the Gods. Women needed a female Initiation and men needed a male Initiation. For each gender, what was a sacred Mystery was largely determined by their attempt to understand their own primordial sexual essence.

Ancient female Initiatory Rites were supposed to imitate the maternal birth process, as well as the process of eternal Rebirth. The Initiation was a way of contacting deep levels of awareness; theirs is a realization that this that makes up the obvious physicality of the world is not true and real. There is a realization of the real and the eternal, which are a different kind of reality. Plutarch, the early Greek Historian describes an inscription about Athena, one of the archetypes of the Goddess. The inscription says: " I AM THAT WHICH HAS BEEN, AND IS, AND EVER WILL BE. AND NO MORTAL HAS REVEALED MY HOLY ROBES." This inscription speaks of the eternal never-changing, ever-changing reality of the Goddess who was and is and shall ever be the same but different. Initiation also represents FREEDOM from the world as it frees the spirit. But the price of that freedom is the willingness to face one's own true dark and light self. To perceive the unconscious rather than the conscious, to touch the Inner Abyss of our own Being, and those parts of us that are a part of our totality. We need to become TRUTH, and know our TRUTH. As long as those areas are distorted, we will not be free!

Initiation is also a process of confronting the Guardian of the Threshold, the Dread Lord of Shadows. The Initiate must be willing to be completely trusting and uncomfortable and face the Shadows. Death and Rebirth are the themes of Initiation, and death is the root of our deepest fears, and the true face of the Shadow, it is the terror behind VULNERABILITY, and during Initiation you are in your most vulnerable state of your entire life, blindfolded, bound, naked and at one with the elements and a lot of strangers.

INITIATION QUESTIONNAIRE

Name: _____

Research done: _____

Time Taken: _____ Date: _____

1. What is Initiation? _____

2. How long must a Seeker wait for Initiation? _____

3. What is a Cowen? What does it stand for? _____

4. How many Initiations are there? _____

5. What degree is the Level of Power and why? _____

6. What is the Password to enter the Magick Circle? _____

7. Why is fasting important before a Ritual? _____

8. What are you skyclad, bound and blindfolded at Initiation? _____

9. What is the Book of Shadows and do you have one? _____

10. What is a Wicce? _____

11. What is the difference between a Wiccan and a Wicce and a Pagan? _____

12. What is the Book of Life and who wrote it? _____

13. What are Bales Fires and when are they used? _____

14. What is the Level of Astrum? _____

15. Why is vulnerability important at the Initiation? _____

16. Who is the principal Ritualist under the High Priest/ess? _____

17. Explain why you think an Initiation is important? _____

18. Are you self-responsible and is it important? _____

19. Why is symbolic Death part of Initiation? _____

20. Are you willing to suffer to learn? _____

THE WICCAN REDE!

"Bide the Wiccan Law ye must,
In Perfect Love and Perfect Trust.
Eight Words the Wiccan Rede fulfill,
An it harm none,
Do what you will!

Lest in thy self-defense it be,
Ever mind the rule of three.
Follow this with mind and heart,
And Merry ye Meet,
and Merry ye Part!"

MAGICKAL
TOOLS OF
A WICCE

Magickal Tools of the Witch

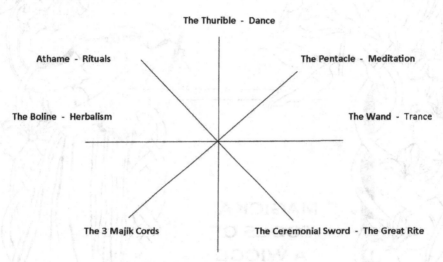

The Thurible - Dance

Athame - Rituals

The Pentacle - Meditation

The Boline - Herbalism

The Wand - Trance

The 3 Majik Cords

The Ceremonial Sword - The Great Rite

The Scourge - Purification and Enlightenment

The Macrocosmic Stellar Three Degree Tools have much to do with the Mysteries of the Magick Circle, which are called the Epagomenes, they are all important and no Magick Circle is complete without them. The Tools also have their correspondences as can be seen above with the Eight Paths of Enlightenment. They are the Powers with which the Wicce develops their skills, necessary to build their Temple of Love and Devotion. Which shall be our Temple of the body/mind/soul. This is sort of restoring ourselves as whole beings, so that we can stand with beauty and with strength.

THE FIRST DEGREE — WICCE — THE TEMPLE OF LUNAR — THE MOON — THE GODDESS

The Thurible – Purification, **Athame** - Illumination, **Pentacle** – Perfection, **The Altar** – Faith, **White Robe** – Freedom, **White Singulum** - Umbilicus and Ladder of the Goddess.

THE SECOND DEGREE — PRIEST/ESS - THE TEMPLE OF SOL - THE SUN — THE HORNED GOD

Boline - Love, **Wand** - Will Power, **Chalice** — Fertility, **Tabard** - Shield of Faith, **Cloak** - Power of Invisibility, **3 Magick Cords** - Sacred Space and Healing.

THE THIRD DEGREE — HIGH PRIEST/ESS — TEMPLE OF ASTRUM — THE STARS — GODDESS AND GOD AS ONE

Scourge – Time; **Sword** – Infinity; **Bell** – Harmony; **Cauldron** – Inspiration; **Scepter** - Control.

THE ALTAR

The Altar is always positioned somewhere safe in your home, so people can view it. But make sure all your Tools are safely put away so people do not touch Consecrated Items. Below is my personal Altar in my home. Which is decorated and changed Seasonally to suit that time of the year. I always have a candle burning in respect of the Goddess and God, and usually upon awakening light the candle, and some incense and meditate for however long I feel is appropriate, whether it be 10 minutes or 1 hour. It depends on the time I have to spare.

An Altar is very personal and should be not too low so you do not have to bend down to it, or too high. The perfect Altar should be the width of your arms wide, and no deeper than you can safely reach. It should be as high as your waist, and if possible have two levels. One level the bottom - to represent everything in Nature physically, and the top Higher Level to represent the invisible within the visible, other-words the spirit of all life, thus representing the Goddess and God.

Flanking each side should be an Altar candle, in the West of the Altar should be a black candle representing the Feminine Spirit - the Goddess; and in the East a white candle representing the masculine spirit - the Horned God. In the centre at the back it would be nice to have a statue of your chosen Goddess and God. Everything else is personal, I always like to have fresh flowers and usually once a week put flowers on my Altar. My mother always had a living plant in the centre of her shrine with a statue of the Virgin Mary in the middle this was her Goddess. The Altar can also be made of anything you want, Oak is preferable, but not a requirement, as it is better to choose a local wood. It is always nice to have an Altar cloth on the Altar, different colours for different Seasons or times of the year, again it is personal choices that make your Altar as grand as you wish or as simplistic but respectful.

The Thurible!

The Censer or Thurible is used to bless or purify our Magick Circle, Home and us. It helps to elevate us from the mundane world with its Magickal aroma's lifting our old factory senses and cleansing and purifying the body, mind and soul. The old Shamanic saying is; *"May our prayers be born upon the rising incense smoke."* The rising incense smoke we can physically see, smell and create a Magickal force field with this combined Element of Air and Fire, even though it represents the east, the Element of Air. Wicces believe that nothing dark or evil can survive in an atmosphere of constructive love and light.

I see many people fighting invisible forces all the time, but do to this only increased its Power. Therefore we should always arm ourselves with Love and Light, combined with the faith in our Goddess. This not only dissolves negative energy but also paralyzes any evil force or entity. If we focus and concentrate on the negative forces within and without ourselves, we realise that it only serves to enforce them and give them more energy, more life. We should always be aware of them, keeping them in check, but never give them the gratification of feeding them with our minds giving them too much attention. We have to starve these forces, to release ourselves from them. If we working 100% on the focus of the good, then all other energies will just fade away.

Our first task then is to Thurify our Magick Circle, this then helps to clear our mind and elevate and insulate us from the outer mundane world. The Incense in the Thurible does this by distracting our consciousness by the mere association of the specified Magickal aroma that is being used. So our Magick Circle then becomes purified of all our outer thoughts and emotions. The Thurible represents Air and is the Symbol of Sacred Space. It aids in contacting certain energies or forces that we need for our Ritual of Spell. It raises our own Vibrations and this part of our Ritual is called; "The Awakening and Raising of the Temple".

No Spell or Word of Power will draw down Cosmic Light, but are Tools to aid in raising our Consciousness to enter the World of Magick. Even the phrase *"Drawing Down the Moon"*, is very misleading, as we do not draw down the Moon but instead open *"Manifest Lunar Consciousness"* and ourselves. When we are working within the Magick Circle we attempt to impregnate this sacred space with certain forces, energies started.

"FOR MY PRAYERS SHALL BE BORN UPON THE RISING INCENSE SMOKE".

Since the beginning of mans awe with Magick, we have used and burned offerings to the Gods. We are not sure how it exactly came about, but I gather it was by mistake. Maybe whilst collecting some wood for a fire, one of our ancestors found either a scented piece of wood, or some aromatic herb or plant, and decided to just throw it on the fire. From here it is a logical step to see how it grew into the beautiful and many varied types of granular gums and resins that we now call incense.

My first Thurible was a "pearl shell" from Broome; I filled it with beach sand to absorb the heat from the burning charcoal blocks. But my next Thurible I purchased at a 'swap meet', it was an old antique silver cake stand, which cost me $3, and for $2 more, I purchased a brass dish to go on top. I put beach sand in that too. The one I used in my Coven (as pictured below) is very special as I brought it in New Orleans at the French Quarter at a friend's Voodoo shop, I paid $160 US and I love it. The Thurible itself is associated with the Air Element, and the incense is associated with the Earth Element and the Charcoal block is associated with the Fire Element. These fire blends are a way of releasing the aroma of incense, the energizing properties of Earth, Air and Fire, plus the grounding and cleansing powers of mineral salts. These Traditional Magickal blends come together in a Natural and effective technique that purifies and Charges any area with Air and Fire, and an aroma to help change the sacred spaces vibrations. Negative energies are drawn into the salts, and the Air and Fire Elements release the Magickal scent clearly and positively.

Resinous blends of incense burned on a charcoal block are stronger and more resinous than regular incense, so use less. This method of releasing fragrance is to be used with caution, and never to be performed unattended, always use care and commonsense whenever dealing with an open flame, remember Wicces and Fire do not go well together (Ha, Ha excuse the pun). Do not use in windy areas, or near flammable substances - to be used with caution and respect.

Here in Australia I discovered many years ago the beautiful aromatic scent of a Grass tree Resin. But there have been over the centuries many different substances used for incense such as Asafetida (Devils Dung), for evil Rites and Banishing's; Wormwood for Necromancy; Musk for seduction; Myrrh for embalming and funerary rites. In general the extracted oils or gums were used instead of the actual plant or wood, the more common of these oils being; Cinnamon, Lavender, Rose, Ylang Ylang, Lime, Cloves, Frankincense, Copal, Myrrh and Benzoin. When you find your perfect Thurible, for static use, rather than to Thurify (perfume) a Magick Circle area, the bowl without the chains is best. The Thurible should be well cleansed and Consecrated, and then a Spell of dedication should be recited like this one I wrote years ago:

"AS I LIGHT THEE PERFUME MAKER,
GOOD-SPIRIT CALLER AND EVIL BREAKER.
AS I KINDLE THIS EARHTLY TOKEN,
POWERS MIGHTY FROM WITHIN ARE WOKEN.
TOOLS OF EARTH, AIR AND FIRE, FOREVER BE,
CONSECRATED NOW BY ME AND THEE!"

PRACTICAL - THURIBLE

Light some incense in your Thurible, using the above suggestions or choose your own, for this experiment, perfumes used should have emotionally wearing associations to you. The atmosphere should be darkened, lit by candlelight. Sit in a comfortable position, in the Center of your Magick Circle, with your Thurible just before you. Concentrate just on your Thurible… just before you. Concentrate on your breathing… inhale…hold…exhale… and continue to draw the vital force from your surroundings… When placing incense upon the lit charcoal block in the Thurible in devotional rituals, it is customary to always offer a prayer to the Goddess, or power that is being invoked. My original Coven use to say this one;

"WE BRING OF YOUR GARDEN, O MIGHTY HORNED GOD,
THE FRAGRANCE ABOUNDS THEREIN.
WE BRING OF YOUR GARDEN O GRACIOUS MOTHER,
THE MAGICK AROMA ABOUNDS WITHIN.
WE FILL THIS AREA OF YOUR PRESENCE.
WE SPEAK YOUR SACRED NAMES,
AND THEREBY SUMMON THE WHISPERING VOICES OF WONDER
FROM ALL THE REGIONS OF YOUR FIELDS
AND ALL YOUR WOODLAND TREE'S.
COME, MIGHTY FATHER, GRACIOUS MOTHER, COME!"

THE MAGICK CORDS

When we are Initiated we are asked to bring four 9' cords, one is to be our Wicces Girdle which is worn around our waist over our robes, it is White and has several specially spaced knots that are called "The Ladder of the Goddess", it is used to trace out and mark the circumference of the Magick Circle. The other three cords are to be our Magick Cords that are used in Binding and Healing Rituals. They are white - representing the Maiden, red representing the Mother and blue representing the Crone. Each is Consecrated with special powers of the triple aspect of our Goddess.

THE BOLINE

The Boline is a Traditional Tool of the Wicce and I have two one, which is only used, within the Magick Circle for cutting, etching, carving, and creating. It has an antler handle and a strong steel blade.

This one I purchased from a store and use it specifically for the ceremonial cutting of my Herbs for Ritual use. It is a small sickle or scythe that is used during harvest time. The Boline does not seem to be mentioned much in the Wiccan world, but is of great importance, especially if you are a Ritualist who wishes to carve candles, make statues of wax or clay, or as in my second one ceremonially harvest your Magickal Herbs and plants. This is a Feminine tool with its Crescent shape, where the Athame is masculine.

THE ATHAME

Where the Thurible is the Element of Air, and represents **PURIFICATION**; the Athame is of the Earth forged in Fire and represents **ILLUMINATION**. On the Path to Illumination or Enlightenment, the Wicce learns that there is much to cut and free themselves from; and that there is much to UNLEARN'. Superstition and ignorance cloud the Wicces consciousness. It is the Will of the Higher Self that is eventually to be awakened. We then set to work developing clarity of Will in the consciousness through the practices of concentration. This step is for the developing Wicce, is a formidable one. It is not merely that attainment of powers of concentration, but mastery of emotional power over the Self. The formula for this is expressed in the Universal Wiccan Rede; *"AN IT HARM NONE, DO WHAT YOU WILL."* Or phased in modern terminology, *"LOVE AND DO YOUR WILL"*, or more simply, *"LOVE UNDER WILL"*.

So the Athame is to become a key to the expression of the Wicces Will, and depends on their Magickal maturity. In any Magickal Ritual you cannot act on your Will and authority alone. You must awaken within the consciousness the Will of Deity. This is done by Invoking the Goddess or God, and so uplifting your consciousness into the Akashic Plane of Spirit, being the Goddess and God. The importance of the work of the Thurible which is used to 'Raise the Vibrations' of the Magick Circle, is paramount if the Will is to change on all Planes. The Athame is therefore an implement that no Wicce is without, well from a ceremonial point of view anyway. From a practical point of view, one does not venture forward in Magickal operations without a Willed Intention, which should come from the Will of the "Higher Self" and not the Mundane mortal. It is very important that the Athame, as a symbol of Will, be well planted in your consciousness, the faculties and corresponding powers symbolized by the Tool.

Thereby you have complete control to Banish that, which has been invoked or evoked. Remember the plight of Disney's 'The Sorcerers Apprentice', who upon splitting the broomstick he had brought to life, found he had two problems to tend with and so on'. Such is the fate of the badly developed Will of the Wicce.

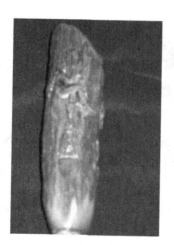 

My family Athame created in the Black Forest in Germany made from Stag Horn and has the Wicce on a Broom and also the Stag God Cernunnos on the handle.

CEREMONIAL BELL

The ceremonial Bell seems to be used less and less in Traditional Covens, but is of importance due to the fact that it signifies that when rang at the beginning of a Ritual, for all to quieten and ready themselves. It is also used to Awaken certain energies or Elemental energies that are welcomed to the Magick Circle.

Is a traditional Buddhist bell that is used by many because it signifies calm, concentration, Attunement, and readiness.

This is a pretty little Bell with a Pentacle etched on it, used by Wicces in their Ceremonies. It is cute and easy to obtain from many Wiccan and new Age shops.

Is the ceremonial bell that I use in my Magick Circle it has been engraved with the Seal of the Breasts of the Goddess, atop with a Crescent Moon. Again this can be purchased easily too.

CAULDRON

The Cauldron is a Tool that no Coven should be without, but is not completely necessary in the workings of every Wicce, as it is used for those into herbal remedies and Potions. We have several Cauldrons that we use; one is for toxic workings, another for herbal workings, and another for Festivals as a stew pot for all to bring something to throw in for Supper and Feasting. Whatever the purpose they are handy to have, but can be quite expensive for the genuine working Cauldron.

FOUR AKASHIC FLAMES

The Lesser Tools of Fire are the Four Akashic Flames/Candles. The Altar also represents the microcosmic Element, the Wicces call forth from within the Magick Circle. This they use within the Magick Circle demonstrating the Hermetic Law, *"AS ABOVE, SO BELOW, AS WITHIN SO WITHOUT."* Flanking the four Cardinal Points of the Circle, they are the Four Akashic Flames of the Four Elements, the macrocosmic forces of Earth, Air, Fire and Water, expressive also of the Four Planes; Physical, Mental, Astral and Spiritual. This is always a reminder to the Wicce', that the work is always effective on all Planes. In my Covens we perform the preliminary Ritual, which I call the *"Warming and Awakening of the Temple"*. Our Man in Black, the Principal Ritualist under the High Priest/ess usually carries out this ceremony. He is also a character called *"Lucifuge"*, and carries a flame "Spirit" into the center of the Magick Circle and onto the Altar. From this Sacred Flame all other Lights are ignited. The Magick Circle is opened in the name of the Goddess; Hecate, Aradia, Diana or Isis; and the Horned God; Pan, Cernunnos or Osiris; demonstrating that Deity is the source of all Light/Knowledge/Power.

How and where did the Athame come into being? The Truth is that during the period known as The Burning Times, where an estimated 9 million men, women and children were forcibly taken from their homes, imprisoned, starved, tortured and finally and horrifically murdered; the Athame had a more horrific purpose, but as horrific as it seemed, it was a necessity in the saving of many lives. The Inquisition proclaimed that anyone who had any exterior markings or protuberances such as birth marks, moles, tumors, warts or any odd markings, these were the markings of the Devil. They believed that these markings were signs of the devil, and in fact were used to suckle the Familiars known as *"Succubi and Incubi"*, to give them life and power in the physical forms of animals or even Wicces themselves. So the Wicces in defense, upon hearing that they may be taken and questioned by the local Inquisitors, would take their dagger and cut the markings from their bodies. Preferring the slow bleeding, and sometimes blood clotting, to the slow torture and eventual death of the Inquisitors. We today, who have reassembled Wicca, reclaim this Tool, as a symbol of Hope and Freedom. It is now used as an added extension to the practicing of Wicce.

The Traditional Athame is black hilted with a double edged blade, the handle is preferably made out of wood or antler, or even stained bone. It should not be a sharp dagger, as it will never EVER cut anything physically. It is an Astral Tool only! Its length should be from the tip of your finger to the base of your palm. It should be as plain as it can be, with no markings whatsoever upon it, and nothing added to it.

It should be clean and virgin. After Initiation certain Magickal sigils are placed on the Athame, but only during the Rite of Initiation. It is used to direct, and to absorb the electro-magnetic energies within the Universe. It is the same with all Tools of the Craft. They are all specially Prepared and Consecrated in the Magick Circle; they are awakened to the connectedness of the Inner Wicce. It takes a long time in being Properly Prepared to hold such a sacred relic that helps us to remember the pain and suffering of our ancestors during the Burning Times. And as we reclaim the Athame and the title Wicce, we will respect both and so the Powers of the Wicce will unfold. When the time is right, the Athame will seek you out and find you.

THE SACRED PENTACLE

Ruling the Higher Mind over the lower Elements of our being of human Nature. It signifies the Awakening of the Cosmic Consciousness and the beginnings of human consciousness, manipulating its environment beyond the Realms of the physical form and perceptions limited into 5 senses. The origins of the Pentagram go far back to remotest historical antiquity, as far back as Pre-Babylonian Sumer. It has been venerated by nearly every culture and civilization. To the Jews is symbolizes the "Pentateuch" - the five Books of Moses. Early Judaic recognized it as pointing out the '5 Stigmata' - the 5 wounds that Jesus suffered whilst on the Cross. It has since survived a variety of titles such as; The Druids Foot, Mirror of Venus, Penta-labrys; Talisman of the Sun; Talisman of Mars; Macrocosmic Man; Shekinah of YHVH; Star of Isis; Celtic Star; The Endless Knot; Pentacle of the Virgin; Star of Knowledge; Pentacle of the Templars; Medieval Churchmen; Wizards Star; Goblins Cross; Devils Sign; Baphomet's Seal; and to the followers of Pythagoras, called it the Pentalpha, being composed of 5 interlaced A's, or Alpha's. Alpha being the first word of the Greek alphabet, we can perhaps view it as shadowing forth unity in the midst of multiplicity.

Those involved in Occult practices could be certain that wherever the Pentacle was displayed, evil had no power at all. Traditionally each of the 5 angles has been Attributed to the metaphysical Elements of Wicca.

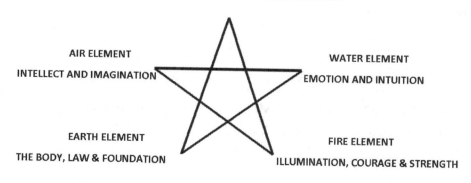

SPIRIT
FAITH WITHIN THE INVISIBLE WITHIN THE VISIBLE

AIR ELEMENT
INTELLECT AND IMAGINATION

WATER ELEMENT
EMOTION AND INTUITION

EARTH ELEMENT
THE BODY, LAW & FOUNDATION

FIRE ELEMENT
ILLUMINATION, COURAGE & STRENGTH

This becomes a graphic betrayal of Spirit ruling over the Elements, and when the Pentagram is placed within the Magick Circle (a symbol of Eternity, totality and unity) its energies are focused and directed. The Inverted Pentagram with the single point buried in the depths of matter, has for many centuries been misinterpreted by the ignorant and those of ill intent, as emblematic of the powers of evil and darkness. However fore the true student of Wicca, it represents Spirit submerged and bonded into the material Elements. Whilst the Inverted Pentagram is representative of Spirits Descent into matter The Pentagram aright, to those of Spiritual Perception represents the redemption of Spirit from Matter by ruling over it. This High Magickal Tool is to be used as a Paten for Ritual Consecrations, especially of salt and water in preliminary Banishing's of the Magick Circle. It is represented as a symbol of authority to the Guardians of the Wicca. All-important Tools may be charged upon this Pentacle, for Consecration before group or solitary consumption. As in all Magick work, ask that your Magick be correct and for the good of all.

The symbols placed upon the Pentacle are placed in a set sequence to represent an ancient Key to unlock the ancient Epagomenes, and the knowledge of the Ancient Ones, when used correctly by those trained properly.

THE GREAT MOTHER: - The Breast of the Goddess - Womb of the Worlds - The Lunar Goddess.

THE HORNED GOD: - Consort of the Goddess - Lord of the Earth and all Nature - Lord of the Magick Circle.

CENTRAL INVERTED PENTAGRAM: - This represents infusion and bonding of the Spirit into Matter, through control of the Earth'.

THE PENTAGRAM: - Power over the Elements - Spirit Rules.

THE KISS - The successes, joys and all the pleasurable experiences in life that encourages us to strive towards perfection.

THE SCOURGE - The pains, sorrows, trials, and difficulties that is essential in the process of self-mastery in the life of a Wicce.

THE MAGICK CIRCLE - The powers and protection of the Magick Circle, the gateway between the Worlds, and enhancer of all True Magick.

INFINITY/ETERNITY - The never-ending cycle of death, birth, life and rebirth. The duality and polarity of manifested existence contained within all encompassing Unity, which is ever in motion.

TRIANGLE OF DARKNESS - Symbol of the Seeker, the Child of Darkness.

TRIANGLE OF LIGHT   - Symbol of the Wicce, the Child of Light.

The Sacred Pentacle is Traditionally made from Bee's wax and Dragons Blood, of which our Coven makes exclusively for Wiccans.

THE SCOURGE

Of all the many Tools in Wicca none is more controversial than the Scourge, the Wicces symbol of Power. Originally it was called the Flail, which separated the wheat from the Chaff, but like many things it has been bastardized down to its present use a whip, a cat of nine tails, etc. It also has some involvement with sexual perversions by the ignorant minds both within and without the Craft. But the true purpose is its original meaning of separating the bad from the good as in the wheat. But on a deeper level, a Spiritual level, it is always used gently for the symbolism of ridding the Initiate of their negativity, and awakening their positivity. Many old Monasteries and Convents used this Tool as a symbol of fear and domination, also for chastisement and the gaining of Sight through flagellation. But in the Wicca it is used for Purification and Enlightenment. Only the older more Traditional Covens use this Tool, as many are not truly aware of its meanings and significance. The High priest or High Priestess makes the Scourge in a ceremonial way, as it is never used by anyone under the rank of High Priest or High Priestess.

The Scourge is made from leather; with the handle being wrapped, attached are eight tails each with 5 knots, totally forty, the number of birth. This Tool is described fully in my next book. But as Douglas Hill comments: *"The ordeal of flagellation seems very important in the face of the fantastic life-span of purification or therapeutic uses of a whip. Flagellations are thought by many to be sexual perversions, but even the devotee's, claiming that the mild birching's they endure are intended to stimulate the circulation and not the libido".*

THE SPIRIT CANDLE

The Spirit Candle or also known as the *"Eternal Flame of the Goddess"* is the first Light that is brought into the Magick Circle, usually by the Maiden on Moon ceremonies or Man in Black at festivals. It is brought into the Magick Circle and presented to the Quarters and placed in the Centre of the Altar. It is then taken to the Centre of the Magick Circle and the Principal Ritualist holds it high and invokes the Light/Life of the Goddess and God and imagines three streams of light descending into the centre of the Hearth Fire which is placed in the Centre of the Circle as they visualize and Invoke, they slowly light the Bale Fire, representing the bringing of Light and Life to the Magick Circle.

After they have done this they then go to the Altar and acknowledge and welcome the Goddess by lighting Her Altar Candle first, and then acknowledge the Horned God and light His Altar Candle. The Spirit Flame is then placed in the centre of the Altar again, prior to the Cleansing and Preparation of the Magick Circle in readiness for the High Priestess and the guests.

"BE TO ME THE FIRE OF MOON,
BE TO ME THE FIRE OF NIGHT,
BE TO ME THE FIIRE OF JOY,
TURNING DARKNESS INTO LIGHT.
BY THE VIRGIN WAXING COLD,
BY THE MOTHER FULL AND BOLD,
BY THE HAG QUEEN SILENT OLD.
BY THE MOON, THE ONE IN THREE,
CONSECRATE THIS MAGICK CIRCLE - BLESSED BE!"

THE CHALICE OF WATER

The Chalice starts out as a lowly goblet for everyday drinking, but when taken and consecrated in a Magick Circle, which is then used only for Ritual as it becomes a Ceremonial Magickal Chalice. The picture of my Chalice here is an 18th Century Chalice from Rome, and is engraved with all the Cup Runes around the perimeter. This Chalice is for Ceremonial Wine. There are two Chalices, which are needed in the Magick Circle, One for Water for Blessings, and one for Wine, for giving Thanks and Offering to the Gods.

The Chalice represents the Womb of the Goddess, and because both water and wine are classed as the "Blood of the Earth", they are important in all our Rituals. The Wine Chalice represents the Goddess, and all within it are Blessings from Her, even water which is the most impure substance on our planet, and which is what every species needs, is a must as it is the vital source of life as we know it. 70% of our bodies are made up of water, and when we mix it with Consecrated Sea Salt, (which is the purest substance found on our planet) when they are mingled it becomes Holy Water. Water that is used to cleanse, purify and banish all negative influences. We should even anoint ourselves in the Magick Circle with the Consecrated Water. The High Priestess always takes a sip of the mingled Salt and Water, to purify herself, in readiness to receive/perceive the Goddess.

The Wine Chalice, with red wine or Port in it also represents the sacredness of the Goddess. It is used in all ceremonies associated with Fertility. And when it is co-joined with the Athame (representing the Horned God/Phallus) represents impregnation of Divine Union being called *"The Great Rite"*, and from here all who partake are blessed by the unification of Goddess and God, and Fertility takes place, such as blessings and new beginnings.

The actual Blessing of the Wine in the Chalice is one of the most SACRED OF ALL RITUALS IN THE CRAFT, and should always be respected with silence and contemplation when it occurs. Visualising the concept of Goddess and God becoming One for the betterment of all Life, so whenever in a Magick Circle, and the wine is being Blessed, please enter the silence, focus and pay respect, as it is an act of Ceremonial Magick at its Highest Level. Even though some things may happen within the Magick Circle that you do not understand, always honor and respect the Ritual as a Mystery, and in time through your respect, dedication and devoutness, you will gain the Insight to understand the Sacred Knowledge of the Wicces, and the Mysteries of the Goddess and God.

This Chalice is used during Large Festivals with large numbers of people available as it holds 4 liters of wine. It has etched around the outer rim the *"History of Avalon and Merlin"*.

This Shell Chalice, which was made in Indonesia, is set in sterling silver and encrusted with precious gemstones. This is my Water Chalice that is used on special occasions.

Besom

The traditional Broomstick or preferably called the besom, is used by the HPs to sweep and cleanse the Sacred Space prior to the casting of the Magick Circle. It is done in a Widdershins manner around the Magick Circle to cleanse and remove all negativity in a Deosil fashion to attract and draw in all positivity. It is used for other ceremonial uses as well, but this is only for High Magick by the High Priesthood. When placed outside your door in this upright fashion means that all is safe within. If upside down or on the ground then it means there is danger within, do not enter.

Ceremonial Sword

The Ceremonial Sword is only used in working full Covens or Churches, by the High Priesthood. It is a significant Tool of the Higher levels of Magick. It is used in the swearing of the oath, discipline, severing bonds, releasing Binding Spells, and also in the Blessing of a hand Fasting.

REGALIA

Ritual Regalia are very important as it separates us from our Mundane lives in civilian clothing. Every Wicce should have either made there own Robe or have someone accepting to make one for you. It should either be in white, green or brown. It is a personal choice; we try to rid ourselves of the colour black because of its negative connotations. We also have what is called Tabards in our Covens, this keeps the Robe clean and protected it is a vestment that goes over the top of the Robe. Cloaks are great but only for winter and those cold wet nights that we need to keep warm so as to not get sick, besides that they have no relevance.

MISCELLANEOUS TOOLS

THE CEREMONIAL DRUM

This is used in our Magick Circles only because of my Shamanic Training in South America. The Drum represents the heartbeat of Mother Earth, and is used for tuning into Nature and for Awakening certain energies. It is also used for Cleansing and raising one's vibrations, and on a deeper level it is used for Healing. We sometimes use it to drum people into our Magick Circle, as it raises their vibrations in readiness for the Ritual.

THE CEREMONIAL HEALING WAND

This Wand I designed and it was made by Shankari, the famous jeweler, and has my mothers and grandmothers hair in it, alongside my own. It is made of solid silver and decorated with Angel Hair (Rutilated Quartz) emeralds, pearls, moonstone, and clear quartz. It is used for Invoking/Evoking spirit energies, for Healing, and more importantly Invoking the Matriarchs of my family.

Wands Traditionally are made from different things the simplest and best is the Natural Branch from a tree (that has never touched the ground, as it must never be Earthed). Rose wood Wands for Love;

Pine and Cedar for Strength: Oak for Deity Invoking: plus many more. It depends on personal choice, but the more elaborate does not necessarily mean the better. I have several Wands. The Wand of Isis for Egyptian Workings: Engraved Ceremonial Wand for Ceremonial Magick: Acorn Tipped Wand for Invoking/Evoking the Goddess and God in Wiccan Ceremonies: Pine cone tipped Wand for Full Moons and Festivals again for Deity: No matter what the Wand always remember it is an extension of yourself, and you must always be PROPERLY PREPARED.

ROYAL SCEPTER

This Scepter is a royal Scepter, which is a 17th Century Arch Druids Scepter from Britain. It is quite lavish and I use it only for Formal Occasions where the Arch Priestess side of me comes out, usually large Festival gatherings when there is VIP's from overseas, and High ordinations of the High Priesthood. This has a Twisted Horn as the staff part, with engraved in Celtic design motifs in silver and gold. It has an Amethyst either side, and in the top is a Meteorite rock from the Moon, which is the power source of this Wand, (with the power of the Stars and what lies beyond). This Scepter is also used as an official Wand for High Magick and for Dubbing of Newly Ordained High Priests and High Priestesses.

HEALING WITH THE OCEAN

Go to the ocean, to make a Sea-sonal ceremony, take with you a couple of small quarts crystals as offerings to Her. Walk (always) barefoot in silence to the waters edge on the shore Walk along the shore until you find a special place that feels Magickal, private and just right to do your Ritual.

When you come to this place, stand and face Sister Ocean... See Her bountiful beauty and majesty... Hear Her voice in the waves that give and take... smell Her salt water fragrance and taste it with your breath... feel Her power and Magickal rhythms... Greet Her with a Ceremonial Invoking gesture... stretch out your arms by your side... raise them up... and face the palms of your hands toward Her...

Call Her by whatever name or names you may know Her... Mother Ocean... Sister Sea... Goddess of the Sea... Yemaja...Aphrodite... Mari... Mara... Honor Her presence, with prayer, spoken or chanted or better still sung... whatever seems appropriate and respectful and beautiful to you...

Give Her your Healing offering... fling one of your crystals into the water as far away as you can... and let Her waves carry it away to Her very heart and to help heal Her and nourish Her... Then step into Her waters yourself... feel Her healing power flow through and ground you as you physically connect with Her... touch Her with your hands and your feet... anoint your face with Her waters... and let Her guide you in how much of your body... to wash in Her and for how long... pay attention instead to being one with the musical rhythms of Mother Ocean... Pay attention to whatever shells or other gifts from Her that she gifts to you... and that flow up to you during this ritual bathing... pick up any that you sense are meant for you... but do not be greedy and leave the rest.

After physically connecting with Sister Ocean... return to the water and let Her waves heal you... then just go to the shore and sit before Her in quiet meditation... Listen to the sounds of Her waves an let them guide your meditation, let them be the music... and focus... let your thoughts… concerns… and pain push away from your conscious mind as you put your attention instead on just being One with the music of the great Cosmic Sister Ocean… Lay down on the shore… if it feels right… to deepen the relaxation of your body whatever protection it needs… such as the Self Blessing Ritual, or the Banishing Ritual of the Pentagram… when you feel completely relaxed… refreshed and attuned to the pulse of Sister Ocean and your meditation by asking Her to guide you on your spiritual quest and how you can bring about a better state of wellness within your day to day life… reflect on yourself radiating wellness and that sense of sharing and gifting of your cosmic primordial oceans that drift within your very being.

When you feel ready… rise up as though completely lifted and elevated physically, mentally, psychically and spiritually… and go to the waters edge… and stand in the water in Pentagram Position… and facing Sister Ocean… chant or sing or silently give thanks for the healing and spiritual insights you have received from Her this day… also thank Her for any shells or gifts that She guided to you to receive from Her…

To close… hold the crystal firmly in the palms of both hands changing it with your blessing of light, love, and healing energies, for Sister Ocean… then kiss the crystal… then gently and lovingly toss the crystal you brought as a second offering and thanksgiving… then depart in silence… feeling completely refreshed and uplifted with your Sea-sonal ceremony.

WICCES TOOLS QUESTIONNAIRE

Name: _____

Research used: _____

Time Taken: _____ Date: _____

1. What is the 1st Degree and what are their Tools? _____

2. What are the macrocosmic Stellar Three Degrees and why? _____

3. What is the Astrum? _____

4. What is the term Skyclad mean and why do we have it? _____

5. What is your favourite incense and why? _____

6. What is the Thurible and what is it used for? _____

7. What is an Athame and what do we use it for? _____

8. What is the Hermetic Principle? _____

9. What are the Watchtowers? _____

10. What is the Akasha? _____

11. What are the Elements an their associated Tools? _____

12. What is the difference between a Pentacle and a Pentagram? _____

13. Explain the five points of the Pentagram? _____

14. Explain the Magick Wand and its uses? _____

15. Who uses the Sword in the Circle and why? _____

16. Why is salt and water so important? _____

17. Explain the symbolism of the Chalice? _____

18. What is a Boline? _____

19. What is the purpose of a Scourge? _____

20. Explain why the Altar is in the North? _____

21. Should every Wicce have a Broomstick/Besom? _____

THE MAGICK
CIRCLE

"And even in this world She teaches us the Mystery of the Magick Circle, which is placed between the world of men, and the world of the Ancient Ones".

So what is a Magick Circle? Simply it is our Wiccan Temple. It is where Wiccans formally worship the Goddess and God. It is the place where most would prefer to honor the Goddess and God and practice their Magickal workings, for here they have the eyes and ears of the Gods of old.

A Magick Circle may be cast indoors, whether for the sake of privacy, or because of severely inclement weather. Where possible, a Magick Circle should be created and cast outside under the stars with an ever-patient gaze of the light of the Moon. A Coven may have its own ritual area that it uses exclusively, in a members backyard for example. Or a Coven may go to one of the many Sacred Sites around their town or city. Covens that work inside usually have a room dedicated to the Goddess and the Horned God, and so it is permanently set up for worship, I actually have an indoor Temple for when there is negative weather and an outer Temple for when the weather is beautiful. Note that this does not mean that the Magick Circle is a permanent creation, the space maybe permanent but the energies creating the Magick Circle on the Astral are closed and banished after every ritual. Every Magick Circle is a *temporary* doorway to the Astral, and is a creation of the personal power of those who have erected and awakened the Magick Circle. If you do not have the knowledge to Properly close down a Magick Circle then invoked Astral entities will remain and create havoc and psychic mischief of those involved. <u>YOU HAVE BEEN WARNED!</u>

A Magick Circle can be raised and awakened at anytime, but is best around the times from the New to the Full Moon. How the Magick Circle is actually erected is taught in my next book (Complete Encyclopedia of Wicca for the Witch Book 2). As a Tool for working on the Astral Plane, the Magick Circle is like the lens of a torch and magnifies all your energies and thoughts and has three main functions:

CONCENTRATION: It provides a comfortable atmosphere suitable for focusing energy to be used in a working ritual.

PROTECTION: Alas, there are malingering Astral Entities that may attempt to tap into ones psyche whilst being open during the rituals.

CONTAINMENT: As energy is raised, it must be contained or 'packaged' until it is ready to be 'sent out' to its target.

There are some symbolical aspects of the Magick Circle that I believe that the Seeker should be familiar with, that relate to Wiccan Philosophy. The Circle is a geometric figure that has no end and no beginning. Nor does birth, death and rebirth, the cycle of Reincarnation. Many things in Nature are in circles such as the seasons, night and day, birds' nests, and many more. Were you to stand upon a flat treeless plain and look up; you would be in the exact centre of a Circle. You are the microcosm within the macrocosm. A Full Moon, or the Setting Sun, symbols of deity appear as Circles in the sky. A Circle defines space in two dimensions, but as we work in three dimensions, would it not be justifiable that we work in a Magick Circle of Three dimensions?

The Magick Circle is actually part of a Magick Sphere or Orb. Half of the Sphere is above ground, and the other half is below ground. The Magick Circle then represents an area where the Sphere cuts the ground. So does the Magick Circle contain and protect; for Magick, both good and bad knows no physical limits, and can, go up or down, as well as out and about and within and without. So why do we not build a Temple with physical walls, a physical roof and great shrines of dedication? Well actually, some do, even in a purpose built Temple, the Sphere/Magick Circle is still cast because it is an Astral Temple not a physical Temple.

A Magick Circle is a place often described as being "Between the Worlds", a common ground where Wiccans, Wicces, Gods and Goddesses can meet and be secure. The creation of the Magick Circle is a key ritual of Wicca; it is comparatively different to the New Religions. Magickally constructed Astral Temples are definitely preferred as a place of worship. The very act of building a temporary Temple with Magick energy helps to create a proper array of emotions spiritually, to aid in raising one's ritual consciousness, awareness and connection. The Magick Circle is like a clearing in a rainforest, a place of peace and harmony, amidst 'the eat or be eaten' chaos of the mundane. As we clear a space for our Magick Circle, indoors or outdoors, we are also clearing our psyches, and becoming attuned to the Magick and Spirit of Wicca. As the Magick Circle becomes manifest, a living thing that surrounds us, it becomes a part of us as we prepare to do the "Great Work" of the Goddess and Horned God.

To cast the Magick Circle without correct knowledge and ritual is highly ignorant and dangerous, in as much, that from the first moment you begin to lay out your Magick Circle, certain factors are released to strike at deeply rooted triggers within your subconscious. As you prepare your Magick Circle with the candles, incense, the Altar, etc.! You have begun to awaken, condition and program yourself to the concepts of eternal primordial Truth. They have always been there, but were released them when you made the preparation for the Magick Circle, the Meeting Place Between the Worlds of Men and the Realms of the Ancient Ones.

Since the dawn of Man, we have not wanted to face the Truth of whom and where we originally came. We wanted to believe that we were made in the likeness of Gods, instead of us creating Gods in our likeness! The Truth of the Intellect is that we came from the oceans of our world and crawled through the swamps and wetlands, and gradually through millions of years of evolution and experiencing life from the lowliest of creatures to what we have aspire to be at the height of the animal kingdom to our present state of heightened awareness.

But even the Magicians of ancient times fear this knowledge, and believed we were not ready to receive this Truth, knowing that man would fear this primordial dark terror that resided in our very deep subconscious. Created new Foundations for their worship, the Magicians of old learned to control this ancient dark terror that could arise and wreak havoc and chaos to mankind.

They gave the sacred Symbol which represented the left-hand Path and was an inverted Triangle and called it the **"TRIANGLE OF DARKNESS"**, (spirit submerged into matter), and is symbolic of the Children of darkness (The Seekers of Wiccecraft), where it has been passed down through the ages to our present neophytes who seek the first steps of Wiccaning. This symbol revealed the dark Knowledge that lies within us all.

When many of the books or Grimoires of Wisdom in the Temples and Alexandrian Libraries had been destroyed by the New Religion, much knowledge was lost but because it was also learned and memorized and was never forgotten, as it has been carried through to the present day as an oral Tradition. The Fellowship of the right-hand Path eventually discovered the secrets of the Inverted Triangle; and had to balance the symbol, so they devised the **"TRIANGLE OF LIGHT"** this was a golden Triangle inside a silver Circle, which is the true symbol of the Wicce. It was here that the Powers of Light and Dark began to take on new aspects as the Initiated Wicce and penetrated deeper into the Mysteries of the Triangles and of the Craft itself.

But the Old Gods have never been forgotten, and false names were used in their place to hide the Truth from prying eyes, especially the ancient kingdoms that sought their secrets. When the Orders of Light and Darkness realized that the whole world was to be engulfed in a world catastrophe (that of the great flood); they together consulted in Unity and great secrecy to discuss the sacred preservation of the Mysteries. After many debates, the Council of Light and Dark combined their esoteric knowledge and their symbology. As a result the two Triangles were interlaced to form a set pattern, which has been handed down to the present day to the High Priesthood as the six pointed star; the Hexagram. This was Unity of the macrocosm and the microcosm inside the Magick Circle. It also represents many other aspects such as dark/light, masculine/feminine, right/wrong, good/bad, truth/deceit, above/below, heaven/earth and many more. Extra-sensory perception is the common inheritance of us all, and forgotten or not believed by most, but the Magickal method of release, one acquires under the careful guardianship of a trained and qualified Priestess or Priest.

After the Great Flood that covered the world, nearly wiping out all of mankind. The ancient Egyptians used the Triangles to represent the **"TRIAD OF DEITIES". "THE TRIANGLE OF DARKNESS",** was adopted and used by the people of Neph-Kham in the lands of Lower Egypt, and led by the Goddess Sekhmet and the God Anubis. The **"TRIANGLE OF LIGHT",** was adopted and used by the people of Khem, the golden lands of Upper Egypt, and led by Amon-Ra and ruled by the Goddess Aset (Isis) and the God Asar (Osiris).

The magician priests of both lands used the **"STAR OF UNITY",** which is where they combined the two Triangles to form this Magickal symbol. All these symbols individually or interlaced have great Magickal significance and Power. As they are all based upon mathematical concepts when placed with the Magick Circle. To these great Anubis Priests of Saiss, these symbols seem ed to be incomplete, so two more Triangles were introduced to make the Twelve Points of the Zodiac, with a sacred and hidden Thirteenth sign being in the centre of the Magick Circle called Ophiucus (Arachne), which corresponded to the Thirteen houses of the Astrological Zodiac. The first of these Triangles was called the **"TRIANGLE OF LIFE",** and was led by Kephera-Ra, and incorporated Hapy and Tuamatef. The second Triangle was called the **"TRIANGLE OF WISDOM",** led by Thoth and supported by Imset and Quebsennuf. The Great Twin Circles of the Magick Circle was now brought together to form the Triangles of **"LIGHT, DARKNESS, LIFE AND WISDOM".**

Thoth, better known by the Greeks, as Hermes Trismegistos was the greatest High Priest and Magician before the great Merlin, some even say he was the true Merlin who was immortal. In his sacred "Book of Wisdom", also known as the "Book of Thoth". He gave to man the greatest knowledge to ever be known, in his Tabulae Smaragina Hermes tablets (The Emerald Tablets) was the knowledge of the Universe, past, present and future. This ancient Book consisted of 78 plates, which later was changed to the 78 tarot cards. Man Tarot readers by the thousands all over the world, many of them are not even aware of the great knowledge that they hold. This ancient **"BOOK OF LIFE",** held the keys to many forms of reality, and many worlds. Sadly man has forgotten the true purpose for their creation, especially as the last gift of the great Thoth himself to assist in the survival of mankind and our Earth.

Use them for meditation and you will find a certain connection between the 78 Tarot Cards and the 72 Genii of the Mercury Zone. Lay them in correct order of the circumference of your Magick Circle, and they will reveal to you the very Magick of the Mysteries of the Magick Circle and the revelations of the Tarot, then you will understand the Cycle of Nature, and penetrate the Mysteries of the Goddess and God.

When you have understood and solved the Mystery of the 72 points of the Magick Circle, you will attribute out of the six remaining cards, four to the Elements (Earth, Air, Fire and Water) and two to polarity (The Goddess and God), these will hopefully unlock and guide you to the hidden secrets of the Book of Thoth.

Learn how to strengthen your Will power, and how to make belief as firm as a rock, in order to be able to increase the power of conviction in such a way that you can directly bring about true Miracles/Magick by working with intent. The letters that accompany some of the Tarot Cards represent secret Keys, as you will learn and realise after being in touch with your relevant Sage or High Priestess.

POWERS OF
THE WICCES
PYRAMID

POWER OF THE PYRAMID

Throughout modern history man has never been in awe of a man-made object as much as the great Pyramid of Giza. It structure, its purpose for being and its very mathematical preciseness is a feat that even modern man cannot duplicate exactly. It surpasses wonderment and perfection, this ancient monument is the largest, heaviest and most perfect structure created on the face of the Earth by human hands. It overwhelms our imagination and defies all explanation within its mystery. Only when you are standing in front of it can you truly get the incredible power of its majesty as even its origin is lost in the shadows of time. The Great Pyramid of Cheops as it is locally called, (supposedly built by the master builder Cheops). Is an embodied tomb not only of Tutankhamun but the very knowledge and legacy of ancient man, which is left within this Immortal Oracle?

Tis perfectly hewn structure is an encoded body of knowledge, mystery, mathematics, astronomy, and unending storehouse of ancient knowledge and wisdom, gifted to man, that one day he will be wise enough to uncover its true Mysteries. It is the true Book of Life and Knowledge, and is the central key search for the how's and why's of our very existence and the purpose of our being. There is an ancient Egyptian saying; **"MAN FEARS TIME, AND TIME FEARS THE PYRAMIDS".** I believe that hidden somewhere within or without the Great Pyramid is its real purpose for being, and if we look hard enough we may just find answers to our own destiny. Does it not then make the Pyramid of Giza the ancient **"PHILOSOPHERS STONE"?**

This photo was taken on my trip to the Pyramids and the Sphinx in 1999.

Recent evidence shows that the Cheops Pyramid has Universal applications. The Pyramidal shape, with the exact ratio's of the Great Pyramid are centered on the true North South axis, reflect, generate, accumulate certain electro-magnetic energy fields. If we leave certain objects in true north-south axis Pyramids with the exacting measurements of the Great Pyramid, Magick Happens. Food, honey, wine and grain have been left within the Pyramids for weeks with remarkable results which included the shortened germination of seeds, increased healthy growth in plants, and even for humans who use the Pyramid (in miniature of course) complete relaxation, improved focus, clarity of mind, ultimate meditative states of bliss, healing and even rejuvenation.

Many always ask why so much attention is focused on the Great Pyramid, when there are hundreds of other Pyramids not only throughout Egypt but the whole world, including; South America, The Himalayas, Siberia, Mexico, Central America, Cambodia, France, England, and yes even here in Australia at a place called Gympie in Queensland. In Egypt alone there are more than 30 major and minor Pyramids, with some still being discovered today, that have been buried by the desert sands of time. We concentrate on this amazing Great Pyramid due to its size, as it is the largest man-made structure ever seen in the world both geometrically and mathematically, and also because of many features that are missing in other Pyramids.

I know and believe that if the ancient knowledge and secrets of the Pharaohs and High Priests are to be uncovered, that it will happen within or around the portals of the Great Pyramid and also the Sphinx herself who stands like a sentinel guardian watching over time and space. This incredible Pyramid is only 10 miles West of Cairo, and stand on a 20 acres leveled plateau that was created by man, with its enormity standing at over 130 feet overlooking the Sphinx, the palm groves and the River Nile. The Great Pyramids base is roughly 13 acres and is level to a fraction of an inch. There are more than 2,600,000 solid blocks of granite, sandstone and limestone, where each weighs from 2 - 70 tons in weight. At present its height stands at over 450 feet, this added onto the 130 feet high plateau makes it over 580 feet in height. All the blocks are so precisely cut that they are never more than 1/100th of an inch.

It has been claimed that the Great Pyramid contains more solid masonry than all the Cathedrals, churches and Chapels ever built in England since the time of Jesus.

Many are not aware that in the ancient writings of Thoth, it states that the Sphinx was a geodetic marker that indicates the Equinoxes and Solstices, and that long ago it held between its giant paws a solid Obelisk Disc of solid Crystal Quartz, this was called the "Djappa Hi", or more correctly in English **"THE STARGATE".** Whose giant shadows used to calculate and compute the correct circumference of the earth and the varied degree's of the Longitudes and Latitudes. To the Children of the Old religion we know it as the Covenant of the Stars and Man, the eternal wisdom and truth of the world, past, present and future, of where we came from and where we will eventually return.

Standing on the steps of the Great Pyramid of Giza, Egypt.

To make your own Pyramid it must be as close to scale as the Great Pyramid as possible for the best results. It must not be placed in a metal base, and it should not be too near any electrical appliances. The Pyramid works better if you tape a hinged base along one edge. The material should be wood, cardboard, or any material that is Natural. The Pyramid must be aligned properly. Draw a square on paper and around the edge of your model, and then draw a north/south line crossing exactly in the centre, under the apex of the Pyramid. Anything placed under the Pyramid, should be ideally placed 1/ 3 of the way up, at the level of the Kings Chamber. With a compass, angle your Pyramid so that one side faces North. Each side is a triangle with the sides 8 7/8", and a base of 9 3/8". Centimeters are the ideal measurement.

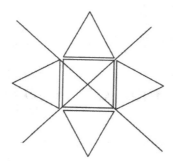

HEIGHT	BASE	SIDE
15cm (6")	23.56cm	22.41cm
31cm (12")	48.69cm	46.33cm
61cm (24")	95.81cm	91.17cm

Cut the sides and assemble the pyramid, glue or sticky tape can be used. To sharpen a blue Gillette razor blade; the blade must be on the side of a matchbox, inside the 6" Pyramid. The box must be directly under the apex of the Pyramid. The blades edges face East and West. The first time the blade is treated, it should be left in place for a week. After those 24 hours between shaves is sufficient.

As a good test before you go to bed, fill two glasses of water from the tap, place one in the Pyramid, and the other outside. In 12-24 hours you will be amazed at the difference in taste, as the water in the Pyramid tastes pure and refreshing.

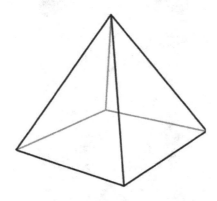

PYRAMIDS OF AUSTRALIA

Standing in a bush land some distance from the town of Gympie in Southern Queensland is a crudely-built 40 meter tall terraced stone pyramidal structure which I believe will one day help to alter the history of Australia - to prove that 3,000 years ago, joint Egyptian and Phoenician mineral seeking expeditions established mining colonies here. It is not the only structure of its kind found in Australia. A second terraced stone pyramidal structure, at least twice the size of the Gympie example, exists in dense bush land near Sydney. There is no doubt these structures are stepped Pyramids, identical to those built by the ancient Egyptians and Aztecs.

I first learnt of the Gympie Pyramid from an old prospector's tales dating back to 1851, when gold was first discovered at Gympie. To the old prospectors, it was just some curious formation to which they attracted no importance. I also learnt that in 1966 a Gympie farmer, the late Dal. K. Berry, ploughed up a strange stone idol, resembling a squatting ape, on his property. These are original clippings from a newspaper.

This idol was ploughed up by Dal Berry. It matches statues in Egypt of the Baboon God Thoth.

Rock carvings that show they are definitely not Aboriginal on the Gympie cliff walls.

This is a very old sketch of the Gympie Pyramid, prior to its growth of trees.

Picture of the Gympie Pyramid from a distance. You can see a clear pointed hill with growth over 200 years old.

Ancient cave etchings of Egyptian Sarcophagus and resting bed found in Gympie.

My theory is reinforced by ancient Aboriginal legends which tell of a race of "Culture-Heroes", who, far back in the "Dreamtime", sailed into Gympie in large ships shaped like birds, to 'dig holes' in the hills and erect the "sacred Mountain" (the Pyramid) and interbreed with some of the tribes. Local Aboriginal tradition indicates the "Culture-Heroes", built the Pyramid for some astronomical purpose.

Gympie now stands 57 kilometers inland from Tin Can Bay. Geologists have shown that until about 1000 years ago a harbor did in fact; exist between Tin Can bay and Gympie. The "Ships" shaped like birds could describe the bird-headed prows of the old Phoenician Triremes.

There are 18 recognizable terraces in the Pyramid. The top four are built from crude slabs of rock up to two tons in weight each; the other 14 terraces are constructed of smaller rock slabs. The Pyramid would have measured approximately 500 meters in Circumference. The Pyramid near Sydney consists of much larger stones than those used at Gympie.

Some years before my first inspection of the Pyramid, a bush walker is said to have found a small onyx Scarab Beetle pendant (an object of ancient Egyptian worship) among rocks near the Pyramid. Aboriginal Cave paintings near Gympie include a hand stencil bearing an Ankh, or "Solar Cross" of the ancient Egyptians, etched into the centre of the hand. Local Aboriginals have pointed out at remains of open-cut copper and gold mines in the Gympie district, which they say, were dug before the coming of the white man.

Near one such site, I photographed a Cliffside carving of a head in profile showing a headdress reminiscent of Phoenician headgear of biblical times. The Gympie area appears to have been extensively mined in antiquity for quite a long period. The large amount of Phoenician and Egyptian pottery fragments ploughed up by farmers thereabouts over the past 100 years implies that a considerable number of people colonized the region. A further search may uncover the location of a former settlement now buried in the district. I believe I know where it is, but I am keeping quiet about this, as to avoid possible vandalism.

In 1985 my partner and I together undertook our first field investigation of the Gympie district, during which we located and made a thorough examination of the mysterious stepped structure, measuring and photographing it. I soon had little doubt that the structure was a crudely built Stepped Pyramid, of the type constructed in Egypt over 4000 years ago. Trees up to 600 years old were growing up on top and through the stonework, which attested to its pre-European origin. Near the proximity of the Pyramid while foraging among rocks I found a small weathered idol carved from local ironstone. The idol was taken to Katoomba Museum, (NSW). The idol has since been compared with Egyptian examples of the God Thoth, in ape form clutching the Tau, or Cross of Life. The Berry idol is unquestionably of pre-Christian origin, as he ploughed it up from a depth of 2 meters below the modern surface soil deposits. An excavation of the site, carried out by a team and me revealed the remains of an ancient hearth containing charcoal and nodules of smelted bronze. That bronze was being smelted at Gympie 3000 years ago implies the presence of a more advanced race than Aborigines

In 1986-1987, I made investigations at a site where enormous stone blocks had been cut from a Cliffside on a large hill, and left abandoned on a flat area nearby, now overgrown with trees at least several hundred years old. A 10 meter wide causeway cut out of solid rock extends from this point down the hillside to what could be remains of an ancient stone wharf on the edge of what is now flat farming land, but which, 3000 years ago, was part of an ancient harbor system. According to Aboriginal legend, a vast amount of 'stone' (minerals) was dug out of the Gympie hills by the strange visitors and shipped out to sea. No doubt back to the Middle East.

If Egyptians and Phoenicians mined Gympie, they certainly had the ships to sail here. Over 3000 years ago their often huge ships/galleys sailed from the Red Sea to trade with the South-East Asian peoples, establishing mining colonies in Malaysia and West Iran. There is evidence that they may have mined copper in the North-West Kimberley's in Western Australian coast 2500 years ago. Local Aboriginals possess Middle-Eastern facial features. It is said Torres Strait Islanders once mummified their dead with methods exactly used in Egypt 2900 years ago. The early Aboriginals of the Gympie district once worshipped a Sun God and Earth-Mother Goddess, handed on to them, they claimed, by the mysterious "Culture Heroes".

Just how long the Gympie colony existed, and why it was abandoned, are questions to be answered.

THE SEEKER

"I DO NOT BID YOU ENTER THE HOUSE OF MY WISDOM,
BUT RATHER LEAD YOU TO THRESHOLD OF YOUR OWN MIND."
"THERE WAS DOOR TO WHICH I FOUND NO KEY,
THERE WAS A VEIL THROUGH WHICH I MIGHT NOT SEE.
SOME LITTLE TALK AWHILE OF THEE, AND ME
THERE WAS! AND THEN NO MORE! OF ME AND THEE!"

THE MAGICK CIRCLE QUESTIONNAIRE

Name: _____

Research used: _____

Time Taken: _____ Date: _____

1. What is a Magick Circle? _____

2. Where can a Magick Circle be cast? _____

3. Why do Wiccans work in a Circle and not another shape? _____

4. What are Elementals and name them, and their Quarters? _____

5. What is Truth? _____

6. Why is it better to work outdoors? _____

7. Explain the Abyss? _____

8. What are the other names for the Hexagram? _____

9. What are the 13 zodiac signs and their names? _____

10. How many cards in the Tarot Deck, and what is their true name? ___

11. What and why is the third Tarot card so important? _____

12. Who created the Tarot? _____

13. What are Genii? _____

14. What are the Four Watchtowers other names? _____

15. What does the Centre of the Magick Circle represent and why? _____

16. Where is the Altar placed and why? _____

17. What are the symbols of the Left-Hand Path and why? _____

18. What is the true symbol of the Wicce? _____

19. Why should we not destroy darkness and evil? _____

20. Who are the Lady and Lord of the Magick Circle? _____

LUNAR CYCLES
AND THEIR
MEANINGS

In ancient times we did not measure our time by days or years but by Months. It is this very Beacon in the night sky that man has disassociated themselves from, wed have lost connection with all of Nature and forgotten Her deepest Mysteries. The Phases of the Moon echo throughout the whole of Nature including us humans. It is the Moon that changes the tides, the seasons and the ebb and flow of the movement of the cosmic oceans within every woman on the planet.

We walk in our concrete urban jungles with heavy feet and downcast hearts, tired and worn out from the pace of the 21st century life. We may consider ourselves brutish masters of the technological society, (which is failing us and destroying our planet, but what price have we truly paid? For many of us life has become mechanical, like the machines, computers and robots that are taking over so much of our lives. Where is the joy, the sense of creativity, of being in harmony with our environment and us? When do our bare feet truly touch Mother Earth?

The Australian Aborigines, the primary people of our land, follow the song lines of Dreamtime and sing their world into being. We sing our world into being with a symphony of negative thoughts, fear, pollution and greed. It is now that we desperately need to reconnect with the Earth - Our Mother - and follow Her Natural cycles to find our own rhythms, to balance out the ever-increasing pressure of our high technology. It will be only through this return to the old ways that we can ever again have the Harmony of the Golden Age. The earth has so much creative energy and so does the Moon; they are both sacred and needed for our survival. We are heirs to the ancient Ley-lines that our Wicces of old traced out, marking and noting where these powerful energy grids were, the Aboriginals knew these sacred grids where the energy fields were created and traced out by our ancestors, who toiled to bring forth a new nation, and the Aboriginals who so love this land and have a history of 40,000 years of Dreaming in this most ancient of lands. We still feel this connection to Nature - haven't you noticed how relaxed, harmonious and creative you feel when you are by the sea or in the country?

Observing and working with the flow of the Seasons, and the cycles of the Moon, we learn tap into a vast reservoir of Natural human knowledge that has been followed by many, for thousands of years. When working with these energies we can more quickly gain insight and resolve areas of discord in our lives. We begin to see *"The patterns that connect"*, the various aspects of our lives flowing like golden webs weaving together our life experiences.

Spring - is a time of rising energy, of rebirth, new life, new ideas and new directions for all.

Summer - represents the flowering of these ideas and new beginnings of the Spring Celebration, and a time to be outdoors, and in Nature.

Autumn - The energies are diminishing, preparing for Winter. It is a time to harvest and gather in the successful components of the previous seasons and sows the seed for the next spring.

Winter - is a time of work going on in the depths, as seeds germinate. It is a time of self-reflection and nurturing.

The **Lunar** cycles follow a similar pattern:

NEW MOON - Is the beginning and birthing of the Full Moon, it is a time for inner reflection, of attuning with Nature and the Moon, quietening your self and listening to your Inner Wicce. At this time we connect with the Goddess and God. We also associate the Communion with deity, elevating our Vibrations in preparation for the Full Moon, connection to the earth and the Moon energies, Creativity and Spells that complete at The Full Moon.

WAXING CRESCENT MOON - It is the time to prepare to welcome in the new. And a time to be Properly Prepared for connection with the Goddess.

FIRST QUARTER MOON - This is the time self-cleansing, self-healing, self-purification, self-awareness, and the time to nurture, at this time we set our goals for the coming Month. This is a power time for affirmations; focus on business, new directions, and positive steps towards spiritual goals.

WAXING GIBBOUS MOON - Time to recharge your energies in readiness for the Full Moon, time of contemplation, meditation, relaxation, of slowing down to take minute vacations of looking at a flower and just being with Nature.

THE FULL MOON - It is the peak of our Month when all Wicces gather to honor and celebrate the Great Mother Goddess and Her symbol the Full Moon. The HPs invokes and calls upon the energies of the Full Moon and awakens the Goddess within. Here we connect with all life and bring all things into balance and harmony. It is the highest time of Goddess Spirituality. It is about Spiritual Insight and Awareness, Creativity, Femininity, honoring the feminine with males as well, time for Powerful Magick, including healing, Nature, learning and the Great Magick that is lent to us at this sacred Time.

WANING GIBBOUS MOON - This is the time we concentrate on what we asked for at Full Moon, of giving it focus and our Will, by sending our thoughts and energies to keep it charged and vibrating, Ready for Fruition.

LAST QUARTER MOON - This is a time of confronting our fears and negatives, of lifting the veils of delusion and releasing the Shadows with Love and Trust. We remain calm and harmonious in what we have received, and learn to relax and have more faith. It is not so much about letting go of our fears and pains, but understanding their deep messages, and how we must learn from them.

WANING CRESCENT MOON - This time we have learnt about our fears and pains, and like the Autumn leaves, allowing their release, so they can nourish our lives with content and understanding.

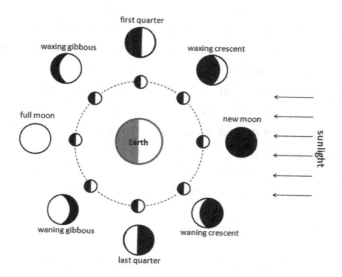

WINTER

"A TIME OF RELF-REFLECTION AND NURTURING"
New Moon in Winter

Natural Awareness: This New Moon notice things in your environment. Are there any flowers out? Which trees are bare or starting to lose their leaves? Is it raining or a clear sky? What is Mother Nature saying to you? What stood out for you this week? What did you notice about your environment and the world around you? Write a few lines and explain what you have seen, thought, felt, sensed, and dreamt.

First Quarter

Draw an outline of a large living leaf that you have collected from your own garden on a page. In this outline list as much as you can of the things you appreciate about Nature, e.g., lovely sunsets, flowers, birds, rain, the ocean, the coldness, the hills, clouds, etc.

Full Moon

Full Moon Meditation

Take a few deep breaths… using the 4 x 4 breathing technique helps get you into the right meditative state… slowly relax every part of your body… and sit under the light and power of the Full Moon… … there is a gentle breeze caressing your face… listen to the breeze ands hear the voice of Mother Nature… you hear the Mothers voice within cool air of the Winters night… the world and most of nature slumbers in dreamtime having left the cares of the day behind… You look up at the magnificent silvery Full Moon… you feel the Moonbeams dancing electrically like sparks of energy through your body waking up your vast creative potential… You know deeply at this time that you have the ability to create the world of your dreams… awaken your Astral Higher Self and begin your creativity linked with the Light of the Moon, nothing is impossible! Now taking a fee gentle breaths slowly return awareness to the here and now

Last Quarter

Release tension by - looking at the blue sky… do this during the daytime wearing something blue and harmonious… burning some relaxing oil or incense… and listen to the sounds of nature helping you to let go and go with the cosmic flow of life. After which enjoy the luxury of a warm, soothing bath... perhaps adding a few drops of your favourite essential oil and flowers.

Autumn

New Moon

If you haven't yet created your own sacred space or Magick Circle, then now is the time to do it knowing that it will bring you joy and connect you to all things Magickal. This special place is your sacred place; so keep it personal and private. During difficult times your Circle can bring you rest, love, harmony, peace. Hope, fulfillment and also be uplifting. To create your special place, choose a place indoors or outdoors but make it yours. If you do not have much room then just make an area of a room a shrine, or Altar. Where objects that have special relevance to your spirituality within the Craft can be carefully hidden away and safe. It could be a shell you picked up while on holiday, a picture of a Nature scene, or it may simply be something you like. During the week add an object that is part of this great land, a rock, crystal, leaves or a flower. Bring Nature into your home.

First Quarter

Surround yourself with people who want you to be everything you can be

Who are the people that bring you support, uplifting positive joy into your life. Write a list of all the people who support you, those that make you feel good about yourself, bring laughter, strength, confidence and encouragement. Call them all to get together with you for a social occasion.

Full Moon

Give yourself the support and empowering uplift you deserve and let go out hang-ups. Make time for some little luxury this week; get pampered facials, massages, whatever your heart needs. Maybe even a small present to yourself, or a bunch of flowers.

Full Moon Meditation

Last Quarter

Rest and relax and enjoy the beautiful person you are

This week make time for rest and relaxation; know that you are a positive, beautiful person. Listen to music, read a good book, see a movie, just let go and take time out from your mundane routine.

Summer

New Moon

We each have within us the child within that we use to be, it is now time to awaken that child and bring their Creativity into being. They live it, they dance it, they sing it, and they play it. Spend a few minutes remembering your childhood and being the child you wanted to be. What was your favourite toy, pet, or person (maybe a grandmother, aunt, neighbor or family friend)? Write some of these things down and reminisce, honor your past as a child, and never forget to play as an adult child.

First Quarter

You can contact this wondrous and creative inner child. Ask your Inner Child to awaken and ask what it is they would like to do as a child without guilt or shyness. Let the child play and misbehave and enjoy their silliness by letting go of the obedient and adult, be the child with courage of convection. Does your Inner child wish for love, nurturing and acceptance, if so simple activities like going to the park, having fun, and being true to who you really are. During the week if you can find a photo of yourself as a young child. And remember to do something childish.

Full Moon

Reacquaint yourself with the enchantment and fantasy of childhood.

Imagine you are the Inner child. Look within for the Magick and search for Faeries in your garden, read some good Faery stories. What tales and songs held enchantment for you? Daydream about these stories and songs. Howe do they make you feel when you hear those songs now, or remember those tales?

Last Quarter

Awaken your Inner child and teach them about relaxation and focus, let them teach you what you did not want to learn as a child but they know. Acknowledge and take ownership of the true Inner child before you changed, what direction would you have taken differently if you could make the decision yourself. What lessons in life can you learn from your Inner Child that they may teach you to be a better adult?

SPRING

Spring is a time of rebirth, new life, new ideas and new awakenings for all.

NEW MOON

For years we have protected the seed. It is now time to become the flower.

Our health good or bad is usually the result of the small everyday choices we make. That extra cup of coffee, piece of cake or hours spent in front of the TV may not seem important but they add up to the demise and ill health of our bodies, minds and attitudes. Today spend five minutes sitting comfortably with your eyes closed. Breathing deeply the 4 x 4 breathe and allow yourself to relax completely, and slowly begin to count your out breaths from one to four. E.g. breathing in, breathing out, 1234, etc. At least one other day this week concentrate on your breathing as above, just focus on your breathing as this is the basis for all meditative states, visualisation and Wiccecraft.

First Quarter

Invest in your health, it will the greatest investment you ever take.

Invest in your health, as it requires your personal in-depth focus and responsibility. Our health is like the greatest investment we will ever take, if we invest wisely in our health our future will be healthy and strong, but if we are lazy and neglect our health then we will have a shortened life of sickness and problems. E.g., just start with a small walk in the park, join a social walking club, eat correct nutritious food, and drink plenty of water. All these and more will radically change your health for the better. Start with this health regime immediately if it is the path of Oneness with nature and the Goddess that you truly seek, as when you are aligned with good health all positive forms attract to you creating a magickal Aura that is healing, elevated and empowering.

Full Moon

Emotions pass like clouds across the sky. They're to be noticed, accepted, acknowledged and allowed to flow on.

Be aware of the subtle influence of the Moon, and how Her rhythms fluctuate and have affect on all of life even you, especially on your emotions. Do you feel more alert, energized, peaceful, spiritual, connected or do you feel a little unsettled, uncomfortable, disconnected, idle, or lazy?

GOLDEN HEALING MEDITATION

Sit or lie down comfortably, taking a few deep breaths 4 x 4 and relaxing completely… know that this is the time for healing… the Full Moon is rising… it is a great golden ball of light coming over the horizon… as you gaze at this golden ball of light you feel yourself being filled with radiant healing energy… as this energy moves deeply through you it helps you release old patterns of fear, negativity and depression… as you relax and release these patterns you are flooded with new energy, new possibilities, new ways of bringing your life into ever increasing balance and harmony.

Last Quarter

Have you taken that first step for better health?

If not, it is now time!

Shadow Work, to remove the blocks that are stopping you from having the success you so richly deserve. Take a deep look at your Chakras and work with and vibrate each Chakra by awakening it with healing divine light. If you have any niggly little doubts about being able to have your Heart's Desire, now is the time to let go of any doubt. Write them down - such as "I can't afford it" or "I can't do it", or "This won't work". "I don't deserve good things" the list is endless. Now tear up the paper and throw it into your Circle fire and as they burn see your negatives and weaknesses dissolving with them. Relax and light-heartedly wait for what you want to appear. You may be surprised how quickly it comes to you if you are devout and true in your request.

PHASES OF THE MOON

EACH OF THE PHASES SYMBOLIZES VARIOUS ASPECTS OF THE GODDESS

The New Moon, the Dark Moon begins the two Waxing Quarters of the Lunar Cycle. Confusingly, however the Crescent Moon, too. This second phase is identified with the Maiden or Virgin. She is described as a young and beautiful woman and is related to the Goddess Artemis or Diana. The Waxing Moon is a time of beginnings and growth. It is traditional to plant herbs when the Moon is in the sign of Pisces, Cancer or Scorpio.

The Full Moon symbolizes the Mother. From beyond the first quarter the Moon is seen as the pregnant woman. Her daily growth to roundness brings Her womanhood into full flower, the Goddess Selene, Isis or Lunar. Full Moon is a time of power, ripeness, and the honoring of helpers and guides.

The Third Quarter or Last Quarter is the postmenopausal woman, sometimes pejoratively called the Crone. As a Goddess, She is the Greek Hecate and the Celtic Morrigan. The Waning Moon is a time for divination, overcoming obstacles, and relinquishing bad habits or thoughts. Customarily, weeding the garden and ploughing the fields are done during this part of the Moon cycle.

In the Anatolian Tradition of Wicca, the Threefold Goddess is divided threefold once more, into nine distinct forms of each Moon.

The Goddess Days of the Moon

Days 1-3   Dedicated to Persephone, the Initiator!

Days 4-6   Ruled by Artemis, the independent one of the wilderness, the impetus behind the newly planted seed.

Days 7-9   Kore rules these lunar days, and She is seen as the Maiden of Menarche, the link between childhood and adulthood.

Days 10-12   Ruled by Hera, Queen of Heaven and Creattrix, representing the power of inspiration.

Days 13-15   Demeter, the morturer, is ruler.

Days 16-18   Dedicated to Gaia, the Earth Goddess.

Days 19-21   In these days the old woman of the Waning Moon is Hestia, She is the Matriarchal Grandmother, ruling and protecting Her family.

Days 22-24   Ruled by Medusa, the terrible Crone of death and spiritual release, the necessary destruction that allows a new cycle to begin.

Days 25-27   Ruled By Hecate, Queen of Annwyn (the Underworld) and the Shades, She is seen as the one who allows departed souls to choose their paths in the next phase of existence and rebirth.

The remaining days of the Moon - the dark days - are those of the unknowable Masked Goddess who is present, but invisible.

FULL MOON
RITUAL FOR THE
SOLO WICCAN

To prepare your Magick Circle you will need. One Magick Circle usually 9 feet if possible smaller can be okay if it is 3 feet or 6 feet, also find the compass points; North, South, East and West of your Magick Circle, and mark them around the boundary of the with appropriate colored candles unlit. The Northern Quarter place your small Altar; and on the Altar in front of the North Candle; a small dish (or Pentacle) with rock salt on it; a Chalice or cup of water; 1 small plate with a Sabbat cake (oatmeal biscuit); and a stick of Incense or granule incense in your Thurible. In the East 3 sticks of Incense or Thurible with charcoal block and incense granules. In the South another Candle and 1 incense stick. In the West a cup of water and a small sprig of leaves, and I incense stick.

When all is appropriately placed, light the 4 Quarter candles and I incense stick at each point as well, starting from the East then going Deosil (clockwise). After which go to the centre of the Magick Circle which is to become your Sacred Temple of the Mysteries, and sit and meditate and clear your mind of all the daily activities, problems and meditate on that which you are about to do. 5-10 minutes should be ample time. Now go to the Altar and imagine yourself as the Earth, the Air, the Fire and the Water, (as you are all of them) now walk Deosil around the boundaries edge of your Magick Circle allowing your energy to make an unseen boundary of protection known only to you. When arriving back to the North pick up the Pentacle of salt holding it high facing North, say.

"This salt is of the Earth, in its purest form, it is pure and sacred and truly Blessed!"

Keeping the salt in your hands walk to the West, and place the salt down
and pick up your Cup of Water, hold it high to the West and say;

"This Water is the Water of Life, it is holy and life-giving and is in all living things!"

Pick up the salt and mix it with the water saying.

"May this pure salt bless this Water of life to work my Will."

Using the sprig of leaves (usually rosemary) dip into the Water, splashing yourself and say:

"As Water Blesses my body, so does the Salt Purify my Soul."

Now walk around the Magick Circle sprinkling the Magick Circle with your Water say:

"May this Consecrated Water purify and bless this Sacred Space, that is My Temple!"

When returning to the West place the Water and the sprig down and walk to the South, pick up the unlit candle and light it from the South Candle and hold it high saying:

"This Flame is the Light of Love, and the Light of the Living
Sun, may it burn forever, within my Heart."

Walk around the Magick Circle holding the candle above the boundary saying:

"As the Light be Cast, may no Shadows last,

Where there is Light, no darkness will remain".

On returning to the South place the candle down and walk to the East, pick up the incense sticks and light it from the point candle and hold it high in the East saying;

"May the sacred breath of Nature, bring the Mothers essence to form this safe Sacred Space."
Now walk around with the incense, moving around your Magick Circle and on returning to the East place the incense stick down. Turn inwards and visualize your Magick Circle taking form, how you perceive it is how it is. Now spread your arms out and say with authority:

"This Magick Circle round, by love abound. Of Water and Air and Nature fair.
Of Earth and Fire and my desire, I affirm thee now, by my inner power.
As it is said, so shall it be done"?

Your Magick Circle is now Properly Prepared, (if it is done with true intent), now sit and enter the Silence and be One with your Magick Circle. When you are finished and feel at One, go to your Altar and pick up your Chalice of Wine, and take back to the centre of the Magick Circle facing the Full Moon. Present the Cup high to the Moon and visualize the Moonbeams entering the cup, then say:

"Lovely Lady of the Night, to you I call with all my Might.
Lovely Lady of the Night, send forth your power to aid my Rite."
(See a glow around your cup and feeling its warmth, drink some and then say;

"As I do receive, so shall I also give?

None Greater than the Triple Goddess!"

Pour a little libation at each Quarter and a little more in the centre if you are outdoors,
if not when your Magick Circle is closed take it outside and offer libations, then
salute the Moon with your cup and then place it back on the Altar. Then pick up the
Lunar Cakes and return to the centre and hold them high to the Moon and say;

"Blessed Be these fruits of the Earth, and as I partake,
May the Knowledge I seek be granted, So Mote it Be"?

Take a Lunar Cake and crumble at each Quarter and also in the centre
and salute to the Moon and replace it back on the Altar. Return to
the centre and facing the Moon holding your arms high say:

"With Devout Love I give thanks and hereby release this my Sacred Magick Circle, and the
energies herein, to be dissolved to enter and heal the Earth. And as it is said so is it done!"

The Rite is now ended.

Blessed Be!

FULL MOON
FOR CHILDREN

The children are gathered into a Magick Circle and they are told to hold hands and spread out as far as they can. They may sit down. Their parents are to sit about a meter behind them. Then the High Priest (the Faery King) will speak to them, saying:

"You are about to become part of the Great Mystery. It is an honor that is not given to just any children. What we have done here by making a Magick Circle and sitting down is only the first step. Each part of the Mystery is more fun than the one before it. We must act very grown up and remain quiet while others are talking and not try to play with each other while in the Magick Circle. The grown-ups who are here tonight are just here to watch. They will not be allowed to join in the Circle. But do not feel bad; they will have their own Magick Circle later. Now I want everybody to stand back up and hold hands again. We are going to chant the Magick Chant that makes us a Magick Circle. And while we are chanting that, we are going to move in a circle this way (Deosil).

> *"THE SUN IS A CIRCLE, THE MOON IS A CIRCLE,*
> *THE EARTH IS A CIRCLE, NOW WE ARE TOO!"*

(Repeat several times)

This is done faster and faster until there is much laughter and giggles, and then we all fall down.

CIRCLE CASTING:

Girl - Sweeping the Circle starting in the East going Widdershins.
Boy - with candle starting in the South going Deosil.
Girl - With Water Chalice in the West going Deosil.
Boy - With salt on Pentacle starts in the North going Deosil.
Boy - With incense in the East going Deosil.

"Once a Month and better it be when the Moon is Full, we come together to have a party of thanksgiving for the good things in our life. The Goddess is the Mother of the Universe. She has given Birth to all things even to God, and all of us are Her children. It is only right that we invite Her to our party.

Long ago, before anybody knew what time, or day, or month, or even what year it was, they spoke to the Goddess in the old language. This we will do tonight, and if She comes, we must make Her our special guest, and give Her a place of honor in the Centre of our Magick Circle. So let us call Her to us now, are you ready to call the Goddess?"

"SHIMA OH MA LA SHIMA"

The children are asked to then close their eyes. The Goddess dressed in something "Faery" will come from the dark to sit in the center of the Magick Circle. Shell will stay seated and then say:

"You have called me, your Mother Goddess. And I have come. Each of you is a child of the Goddess and is very special to Me. You see me now in this form. But I can appear to you in many forms. You can see Me in the flowers of the field and in the waves of the sea, the flight of Birds and the Wind in the trees. You will find Me in the kindness of all people and the beauty of all places. I am with you always, and I am everywhere, always watching over you."

Now She takes a sweet Sabbat Cake and places it in the mouth of each child saying:

"All that you dream will come to be, for Blessed are My children, Blessed Be!"

Then the Goddess asks that they close their eyes as the Goddess steps to the outside of the Magick Circle and the children then stand up, and hold hands and chant;

"EARTH AM I, WATER AM I,

FIRE AND AIR, AND SPIRIT AM I."

(Repeat)

"THE SUN IS A CIRCLE, THE MOON IS A CIRCLE,

THE EARTH IS A CIRCLE, NOW WE ARE A CIRCLE TOO!"

The Goddess circles Widdershins and then disappears. Everybody closes the circle with a finger pointing in the Air saying:

"BLESSED ARE THE WITCHLING CHILDREN, BLESSED BE!"

Everyone bring their finger down to the ground and closes the Magick Circle.

THE WICCAN PRAYER

"May we work and Will together,
May we reap the fruits of Fellowship?
How ruff and course our garden can become,
If we let the weeds of contempt & pride divide us!
Weeds will always grow back,
And there is danger!

That we may give up the struggle for hopeless,
I nearly did, but no more!
We will work energetically in this time for us,
And the hopeful opportunity of a spring to come!

I will Nurture the seeds of warmth,
And Love for one another,
And blossoms of trust will surely come in time
And shared experience, to uproot the weeds of fear,
May our love be as perennial as the wild flowers?
Blessed Be!

MOON PHASES QUESTIONNAIRE

Name: _____

Research used: _____

Time Taken: _____ Date: _____

1. What is the Moon? _____

2. Why is the Moon important to Wicces? _____

3. What are the phases of the Moon? _____

4. What is the Craft name for the Full Moon? _____

5. Why do Wicces meet at the Full Moon? _____

6. How many Full Moons in the year? _____

7. When does a Blue Moon occur and when is the next? ____

8. What is a Blood Moon? _____

9. What are the 13 zodiacs associated with the Moon? ____

10. What is the Charge of the Goddess? _____

11. What is the best time of the year to let go? _____

12. When is the fertile time of the year and why? _____

13. What are an Equinox and a Solstice? _____

14. What is the least important phase of the Moon to Wicces? _____

15. By drawing the phases of the Moon, which is which? _____

16. Which Month is the most Magickal and why? _____

17. When is the Harvest Moon? _____

18. What is more important a Moon or a Festival? _____

19. How many Moons and Festivals in the year? _____

20. What date does the next New and Full Moon arrives? _____

MAGICK OF THE
ASTRAL PLANE

Throughout the 18th century belief from the Occult and Esoteric Fraternities and Lodges was strong in the Astral World and the Astral Body and its ability to project and travel, these beliefs seemed to have disappeared but again reappeared with the awakening of the Spiritualist and Theosophical movements in the mid 19th century. It is only in the past 60 years, however that techniques of Astral Projection, deriving from the writings of Oliver Fox, Sylvian Muldoon and Herward Carrington, have become widely known and accepted in the Western world. Oliver Fox discovered what he termed for himself the "Pineal Doorway".

Dangerous experiments were induced on people by reducing them to a catatonic state near death, but this became too dangerous, but with the uses of certain drugs in the 60's and 70's, many were awakened to this Astral Doorway without even knowing what it was, LSD was the bigger trigger for this, that is why it became so popular, but it too became quite dangerous as it was the drug that was in control and not the trained individual. This ancient method was used by Wicces a long time ago, but they had the skills of Natural Lore to be able to control such Astral projections and travels. They had hallucinogenic recipes for Magickal Flying Ointments, which they anointed their bodies and with a disassociation of consciousness flew to the Sabbats.

These methods sometimes had tragic results that related to death. On of the greatest Occultists of the time was Stamislas de Guita who used this form of experimental Astral Travel; here are two of the recipes that they used. (THESE ARE DEADLY SO DO NOT TRY)

1.

Lanolin 5 oz. - Hemp flowers 1 handful Hellebore - 1/2 handful
Alcohol - 1/10 oz. Laudanum - 1 1/2 oz. Betel Nut - 1 oz.
Catharsides - /50oz.

2.

Hashish - 1 oz. Poppy flowers - 1 handful Tincture of Cinquefoil - 1/50 oz.
Tincture of Henbane - 1/2oz. Tincture of Belladonna - 1/2oz. Tincture of Cannabis - 8oz.

Before we commence any further onto detailed descriptions of the (tried and true) methods of Astral Projection and Travel. It is well worth considering whether Astral visions are of projective reality. This is an answer that each Wicce must answer for themselves. J.F.C.

Fuller who wrote has expressed my beliefs and that of many Spiritual Occultists past and present wisely:

"The truth is it does not matter one rap by what name you Christian the illusions of this life, call them substance or ideas, or hallucinations. It makes not the slightest difference, for you are in them, and they are in you, and the less you consider their names the better; for name-changing only creates unnecessary confusion and is a waste of time."

Both Magick and Visions are a part of the true study of Magick and Wiccecraft, and the differences are varied.

"THE CLEARER THE VIEW, THE MORE PERFECT THE VIEW, THE CLEARER THE VISION THE MORE PERFECT THE VISION".

We each see and believe different things, and everything is different from differing angles, the hawks eyes are keener than an owls, and a trained Wicces perception is keener than one who has not been trained. Only the individual Wicce can therefore judge their own visions, for they belong only in their Universe, and can never truly be understood, and this can only ever be experienced. The trained Wicce has a much truer and deeper Inner Vision than untrained visions. This training teaches you how to be in and of the Astral and how to perceive and see and feel the Invisible within the Visible.

To the Aboriginals of my country an to Wicces we know that Dreams are real, we know that Magick is real, we also know there are many who claim the knowledge and skills of Astra Travel, but usually have only ever experienced what we term mental Travel, and not the genuine form of Astra travel, which takes years of careful training to master. Truth can be real, but represents something different for each individual.

There are three basic forms of Projection, that often-confused one with the other, these are:

MENTAL PROJECTION: Concerned with exploratory acts of Scrying, and the using of symbolic doors as an aid to understanding a particular part of the Astral Plane. This is Projection by symbol of the mind.

ASTRAL PROJECTION: (Proper) This is where the actual Astral Body projects from the Physical Body, and travels as distance away from it, it can also move back and forth through time and space as there is no restriction on the Astral Body.

ETHERIC PROJECTION: This is the dangerous one as stated before used by taking of drugs etc. It is where the Physical Body is reduced to state of catalepsy (this is where the heart slowly so much that the heart beat is quietened and nearly ceases completely). What does extend from the Physical Body is the Etheric Substance called Ectoplasm, which is a visual form of energy that is seen and felt.

Of these three types of Projection, the second; Astral Projection is most often referred to. This brings us now to the proper technique of Astral Projection. There are a number of these outlined in modern writings on Projection. But many of those techniques have not yet appeared in print, and are extremely effective if persevered every day, usually take approximately 3-4 weeks of serious dedicated and practice. Here is a list of books that I have found quite interesting and which have enabled me to achieve my means to Astral Projection and Travel.

Journeys out of the Body - Robert Monroe

Man Outside Himself - HP Blattsby

Astral Projection - Oliver Fox

The Projection of the Astral Body - S. Muldoon and H. Carrington

TECHNIQUE

This is one of the easiest and safest for the beginner. It uses the Tattwa symbols, their attributions to the body, Elements and Sephiroth of the Tree of Life as follows; it is slower and takes more concentration and training but more effective and will continue working effortlessly, the more skilled you become the easier it will become.

ELEMENT	TATTWA	SEPHIROTH	BODY
Spirit	Akasha	Kether	Crown of the Head
Air	Vayu	Daat	Throat
Fire	Tejas	Tiphareth	Heart
Water	Apas	Yesod	Genitals
Earth	Prithivi	Malkuth	Anus or Feet

As you have already used the Middle Pillar Exercise you should now be familiar with the idea of corresponding the Sephiroth to certain parts of the body, along with vibration and toning certain God names. This technique is applied to the Daat Centre (Throat Chakra) by concentrating and visualizing Vayu (Air Element) on the throat at the back of the neck with certain Magickal vibrations. Although the Astral Body vibrates out of the whole Physical Body it is the Throat Chakra that is in resonance and connection of the two, well from a theatrical point of view anyway. When you become more familiar with the Sacred Tree of Life and its very Sephiroth, Daat is ascribed to the Throat Chakra. It is in fact the very Portal to another dimensional reality.

With practice this will amaze you when the time comes at how much it will reveal to you and show you. Here are steps in order:

1. Assume a seated position, the back always straight… your neck slightly falling back… knees together… making sure that there is no tension… feet together… so that if you fall asleep your position hopefully would not change. The most important thing is to

be completely relaxed and comfortable, do your 4 x 4 breathing to take you to that state of relaxation…

The usual position of lying is not a good position for Astral Projection as you generally get too relaxed and fall asleep…

Close your eyes…

2. Perform the LBRP in your mind from this seated position…visualising yourself as a robed Wicce moving Deosil around your Magick Circle… Visualize yourself in your Third Eye standing up in your robes and holding aright your Athame. Projecting your consciousness into this mental image of yourself… try to see through this images eyes as if they were your actual sight… In your Mental form go to the East, and "FEEL" being in the East… Look around and notice everything in your Magick Circle… Begin your Ritual when focused and comfortable… moving Deosil doing your LBRP… feel this image and everything in the ritual including its Power and Energy… before finishing again look around your Magick Circle as being the Mental Figure… now it is time to return back to your sitting body by standing behind your body and looking at the back of your head… slowly allow yourself to be absorbed into it safely and comfortably… this is the technique to start you on your Astral Journey's…

3. Do the Middle Pillar Exercise!

4. Now strongly visualize the Vayu Tattwa symbol, which is a ball of electric light radiating in an electric blue colour… this ball of light is four inches in diameter and is situated at the Throat Chakra…

5. Vibrate the God name attributed to Daat, "YHVH Elohim". (Yode hay vaw hay ee lo kheem)

6. Now focus all your attention of the nape of your neck… and sense a feeling of tilting as though gently falling in one direction… (The natural reaction is to counteract this by jerking yourself in the opposite direction as to stop you from falling) but it is your Astral Body slightly moving out and away… allow this to happen; you may also experience and vibrating wave sensation in the Throat Chakra… this goes up and down… and can gradually get faster and faster. Just notice it and accept it… You may also feel a dull aching in your Throat Chakra but is less common than the other two…

These signs have to notice and ignore or fought a little but with not too much intensity or focus. Or you will connect more with your Physical Body and not your Astral Body. Try to relax your thoughts and keep yourself focused of your desired goal of achieving Astral projection. Continue your concentration of your Nape of the neck and regulate the vibrations and slowly feel the detachment from your Physical Body.

7. When your actual projection starts… do not roam away from your Physical Body… remain in constant visual of your Body at all times… just experience and get use to the sensation and feeling of the freedom and the floating of your Astral Counterpart.

8. When you have truly experienced this sensation… allow your Astral Body to gently return back to the Physical Body… just think about it and it will happen… as the mind is powerful, and it is only the thought that will bring you back to your home-body. Slowly just slide into its being… and remember this experience and make sure your write down in your Book the details of your complete experience from start to finish. As this will make it easier the next journey you take on your Astral Travel.

9. Close now with the Middle Pillar followed by the LBRP. Also project with your mental image to do the work for you. If you continue to practice this ritual often, it will take you about 2-4 weeks to succeed and do it easier and simpler. But your first is always the most incredible in believing in your abilities and the Magick of Astral.

PRITHIVI - EARTH   APAS - WATER   VAYU - AIR

YELLOW SQUARE   SILVER CRESCENT   BLUE CIRCLE
TEJAS - FIRE   AKASHA   - SPIRIT VAYU OF PRITHIVI

RED TRIANGLE   BLACK OVOID   YELLOW SQUARE WITH
A BLUE CIRCLE IN THE
CENTRE

Astral Questionnaire

Name: _____

Research Used: _____

Time Taken: _____ Date: _____

1. What is the Astral? _____

2. What is the 'Pineal Doorway'? _____

3. Where is the Occult capital of the world? _____

4. Do we need to connect with the Astral for Healing and why? _____

5. What is Vayu? _____

6. Where and what is Malkuth? _____

7. What is the Kabala? _____

8. What is the difference between Mental and Astral Projection? _____

9. What is the Aura? _____

10. What is the Drawing Down of the Moon? _____

11.What is the Athame? _____

12. What is the Higher Self? _____

13. Why is the Astral so important? _____

14. What Element is the Athame? _____

15. What is the Warming of the Temple Rite also called? _____

16. What is a Spirit Flame? _____

17. What is Enlightenment? _____

18. What is a Spell? _____

19. What is the Wiccan Caveat? _____

20. What is the Magick Circle? _____

21. What is your favourite Tattwa and why? _____

NATURES
SECRETS OF
HERBALISM

THE DR BACH SYSTEM OF WILDFLOWER MEDICINE

THE RESCUE REMEDY – THE FIRST-AID OR EMERGENCY REMEDY

This Magickal blend is of five different Remedies, which Dr. Bach uses in all cases of emergency. No first aid kit is complete without it. I always keep a bottle in the draw of my bedside table and in the first aid kit. It is used for a myriad of purposes, even just to keep a patient relaxed and comfortable whilst the doctor has been sent for. It has a genuinely strong effect and used in cases of shock, stress, anxiety, fractures or falls, acute illnesses, fainting, dizziness, cuts, sprains and bruises, strong pain, nightmares, even aids in panic attacks. I believe that anyone over the age of 50 should have this close by as it acts strongly as a relaxant and carminative. All midwives will also find it invaluable for mothers and their infants.

THE FIVE REMEDIES ARE:

ROCK ROSE   for terror, extreme fear, panic, either in the patient or in those around.

STAR OF BETHLEHEM   for the after-effects of shock, mental or physical.

CLEMATIS   for unconsciousness, coma, fainting, giddiness, all of which indicate a temporary lack of interest in the present.

CHERRY PLUM   for the fear of the mind giving way, insanity, brainstorms, hysterical conditions, suicidal tendencies.

IMPATIENS   for extreme mental tension and irritability resulting in muscular tension and, hence, pain.

PREPARATION OF THE RESCUE REMEDY:

To prepare the Rescue Remedy add two drops from each of the five remedies above to a half or one ounce bottle of Brandy or Vodka. This will keep potent and remain clear indefinitely, even if not used for quite some time. Label the bottle "Rescue Remedy", or "First Aid Remedy" and cork tightly.

DOSAGE: Three drops in a cup of cold water to be sipped very frequently, as the patient improves, every quarter of an hour, every half hour, every hour or as necessary.

If the patient is asleep or unconscious, then place a small drop of the rescue remedy on the lips, gums, behind the ears and even on the wrists. If there is no water available just place a few drops into the palms of their hands for them to suck up.

FOR EXTERNAL USE: Add six pints to a pint of warm water if possible but if not cold will do. Then with a cotton ball bathe the part that is affected, or even use as a compress. Rescue remedy is also helpful with Bronchial chests by placing on a swap onto the chest. If severe back pain place a compress of it on the lumbar region or the region where the pain is.

FOR ANIMALS: Three drops in a little water given by mouth, or three drops in the drinking water or sprinkled over the food.

Introduction to Herbs as Medicine

The ancient tradition of herbs and their properties is based on verbal traditions that have been passed down from Shaman to Shaman, Sage to sage, Wicce to Wicce, then later with the knowledge of writing it was written down in powerful artistic manuscripts. But through much translation, certain factors have been lost. It was only instinct, intuition, and pure luck in some cases, which created the histories supply of medicines both herbal and even the pharmaceutical allows its essence to be in their many medicines of today, even though they are a hundred times more expensive, and have lost the original spirit of the Natural life of the Plant.

Contemporary herbal medicinal practices are based on ancient Shamanic and Pagan traditions, and a more recent understanding and knowledge of healing and health. The uses of some herbs have changed considerably, while others have changed very little over the millennia. Nearly all the Herbs in use today are native to the lands, which border the Aegean and Mediterranean Seas. Most of them come from the original Persia, which sadly has been lost today due to the warring in those lands. Some from India and Pakistan, Much from China, even Australia has plenty of Herbs and plants used for healing. Most of the common weeds (Herbs) are of Europe and America. Many practices follow the European customs of Herbalism.

HISTORY OF EUROPEAN HERBAL MEDICINE:

To place herbal medicine in the context of the 21st century, a brief study of its history will help connect traditions to current usage. Ever since Neanderthal man we have used flowers, leaves, barks, twigs and roots as a conscious use for medicinal and fragrant purposes. Even the Chinese have recorded their herbal culture for over 5000 years, as did the Sumerians and Persians. One of the oldest recorded documents describing herbal medicine is the Pharmacopoeia "between 2730 - 3000 B.C."

The ancient Egyptians and their Magickal Priest/Herbalists were admired worldwide and respected for their advanced knowledge of healing and Magickal skills. An ancient Papyrus of 2000 B.C. Documents that they believe that disease and injuries were not caused by Magick and Curses but due to natural causes. Within this ancient papyrus were hundreds of ancient formulations of ancient herbal medicine and Practices. The most famous to come out of Alexandria was not only their magnificent library but the Medical College of Thoth which was established in 332 B.C. Within its confines were learned Priest/Physicians including Galen, but sadly due to the great fires of Alexandria not only was the most elaborate Library the world has ever known been destroyed but also nearly all the archives of the Medical College.

When we look at Greek medicine we always hear the name Hippocrates, his great botanical knowledge and skills of Natural Medicine was taught in his great Medical Colleges which were only available to males as females were never permitted to learn or have knowledge of any form. Throughout thousands of years it has been the Greeks that took the ancient arts of Herbal medicine through the ages to the present Pharmaceutical evaluations and remedies. Hippocrates influenced the whole world with his attitudes to healing and good health but the usage of herbals. He believed strongly in the certain properties of Herbs elevated the Immune System and protected man against ill-health and formulated herbal diets to help the natural body fight against all forms of illness both within and without.

With the introduction of printing with presses in the 15th century, many became learned readers, which established more and more books of knowledge, as man became hungry for knowledge and books gave him the ability to learn from home. Many of the first books that were ever printed were the classic Herbals of Hippocrates who lived between 460 B.C. - 370 B.C., which meant he lived to the ripe old age of 90 years, which was unbelievable in that day and age, he must have been taking his own advice on herbs. His first book published was called " The Materia Medica of Diorscorides".

With the discovery of the Americas, the Europeans discovered many new and exciting botanicals, both edible and medicinal. These great finds started the explosion of Botany and the plant, herb; spice trade became the biggest moneymaker of the time. But in the travel many plants lost their original meanings and explanations as they did in translations from one language to another.

Herbalism changed drastically due to a Swiss-German Paracelsus (1493 - 1541) who was a chief Physician, Herbalist and Botanist. He introduced to the world chemical research and defined what is now termed the 'active principal' of a plant. But in doing this he changed the Natural energies of the down to earth Herbalist into a chemical Pharmacist. Where medicines became empty of spirit and fool of negative side affects. He extracted basic substance from the plant that Mother Nature took millions of years to formulate; he then formulated new ways to prepare the plants. This rapid development of Chemistry made them drift apart from natural to unnatural.

Natural Botanicals last for millions of years but then they were thrown out the window when the first synthetic drugs were formulated in the mid 1850's. From here it basically tried to destroy the herbalist and Natural practitioner where it took over the world in the latter years of 1945. Now huge pharmaceutical companies are trying to destroy Herbal medicine and Naturopaths by debunking their remedies as "Old Wives Tales" and dangerous. But they could not stop man seeking the Truth, as Truth always comes out, and many Natural Medicines and Herbalism have continued. We now see the Pharmaceutical companies having their huge lines of Natural medicines on shelves in Chemists covering all aspects. But with a difference, the Herbalist charges for the Herb usually ($2-$5) for the Natural herb, more for tinctures. But the Pharmacist charges a small fortune for the same thing because they are placed in capsules etc.

In my new book *"Complete Encyclopedia of Herbal Medicines of the World"*, covers all known Herbs of Europe, Britain, Africa, Polynesia, Australia, North and South America, Middle East, India and Asia. It shows you what they look like through beautiful artistry and explains in every detail their benefits and uses.

REMEDIAL HERBAL CLASSIFICATIONS

Abortifacient	These are most likely to induce miscarriage, it is considered highly dangerous during pregnancy. Know Abortifacients include Blue Cohosh, Ergot, Golden Seal, Parsley, Tansy (oil), and Valerian.
Alterative	Their function is as a tonic to aid in renewal and healing some' Burdock, Elder and Red Clover.
Anaesthetic	Cause the nerve endings to lose sensation, making them less aware of pain include; Birch bark, Clove (oil), and Mandrake.
Anodyne	Also alleviates pain but may be narcotic including Belladonna, Coca leaves, Henbane, White Willow Bark, and Wintergreen.
Anthelmintic	deter the existence of parasitic worms, common in undernourished people include Flax Seed, Tansy and Wormwood.
Antiemetic	these are carminative's and stomachics, they alleviate nausea and can stop vomiting; Clove, Frankincense, Nightshade, Spearmint, Ice crushed and taken internally may also be useful.
Antiseptic	prevents the wound or sore from becoming infected: Basil, Eucalyptus, and Thyme.
Antispasmodic	calm the muscles, stopping spasms and convulsions: Blue and Black Cohosh, Chamomile, Eucalyptus, Lobelia, Skullcap and Valerian.
Aperient	similar classification to Laxative, reducing a natural movement of the bowels; Dandelion and Rhubarb.
Aromatic	a pleasant fragrance. Allspice, Anise, Catnip, Cinnamon, Clove, Coriander, Elecampane, Ginger, Lemon peel, Peppermint and Yarrow.
Astringent	these cause the tissue to contract and tighten pores. Agrimony, Alum Root, Bayberry, Blackberry, Comfrey, Nettles, Sage and White oak Root.

Bathing Herbs	Lovage and Heather.
Cardiac	a distinctive effect on the heart. Foxglove, Lily of the Valley, Rosemary, Tansy, and Yarrow.
Carminative	good for digestion, gas cramps and tension: Allspice, Aniseed, Angelica, Catnip, Cloves, Dill, Elecampane, Fennel, Ginger, Peppermint, Spearmint, Valerian and Yarrow.
Cathartic	for a dramatic release of the bowels. Boneset, Broom, Castor (oil) and Mayapple.
Constituents/ Vitamins	Vit A-Dandelion and Alfalfa, Vit B-Bladderwrack and Okra, B12-Alfalfa, Vit C-All Citrus, Vit D– Watercress, Vit E-Alfalfa.
Demulcent	soothing herbs. Arrowroot, Comfrey, Liquorice Root, Marshmallow Root, and Slippery Elm.
Deva	to describe the energy field of an herb.
Diaphoretic	to perspire used in mild fevers. Angelica, Boneset, Camphor, Catnip, Marigold, Pennyroyal and Yarrow.
Diuretic	to aid in the flow of urine, and cleansing the kidneys. Agrimony, Asparagus, Burdock, Dandelion, Elder, Fennel, Piper Methystum and Uva Ursi.
Emetic	cause the stomach to contract and induce vomiting. Boneset, Elder Root, Lobelia, Mustard and Vervain.
Emmenagogue	stimulates the menstrual flow. Blue or Black Cohosh, Ergot Motherwort, Pennyroyal, Rue and Tansy.
Emollient	for external use will soften roughness. Linseed, Liquorice, Marshmallow and Comfrey.
Expectorant	to loosen phlegm, which collects in the lungs. Boneset, Benzoin.
Febrifuge	treats fever and lowers temperature. Boneset, Sage, Tansy and Wormwood.
Fixative	used primarily as a carrier of another. Elder Flower.
Haemostat	quicken the coagulation of blood. Corn Ergot, marigold, Sage and Cobwebs.
Hepatic	works on the liver to function easier; Agrimony, Celandine, Dandelion, Peony and Tansy.
Irritant	Irritates the skin. Bryony, cayenne, Poison Oak, Mustard, Nettle.
Laxative	stimulates the bowels. Boneset, Dandelion, Liquorice Root, Mandrake, Mountain Flax and Rhubarb.

Liniment	making of oils or creams. the mints.
Narcotic	self-explanatory.
Nephritic	Herbs that affect the Kidneys.
Nervine	calming of the nerves and soothes emotions. Chamomile, Cinquefoil, Fennel, Hops, Lavender, Marigold, Rosemary, Tansy and Verbena.
Nutrient	high in vitamins and minerals. Comfrey, Dandelion and Nettles.
Pectoral	works upon the lungs and chest for congestion. Aniseed, Coltsfoot, Irish Moss, Marshmallow, Mullein and Wild Cherry.
Purgative	strongest of the laxative herbs. Bitter Apple, Black Root, Boneset, May Apple, Mandrake and Senna Leaves.
Refresherant	relieves thirst, and sensation of coolness. Aconite, Catnip, Chickweed and Wormwood.
Rubefacient	for painful joints, arthritis etc. Cayenne and Nettles.
Sedative	a tranquilliser relaxes nervous tension. Black Cohosh, Chamomile, Jasmine and Valerian Root.
Stimulant	to quicken the pulse. Bayberry, Cayenne, Cinnamon, Eucalyptus, Horseradish, Mustard, Peppers, Tansy and Wintergreen.
Stomachic	helps the stomach with poor digestion. Angelica, Chamomile, Dill, Pennyroyal, Peppermint, Sage and Wormwood.
Styptic	similar to Haemostatic to stop bleeding. Avena, Nettles, Sage and Cobwebs.
Sudorific	to induce sweating; Cayenne, Germander, Marigold, Vervain and Yarrow.
Tonic	a sense of well-being. Agrimony, Bayberry, Blackberry, Boneset, Catnip, Cayenne, Chamomile, Dandelion, Nettles, Peppermint, Sage, Tansy, Wormwood and Yarrow.
Volatile Oil	their ability to evaporate easily.
Vulnerary	effective in treating wounds. Comfrey, Marshmallow and Tansy.

THE PRIESTHOOD
OF WICCA

The criteria for advancing into the Wiccan Priesthood vary upon the individual Church/ group/Circle or Coven that you are entering into. Make sure that you are sure of the commitment that you will be making as a Priest or Priestess of the Wiccan community and how best to serve the community as a whole. Entering the priesthood is not about self-ego it is about what is your best ability or skill that you have on offer. The qualifications of every Wiccan Priest or Priestess are important, and also the years of their dedication in training, service and character to and for the community. Many legal Wiccan institutions have formulated excellent Clergy training programs based upon the needs of their respective Traditions, visions and Mission Statements, what is also important is to know what the inner and outer community are in need of. For more details into a true and legal Priesthood and their Clergy training contact such forward thinking such as; The Aquarian Tabernacle Church (ATC), Church of Wicca, Covenant of the Goddess, Henge of Keltria, Fellowship of Isis, even the contacting of the Interfaith Council can help advise where is available. Correct leadership is what you need to look carefully for, as there are some that are not so genuine.

Within most of the legal organizations of Wicca there has been much discussions about what it is that makes a good Priest or Priestess, their qualities, qualifications, ethics and moral standards, and their need for assistance to the outer community. There are many guides and criteria for the right sort of Clergy, but importantly it is about their Spiritual side of there more so than their more mundane Nature. The community, whereas Initiation as a Wicce is for the self, Ordination is for higher calling of the Wiccan Community. Fundamentally the knowledge basis must be there, as any and all questions asked should be given an honest and knowledgeable true answer without hesitation or false information.

But they must always be striving for internal growth that will in time manifest in their actions, words and relationships. Their normal home life must be organized and structured with a spiritual discipline above the norm. Their home life shows and dictates their spiritual life. Therefore I warn those seeking Ordination that the internal work on oneself is far more important than the outer observance of the scholarly work. Wicces must be able to show, in their own way, what they have done in this area and how they have progressed. We expect our Clergy to have their own personal lives in reasonable good order - substance addicts, welfare dependents, prisoners, homeless people whose personal relationships are in turmoil, need to address these issues before they can expect to serve others! They are not rejected but helped to elevate their issues prior to being accepted on a deeper level.

THE REQUIREMENTS

THE WICCANING/BAPTISM:

The primary training starts with an Outer Court, (Seeker Training as in this book1) also before being Wiccaned you must denounce all other rites of Baptism entered into. Commence with 1 year training. The requirements are:

- To have successfully completed the Outer Court Lectures/Lessons (adults only). Book 1.
- To have commenced with their "Nature Diary", observations of Nature. Book
- To have commenced with their "Nature Diary", observations of Self. Book
- The Seeker must be interested in the Goddess Mysteries.
- The Seeker must see them as a Wiccan and adore Nature.
- The Seeker must have expressed to learn more of the Wiccan Mysteries.

INITIATION AS A WICCE:

After being Wiccan for at least a year and being involved meeting and knowing the Wiccan community, and doing the Advanced Wiccan Training Studies within a Coven/Circle, they must then ask for Initiation, which will make them of the Priesthood at the lesser level as a Wicce. 1-2 year training and dedication is required. The requirements are:

1. The Wiccan must have been Wiccaned into the Craft.
2. They must have attained the age of 18 unless special circumstances arise.
3. They should have completed their yearly Nature Diary in full.
4. Should have a good knowledgeable background of the Wiccan history and that of the Coven.
5. They must be aware that as an Initiate they are entering the Inner Circle, and shall be responsible for their actions.
6. They must know by heart the Self Blessing Ritual.

7. They know and perform the LBRP (Lesser banishing Ritual of the Pentagram).
8. They must have written their own Charge of the Goddess (Their words to and from the Goddess)
9. They must wish to dedicate their life to the Goddess and God of the Old Religion.
10. They must be proficient in Meditation.
11. They must sacrifice at least one bad habit prior to Initiation (permanently).
12. They must write a letter of asking to the High Priest/ess of the said Circle they wish to be Initiated into asking for Initiation.

ORDINATION FOR THE PRIESTHOOD:

This is the primary requirement for those who wish to become Priests and Priestesses.

1. The Wicce must have been Initiated for a minimum of 1-2 years.
2. They must be proficient of all other levels and requirements up to this level.
3. They must have a good working knowledge of all aspects of The Eight Paths of Enlightenment.
4. They must be able to perform and carry out a Wiccaning to the lesser degree.
5. They must have good knowledge of the Principals of Ritual Construction.
6. They must be capable of forming and running under supervision a new Coven/Church/Circle.
7. They must have an understanding of the significance of the Second Degree Ritual and its symbologies.
8. They must have a desire to Worship within the Wicce and take on all the responsibilities of a Priest/ess for the Church and the Community as a whole.
9. They must have chosen one of the Eight Paths to specialize in.
10. They must have successfully completed at least one act of Ceremonial Magick.

TRAINING OF THE PRIEST/ESS

- They must be an active member of the their Coven for at least 2-3 consecutive years, having served in the following duties; management of Church programs, functions, and activities, as well as studied towards qualifications for Priesthood.
- Thorough familiarity with the Coven and its subsidiary branches;

- Adequate religious/Magickal training to show competency, leadership and originality. Studies should include as much as possible of the following subjects; mythology, cosmology, psychology, ecology, mysticism, trance-work, biology, art, history, music, dance, literature, theatre, comparative religion, ritual design, and construction, psychic development, herbcraft, medicine and healing, and etiquette.
- Personal therapy to clear out the cobwebs in the Wicce's personal life and history.
- An in-depth investigation of at least one other particular religious or Magickal Tradition. A study of particular healing Traditions with a Spiritual focus could in some cases also suffice.
- Intimate familiarity with the Earth in Her more Natural forms, including the ability to survive in relative wilderness, with at least a minimum of country skills. This would be demonstrated by undertaking a solitary vision quest of at least 3-9 days duration.
- Willingness to serve, with proof of dedication through past service.
- Ability to create and lead effective rituals, ceremonies, Rites of Passage, events and meetings.
- Administration of Ministerial energies to the public. This may include pastoral counseling, Ministering to the ill and dying; creating rituals, writing articles; giving interviews, teaching, and ecological and political activities.

High Priesthood:

As for how Priest/esses of the Coven are expected to function in their Priestly duties and capacity, the following points are taken from the Coven Membership handbook:

- Establish a link between the Gods and the community, and help people make that link themselves.
- Administer Sacraments, meaning to be able to perform the Rituals of this Religion.
- Articulately communicate the body of Lore or Doctrine of the Coven to anyone.
- Teach what you know; and know WHAT YOU TEACH!
- Take responsibility to make things happen;
- Put fires out effectively;
- Have a sense of presence, that is inspiring to others.
- Create original material.
- Have personal credibility through lack of hypocrisy.
- Think on your feet and be able to 'wing it' when necessary.

- Effectively lead others without using "power over";
- Evoke a sense of affection and respect;
- Maintain clarity of vision for the community;
- Be able to deal with administrative issues effectively, appropriately and timely.
- Be willing to serve others before 'laying out your own trip'.
- Be able to raise power Magickally;
- Lead regular services.

After due consideration the High Priestess may select various High Priests to be her consorts. These must have attained a degree of Spiritual progression to be able to take the chosen few out of the rank and life to progress them to the Inner Mysteries, which lies beyond the Third Degree.

The High priesthood are the Elders of our Community and must be sufficient in Wiccan/Pagan knowledge, therefore being capable of teaching the kernel essence of their Spiritual, Magickal and Mystical knowledge. I advise many to seek out as many books especially old manuscripts, learning from as many diverse Wiccan people as possible to get a Broadview of every pathway of Wicca, as there are many. The High Priesthood or Elders are the specialists and must have the knowledge and skills of the Wicca on all levels at their hands. They must guide everyone, showing that they too have in the past failed and succeeded to varying degrees, and probably will again. It is how we learn from our mistakes that are important. They should be able to communicate openly and honestly with all members and help in rectifying any negatives, doubts, mistakes or failings.

When they get to the Rank of High Priest or High Priestess they usually then hive off and form there own Coven or Church to aid in the growth of the community. In Traditional Covens, we continue the old ways and try not to change too much. Remember to always bathe or wash and fast prior to entering the Magick Circle, for being fresh in body, you will be fresh in mind and so be better to receive and contribute to the efforts of the group, for in all these things:

"PROPERLY PREPARED YOU MUST ALWAYS BE!"

Naturally when you have formed your new Coven you will attract many new members, especially those that live nearby. But always be careful not to just except everyone as a numbers game, as you need to start slow, and grow slow. This creates stability and deep fellowship. Usually it is the decision of the HP and the HPs who decide whether they will fit in the confines of their

Magick Circle. Some people will outwardly show signs of devout interest, and may not be there for the right reasons. But many are truly searching for right reasons and are Spiritual devout. A full working Coven or Church is not for spectators, it is about everyone being involved and assisting where needed, this will show dedication, harmony and fellowship.

There may be many failures when first starting your own Magick Circle, but in time and sincerity your Coven will work well and be cohesive, it will take time, but it will happen if the energies are balanced and real and remember;

"KEEP PURE YOUR HIGHEST IDEALS, STRIVE EVER TOWARDS IT, AND LET NAUGHT STOP YOU OR TURN YOU ASIDE, FOR YOU ARE A CHILD OF THE GREAT MOTHER."

The Priesthood Questionnaire

Name: _____

Research Used: _____

Time Taken: _____ Date: _____

1. What is a Priest/ess? _____

2. What is the symbol of the Priesthood? _____

3. How long must a Wicce wait minimum before becoming a Priest/ess? _____

4. What is the difference between Initiation and Ordination? _____

5. What is an Elder? _____

6. What is the difference between a Hag, and Elder and a Crone? _____

7. Who is titular head of a Coven and why? _____

8. What other term is the Arch Priestess and why? _____

9. Which level is the Level of Divine Love? _____

10. What is ecstasy in a spiritual sense? _____

11. What is the fifth Level? _____

12. When can a new circle be formed and hived off? _____

13. Why do we still have Initiations? _____

14. How do you see the role of a Priest/ess? _____

15. What is your destiny within Wicca? _____

16. Why are some Temples skyclad and others not? _____

17. What has been your favourite Outer Court Lecture and why? _____

18. Is every Magick Circle different and why? _____

19. Why is it important to have Hierarchy? _____

LISTENING,
LEARNING AND
UNDERSTANDING

Well my dear little Bunnies', you are now familiar with the basic understanding of Wicca and you have read and understood this Seekers Book 1; read its pages that describe the Wiccan Tradition of Elphane, which is of service to the community as a whole. But you need to understand why I created the Church of Wicca, and what were its basic foundations, these are my words to the Seekers and Students of the Ancient Religion of Shamanism and the New Religion of Wicca. And that you are reading this today, means that you have, of your own accord, are interested in stepping forward into your Wiccan future, into the Great Mysteries of Wicca; the very foundation of Wicca, the Church of Wicca and the ATC. But there are some things you need to know regarding true studentship with a Mentor, and the study of the ancient ways in any form.

First you will note, I said Mentor, and not teacher. A Mentor is more than a teacher. The word Mentor originates from the ancient Greek as a person in mythology actually named Mentor, who was both friend and a counselor to Odysseus and Telemachus. Mentor is defined as 'as a wise and faithful counselor' in the Webster Unabridged Dictionary, and that is what the Priesthood should accept the responsibility for; to counsel you and guide your steps of learning as far as you wish, to teach you what Mysteries I know, and to assist you in finding out the rest on your own. Part of what I offer do is help guide you how to acquire TRUE KNOWLEDGE, and how to get your own answers to your questions; in short, how to survive on your own, without us. My method can be best described as 'independent knowledge for independent minds'. I am not interested in acquiring students as a sign of status in the Wiccan or Pagan community. I am interested in helping you to go out into the community as a True Being of Light, not just as a Wicce or a Priest/ess; but to successfully begin, nurture and maintain your own Spiritual Family. My goal is for the Wiccan/Pagan Traditions to not only survive, but also thrive in a positive structured manner; and to live on as publicly accessible religious Paths for everyone long after all of us have stepped through the veil with this incarnation.

Priesthood training, in many good Traditions can be had from many competent, honest, sincere Mentors. Occasionally with some pretend teachers, Initiation can be had, just for the asking, and one can move through the degrees very easily and swiftly, without any real training, like floating down a river, and not in control. Gaining no knowledge but status! In a genuine formal training, know the liturgical format for the basic of rituals and ceremonies and True Magick.

But is it sufficient training to go out and successfully establish and administer a recognized and legally protected Circle/Coven/Church/Congregation/Spiritual Family; counsel people in real-life crisis situations, and minister to the Spiritual needs of others?

There is a lot more to it than a simple Full Moon Ceremony, Handfasting or Initiation, very much more indeed! It takes many years of dedication as the student to eventually become the teacher. And so you must be sure this is what you truly want for yourself, for it involves a time long emotional commitment of time by both the student and the Mentor. For that reason, If you seek only basic training and do not continue at home with further study and learning, and do not wish to enter with a Coven or Church, then read my series of Complete Encyclopedia of Witchcraft Series and it will give you all the basic knowledge and skill that you will require, but alas it will not give you the fellowship nor the one on one ability to learn with a true Mentor. If your interests truly run much deeper, I can help; provided you are sincere in your commitment. I can eventually recommend you to fellow Wiccans in the your that are sincere and true to the Craft and the community. I fully expect you to fully understand the responsibilities you will be assuming regarding your choice, and to honor those commitments.

Not every Student/Seeker who seeks the Truth receives it. As there are many obstacles in our 21st century mortal lives, and to try and devote our lives in two separate worlds at the same time, can be quite tiring and stressful. But we need to keep alive the ancient Tradition of my Mentors, my teachers, my shamans, my High Priests and High Priestesses, My mother and father, my ancestors, and more. To train effectively, a Mentor must be strict, yet loving; willing to take the less popular role as emissary of that which empowers Seekers with the Tools of discipline, faith, strength, conviction, sincerity, loyalty and character. You must be capable of weathering the worst storms and tests of faith, occasionally from within.

Good luck on your path ahead, and hopefully it will, like it did for me, leads you home, home to your true Spiritual Family.

Brightest of Blessings

May the Goddess hold you firmly in the palms of Her hands and always close you Her heart!

RECOMMENDED
READING LIST

The Complete Book of Witchcraft	Raymond Buckland
Spiral Dance	Starhawk
An ABC of Witchcraft	Doreen Valiente
Goddess in my Pocket	Patricia Telesco
The Goddess Path	Patricia Monaghan
To Stir a Magick Cauldron	Silver Ravenwolf
Teen Witch	Silver Ravenwolf
The Witches Calendar	Llewellyn
Dreaming the Divine	Scott Cunningham
The Goddess Companion	Patricia Monaghan
Green Witchcraft 1 & 2	Ann Moura
To Light a Sacred Flame	Silver Ravenwolf
Wicca, Guide for the Solitary Practitioner	Scott Cunningham
Living Wicca, Guide for the Solitary	Scott Cunningham
To Ride a Silver Broomstick	Silver Ravenwolf
Encyclopedia of Magical Herbs	Scott Cunningham
The Truth About Witchcraft	Scott Cunningham
The Secret of Letting Go	Guy Finley
Covencraft	Amber K
Earth Magic	Marion Weinstein
Family Book of Wicca	Ashleen O'Gaea
Natural Magic	Doreen Valiente
Principles of Wicca	Vivienne Crowley
365 Goddess	Trish Telesco
Wicca, The Old Religion	Vivienne Crowley
The Witches God	S & J Farrar
The Witches Goddess	S & J Farrar
The Witches Bible 1 & 2	S & J Farrar
The Spell of Making	Blacksun
Moonmagic	D. Conway
The Power of the Witch	Laurie Cabot
Never on a Broomstick	Donovan

The Truth About Witchcraft	Hans Holzer
Magick Made Easy	Trish Telesco
The Golden Bough	Sir James Fraser
Witchcraft Today	Gerald B. Gardner
Witchcraft, the Sixth Sense and Us	Justine Glass
The Pickingill Papers	WE Liddell & Michael Howard
Born in Albion	David Williams & Kate West
Aradia: Gospel of the Witches	Charles G. Leland
Fiona Horne: A Personal Journey	Fiona Horne
Witch: A Magickal Year	Fiona Horne
Pans Daughter	Neville Drury
The God of the Witches	Margaret Murray
The King of the Witches	June Johns
Witchcraft, Ancient and Modern	Raymond Buckland
What Witches Do	Stuart Farrar
The White Goddess	Robert Graves
Positive Magic	Marion Weinstein
The Rose-Cross and the Goddess	Gareth Knight
The Master Book of Herbalism	Paul Beyerl
The Mystical Qabala	Dion Fortune
Magick: An Occult Primer	David Conway
Techniques of High Magic	Francis King
Magick in Theory and Practice	Aleister Crowley
Ceremonial Magick	A E Waite
Practice of Magickal Evocation	Franz Bardon
When God Was a Woman	Merlin Stone
Lid Off The Cauldron	Patricia Crowther
The Rebirth of Witchcraft	Doreen Valiente
Drawing Down the Moon	Margot Adler
Witchcraft from the Inside	Raymond Buckland
The Holy Book of Women's Mysteries	Z. Budapest
Eight Sabbats for Witches	S & J Farrar
The Witches Way	Doreen Valiente

The Great Mother; An Analysis of the Archetype	Erich Neumann
Astral Voyages	Dr. Bruce Goldberg
Herbal Almanac	Llewellyn
Daily Planetary Guide	Llewellyn
Hereditary Witchcraft	Raven Grimassi
Halloween	Silver Ravenwolf
Chakras for Beginners	David Pond
Creating Magickal Tools	C & S Cicero
Shamanic Guide to Death and Dying	Kristen Madden
Astral Projection For Beginners	Edain Mc Coy
Aura Energy	Joe H Slate
In Praise of the Crone	Dorothy Morrison
A Garden of Pomegranates	Israel Regardie
Practical Candle Burning Rituals	Raymond Buckland
Magickal Herbalism	Scott Cunningham
The 21 Lesson s of Merlin	Douglas Monroe
Tarot Spells	Janina Renee
Celebrating the Crone	Ruth Gardner
Ariadne's Thread	Mountainwater
Maiden, Mother, Crone	David Conway
Every Woman a Witch	Kisma Stepanich
Grandmother Moon	Z Budapest
Malleus Malificarum	Sprenger and Kramer
Moon Magick	David Conway
Pagan Book of Living and Dying	Starhawk
Way of the Strega	Raven Grimassi
The Dark God	Nicholas Mann
The Wheel of the Year	Pauline Campanelli
The Underworld Initiation	RJ Stewart
Wicca for Men	A J Drew
The Complete Book of Witchcraft	Israel Regardie
Initiation into Hermetics	Franz Bardon
The Ritual Magick Workbook	Dolores Nowicki

Mastering Witchcraft   Paul Huson

History of Magic   Eliphas Levi

Bubble, bubble toil and Trouble   Patricia Telesco

Spinning Spells, Weaving Wonders   Trish Telesco

Language of Dreams   Trish Telesco

THE WICCES
CALENDAR

JANUARY:

World Peace Day	1 January
Sir James Fraser author of "The Golden Bough".	
Fiesta of the Black Nazarene in Manilla, the Philippines.	1-9 January
Nativity of The Goddess Inanna, Sumerian Goddess of Heaven and Earth	
2 January	
Advent of Isis from Phoenicia	
Earth is at Perihelion to the Sun, closest to the Sun than any other time of the year.	
Women's Fertility Festival, Pueblo Deer Dancers	3 January
Aquarian Tabernacle Church Australia by Lady Tamara Von Forslun 4 January 1994	
Day of the Goddess Isis and Hathor	
Doreen Valiente	4 January 1922 - 1 September 1999 *
Sir Isaac Newton	4 January 1643 - 31 March 1727
Eve of the Epiphany of Kore and Paeon.	5 January
Ritual to the Goddess Venus	
Feast of the God Poseidon	
Night of La Bafana who brings gifts to children, lump of coal if they have been bad	
Day of the Sacred Triune, Maiden, Mother and Crone	6 January
The Beatific Vision of the Goddess 6 January	
Arrival of the magi to Christs Manger in Bethlehem	
Joan of Arc	7 January 1412 -

Decrees of the God Sokhit and the
Goddess Sekhmet (Justice and Law)

Magical Day of the Seven Herbs

Magical Day for healing with Herbs

Old Druids New Years Eve   8 January

Samuel Macgregor Mathers   8 January 1952 - 19 November 1918

Day of the Goddess Justicia, bringing
justice to the world

Day to Honour all Midwives

Day of Antu - Isis searches for Osiris   9 January

Day to gather Yarrow to dry for insect
sachets for dog's collars

Dirge to the Goddess Isis and Nephthys

Plough Day - until 1980 it was illegal to
plough the fields before this day 10 January

Securitas - Invoke when threatened

The Juturnalia   11 January

Day of the Goddess Carmenta - Goddess
of childbirth

Day of the African Mother Goddess   12 January
Oddvdva

Basant Panchami Day - Day of Wisdom
and Art

Day of the Goddess Sarasvati

Final Witchcraft law Repealed in Austria   13 January
in 1787

Festival of the God Faunus (St.
Valentines Day)

Day to bathe for purification in the   13 January
Ganges River

Blessing of the Vines dedication to the   14 January
Gods of Wine

Official Confession of error, made in 1606 by the Jurors of Salem Witch Trials	14 January
Hindu Festival - Makar Sankranti	14 January
World Religions Day	15 January
Day of the Goddess Vesta	
Feast of the Ass	
Day of the Goddess Concordia	16 January
Honour the Gods of the Eight Winds	
Day of the Queen of the Universe in France	16 January
Day of Rest and Peace - dedicated to the Goddess Felicitas	17 January
Women's Festival Honouring The Goddess Hera	18 January
Dorothy Clutterbuck	19 January 1880 - 12 January 1951
Day of Honouring the Goddess Minerva	19 January
Blessing of the Waters	
Dorothy Clutterbuck who Initiated Gerald Gardner	
Blessing of the Waters and all Water Goddesses	
Grandmothers Day	20 January
Festival of Peace and Harmony	
Feast of the Goddess Hecate	21 January
Day of St. Agnus	
Day of the Goddess Yngona (Denmark)	
Day of Visions	
Sir Francis Bacon - Philosopher	
Rasputin's Birth	
The Herb Mullein to be infused in olive oil for ear drops	22 January
Day dedicated to the Goddess Mawu	

Beginning of Aquarius

Marija Gimbutas

23 January 1921 - 1994

Day to honour the Goddess Hathor by having a milk bath

23 January

Day of the Goddess Venus

Sementivae Honour the Earth Goddess Terra

24 January

Blessing of the Candle of the Happy Women

Tu Bi-Shivat - Hebrew holiday showing respect for trees and growing things 25 January

The Shekinah - Sarah and Esther

25 January

Celebration of the Triple Moon

26 January

Day of the Goddess Cerridwen and Copper Women

Day of the God Alacita, god of Abundance

Dedicated to the Goddesses of the Grain and Harvest

Gamelion Noumenia honouring all Deity

28 January

Up Kelly Aa (Scotland) Norse derived fire Festival to sacrifice to the Sun

Peace Festival

29 January

Day of the Goddess Hecate

Feast of the Goddess Charites

30 January

Dedication of the Altar of peace and Harmony

Purification ceremony dedicated to the Goddess Yemaya

Zsusanna Budapest Witch and author

30 January 1940 - 14 March 2008

Dr Frian - Alleged HP of North Berwick Witches, executed in Scotland in 1591

31 January

Feast of the Goddess Aphrodite	31 January
Candlemas Festival	
Festival of the Goddess Brigid	
Day of the Goddess Hecate	

FEBRUARY:

Festival of Lughnasadh Southern Hemisphere	1 February
Festival of Imbolg Northern Hemisphere	
Festival of the God Dionysus	
Festival of the Goddess Februa	
Ethnic Equality Month	2 February
Original Ground Hog Day	
Day of the Goddess Ceres and Proserpine	
Day Dedicated to the Horned Gods	
Lesser Eleusian Mysteries	3 February
Day dedicated to the Goddess Demeter and Persephone	
Halfway point of Summer in the Southern Hemisphere	
Lantern Lighting Ceremony Festival	4 February
Day of the Goddess Maat	5 February
Day to Honour Air Spirits	
H. R. Giger	5 February 1940 - 13 May 2014
Feast of St. Agatha - Patroness of Fire Fighters	
Day of the Goddess Maat - Goddess of Wisdom and Truth	
Festival of the Goddess Aphrodite	6 February
Day of the Goddess Artemis	
Day of the Goddess Selene	7 February
Stuart Farrar passed into the Summerlands 2000	

Death of Thomas Aquinas 1274 - whose writings refuted the Canon Episcopi

Day to honour all Moon Goddesses

Chinese New Year   8 February

Eliphas Levi   8 February 1810 - 31 May 1875

Celebration of the Goddess Kwan Yin   9 February

Day of the Goddess Athena   10 February

Festival of Toutates

Feast of Our lady of Lourdes - visitation of the Goddess   11 February

Day of the Goddess Persephone

Day of St. Gobnat

Day of the Goddess Diana   12 February

Day dedicated to the Ancestors   13 February

Day of the Goddess Vesta

Betrothal Day (later adopted by Christians and changed to St. Valentines Day)   14 February

Women's plea to the Goddess Diana for children are granted this day

Heinrich Cornelius Agrippa   14 February 1486 - 18 February 1535

Day of the Goddess Rhiannon   15 February

Pope Leo X issued the Bull Toensure - that secular courts would carry out executions of Witches condemned by the Inquisition in 1521.

Day dedicated to the Goddess Juno Februata

Day of Lupa - The She-wolf

Day of Honouring Light   16 February

Christ accepted as the God Quetzalcoatl in South America   17 February

Festival of Women - dedicated to the Goddess Spandermat   18 February

Birthday of Ramakrishna - Hindu Mystic

Day of the Wicces Sacred Tree - The Ash

Day of the Goddess Minerus   19 February

Birthday of Copernicus - Astronomer

Day of the Silent Goddess Tacita - averter   20 February
of harmful gossip

Healing Day of the Goddess Kwan Yin   21 February

The Sun enters into Pisces

Holiday of St. Lucia - Goddess of Light   22 February

Sybil Leek   22 February 1917 - 26 October 1982

Day of Blessing Land Boundaries   23 February

The Regigugium -   24 February

Flight of Kings, when the Year King is
sacrificed and successor crowned by the
Goddess

Day of the Goddess Nut   26 February

Shrove Tuesday - the first day of Lent

Day of the Goddess The Morrigan   27 February

Time of the Old Woman

Anthesterion Noumenia honouring all
Deity

The Great Wicces Night   28 February

Sabbatu - cakes and wine offered to the
Goddess for Prosperity and Luck

Leap Year - when women rule the Earth
and can ask men for marriage 29 February

Day of the Goddess St. Brigid

MARCH:

The Golden Dawn Founded   1 March 1888

The Covenant of the Goddess Wiccan
Church was formed in 1975

Day of the Goddess Hestia

First Day of Autumn

Bale Fires are lit to bring back the Sun

Festival of the Goddess Rhiannon   2 March

Day of the Goddess Spider Woman

Women do not work on this day or the
Goddess will send storms to destroy

Doll Festival for young girls   3 March

Founding of the Church of All Worlds   4 March 1968

First Wiccan church to Incorporate
in USA

Festival of the Goddesses Artemis and
Diana

Feast of Flowers dedicated to the Goddess
Flora and Hecate

All Souls day – Greece

Navigum Isidis of the Goddess Isis who   5 March
opens the seas to navigation

Laurie Cabot Official Witch of Salem   6 March 1933 *

Junoalia — Celebration of matrons and
young girls

David J Conway author   6 March 1939

Day of the Goddess Ishtar   7 March

Ceremony of Peace

Day of the Goddess Juno

Birthday Celebration of Mother Earth   8 March

Day of the Goddess Ilmatar

International Women's Day

Mothering day - original Mothers Day   9 March

Feast of the Year Goddess - Anna Perenna   10 march

Day of Our lady of Lourdes - appearance
of the Goddess Persephone 11 March

Festival of the God Marduk   12 March

Day of the Goddess Demeter

Discovery of the Planet Uranus - 1781   13 March

Bale Fires are lit to call in the Rain	
Birthday of Ronald Hubbard - Creator of Scientology	
Jacques de Molay - Head of the Knights Templar	14 March
Festival of the Goddess Ostara	15 March
Pete Pathfinder becomes the first Wiccan Priest elected as President of the Interfaith Council, 1995.	
Day of the Goddess Levannah	16 March
Day of the Goddess Morrigan	17 March
Feast of Liberalia - Women's Festival of the God Bacchus and the Maenads	
Festival of the God the Greenman	
Sheelah's Day - The Goddess Sheelah-na-gig of Sexuality	18 March
Birthday of Edgar Cayce	
Manley Palmer Hall	18 March 1901 - 29 September 1990 *
Marriage of the Goddess Kore to the God Dionysus	
Quinquatrus Festival of the Goddess Minerva`	19 March
Lesser Panathenacea - dedicated to the Goddess Athena	
Criminal Witchcraft Stature enacted under Queen Elizabeth - 1563	
Day of the God Aries	20 March
Day of the Goddess The Morrigan	
World Forest Day	21 March
Day of the Goddess Athena	
Day of the Autumnal Equinox Southern Hemisphere	

Mandate of Henry VIII against Witchcraft enacted in 1542, repealed in 1547

Birthday of the Goddess Athena — 22 March

Rev. Pete Pathfinder Founder of the Aquarian Tabernacle Church 22 March 1937 - 2 November 2014

Day of Fasting — 23 March

Day of the Goddess Ishtar

Day of the Goddess Bellona - Witches Power day — 24 March

Lady Day - Feast Annunciation of Mary — 25 March

Pope Innocent III Issues the Bull establishing the Inquisition in 1199

Day of the Goddess Ceres (named for cereals) — 26 March

Feast of Esus the Hunter

Day of the Goddess Ceres, who lends her name to breakfast cereals

Day of the Goddess Hecate — 27 March

Birthday of Rudolph Steiner

Elaphabolion Noumenia honouring all deity — 28 March

Death of Scott Cunningham in 1993

Birthday of Kwan Yin Goddess of Mercy - Healing Day

The Delphinia - dedicated to the Goddess Artemis — 29 March

Festival of the Goddess Athena — 30 March

Anita Festival

Festival of the Goddess Aphrodite and the God Hermes — 31 March

Last Witch trial in Ireland in 1711

Day of the Goddess Hilaria

Day of the Goddess Rhaeda

APRIL:

Veneralia Festival of Peace	1 April
Day of the Goddess Hathor	
April Fools Day	
Feast of Ama - Goddess and Patroness of Fishermen	2 April
Birthday of Hans Christian Anderson	
Descent of the Goddess Persephone into Annwyn	3 April
Day of Ceralia - Seed Day	
Day of the Goddess Ceres	
Descent of the Goddess Persephone into Annwyn	
Honouring of Aesculapius The Great Healer	4 April
Day of Megalesia of the Goddess Cybele	
Day of Fortune	5 April
Birthday of Kwan Yin	
Birthday of Harry Houdini the Magician	6 April
Stanislas de Guaita Occultist and author	6 April 1861 - 19 December 1897
World Health Day	7 April
Church of All Worlds Founded in 1962 in the USA	
Day of Mooncakes	8 April
Day of the Goddess Ata Bey's	
Empowering of Women day	9 April
Day of the Amazon Goddess of Women	
Day of the Goddess Bau - Mother of Ea (The Earth)	10 April
Day of Kista - Spiritual Knowing	11 April
Day of the Goddess Ceres	
Day of the Goddess Anahit - Armenian Goddess of Love and the Moon	

Anton La Vey Founder of the Church of Satan USA	11 April 1930 - 20 October 1997 *
Day of the Goddess Chy-Si-Niv Niv	12 April
Festival of Change	
First Confession of Witchcraft by Isobel Gowdie in 1662	13 April
Blessing of the Sea	
Festival Honouring all Nordic Deity	14 April
Adoption of Principles of Wiccan belief at the 1974 Gnostica Witch Meet	
Day of the Goddess Venus	
Birthday of Elizabeth Montgomery (Bewitched)	15 April
Bernadette sees the Goddess at Lourdes	
Day of the Goddess Luna, Tellas and Venus	
Day of the Goddess Luna	16 April
Margot Adler Author and HPs of Wicca	16 April 1946 - 28 July 2014
Day of the Goddess Isis (Aset)	17 April
The Chariot Festival	
The Rain Festival	
Day of Honouring the Air Element	18 April
Day of Temple Offerings to the Goddess in Bali	19 April
Day of the Goddess Hathor, Isis and all Horned Goddesses	20 April
Astrological Beginning of Taurus	
Feast of the Goddess Pales	21 April
Roma Dea Roma	
Day of the pastoral Goddess The Perilya	
Earth Day	22 April
The Rlenteria	
The First day of Winter	

Clothes Washing Day

Festival of the God the Greenman   23 April

Pyre Festival of the Goddess Astarte,
Tanith, Venus and Erycina

Birthday of actress Shirley Maclaine   24 April

Children's Day

First Seasonal Wine Festival of Venus
and Jupiter

Day of The Goddess Robigalia of Corn   25 April
and harvest

Passover originally dedicated to the
God Baal

Day of the Goddess Yemaya   26 April

Birthday of William Shakespeare

Mounikhion Noumenia Honouring of
all Deity

Feast of St. George originally derived   27 April
from the God Apollo, the twin of Diana

Festival of the Goddess Florala (Flora)   28 April

The Ploughing Ceremony   29 April

Women's Day in Nigeria

Walpurgas Nacht (The Wicces Night)   30 April

Samhain (Halloween) Southern
hemisphere

Beltane (Northern Hemisphere)

Remembrance Day

May:
**May is dedicated to and named after
the Goddess Maia.**   1 May

May Day and Samhain day dancing with
the Maypole for fertility to the Earth

Day of the Goddess Maat The Goddess
of Truth

Day of Moon Goddesses Asherah, Damia, Latona, Bona Dea and Dea Dia	
Day of Ysahodhara the Wife of Buddha	2 May
Festival of the Goddess for public welfare Bona Dea	3 May
Chloris Tarentia	
National day of Prayer	4 May
Festival of the Goddess Cerridwen	
Veneration of the Sacred Thorn (Moon Tree)	
The beginning of Hawthorn Moon	
Rain Ceremony	5 May
Day of the Goddess Maat of Truth	
Birthday of Sigmund Freud	6 May
The Goddess visits Mut, Mother of Gods and Goddesses	
Festival of the Earth Spirits	7 May
Hathor Visits Anukis the Goddess of the Nile	
Festival of the God Apollo	
Furry Day	8 May
Morris dancing for Maid Marion originally the Goddess Flora	
Day of Honouring the Great White Mother	9 May
Joan of Arc canonised 1920	
Day of Ascension	
Day of Tin Hau the North Star	10 May
Celebration of the Goddess Anahit	
World Nations Reduce Greenhouse Emissions	
Day of Russali, the Triple Goddess - Ana, Badb and Macha	11 May
Shashti - The day of the sacred Forest	12 May

Founding of the Church of Wicca in Australia by Lady Tamara Von Forslun 13 May 1989

Procession of our lady of Fatima

The Goddess as a Young Maiden (Persephone, Athena, Artemis and Diana)

Time of the Midnight Sun 14 May

The Panegyric of Isis - Her finding Osiris

Honouring the Great Stag 15 may

Honouring the Queen of Heaven 16 May

Festival of the Goddess Hathor 17 May

Goddess with Child

Festival of the Horned God 18 May

Feast of the Horned God Cernunnos

Day of Nurturance

Day dedicated to the Goddess Pallas Athena

Festival of the God Pan 19 May

The Goddess Hathor arrives at Edfu in Neb

Festival of Springs and Wells

Beginning of Gemini

Day dedicated to Night and Day being Equal 20 may

Birthday of the Bard Gwydion Penderwen 21 May

Biological Diversity Day 22 May

Adoption of the Earth religion Anti-Abuse Act 1988

Day of the Rose 23 May

Celebration of the Birthday of the Goddess Artemis 24 May

Festival of the Triple Goddess 25 May

Sacred Day of St. Sarah for Gypsies

Thargelion Noumenia honouring all deity	26 May
Day of the Warrior	
Morning Glory Zell HPs and author of Wicca	27 May
Night Time Healing Ceremony	
Scourge of Pythia - Seer at Delphi, the Delphic Oracle of the Goddess 28 May	
Feast of the Oak Apple	29 May
Family Day	
Blessing of the Fields	30 May
Death of Joan of Arc 1431	
Thargelia Honouring the Goddess Artemis and the God Apollo	31 May
Honouring of Joan of Arc in Commemoration 1412 –1431 (19yrs of age)	
Pucelle of the Goddess	

JUNE:

June named after the Goddess Juno.	**1 June**
Festival of Opet in Egypt	
Feast of the oak Nymph	
Day of Epipi the Goddess of darkness and Mysteries	
Festival of the Goddess Ishtar	2 June
Birthday of Alessandro of Cagliostro Alchemist and Heretic	
Marion Zimmer Bradley author Mists of Avalon	3 June
Buddhist Blessing for young girls	
Free Women's Festival Skyclad (nudity)	5 June
Alex Sanders King of the Witches	6 June 1926 - 30 April 1988 *

Leave Cakes at Crossroads for the Goddess Artemis for luck	
Vestalia Festival of the Goddess Vesta	7 June
World Oceans Day	8 June
Day of the Goddess Rhea	
Mater Matuta Festival Honouring all Mothers	9 June
Day of the Goddess Venus	10 June
Lady Luck Day	11 June
Dolores Ashcroft-Nowicki HPs and author	11 June 1929
Grain Festival to the Goddess Ashtoreth	12 June
Gerald B. Gardner Founder of Gardnarian Witchcraft 13 June 1884 - 12 February 1964	
William Butler Yeats author	13 June 1865 - 28 January 1939
Day of the Goddess Epona The Horse Goddess	
Day of the Muses	
Starhawk HPs and author	14 June 1951
Lesser Quinquatrus of the Goddess Minerva	
Day of Our lady of Mount Carmel	15 June
Feast of the Water of the Nile	16 June
Night of the Goddess Hathor	
Day of the Goddess Eurydice the Goddess of the Underworld	17 June
Day of the Goddess Danu	18 June
Birthday of King James 1st of England	19 June
Day of all Hera's Wisewomen dedicated to the Goddess within	
First day of Cancer	20 June
Midwinter Solstice (Southern Hemisphere)	21 June

Midsummer Solstice (northern hemisphere)

Festival of the God Herne the Hunter	22 June
Final law Against Witchcraft Repealed in England in 1951	
Day of the Faerie Goddess Aine	23 June
Day of the Burning Lams at Sais for the Goddess Isis and Neith	24 June
Janet Farrar Alexandrian HPs and author	24 June *
Day of Praises to the Goddess Parvati	25 June
Skirophorion Noumenia Honouring all Deity	26 June
Stuart Farrar Alexandrian HP and author	26 June 1916 - 7 February 2000 *
Day of Honouring all Corn Mothers	27 June
Scott Cunningham HP and author	27 June 1956 - 28 March 1993
Birthday of the Goddess Hemera the Daughter of Ayx	28 June
Day of the Sun God Ra	29 June
Day of Aestas the Goddess of Corn	30 June

JULY:

Named after Julius Caesar.	**1 July**
International Save the Species protection day	
Day to Honour all Grandmothers	
Day of the Goddess Selene	
The Coldest Day of the Year	2 July
Day of the Witch Gaeta	
Day of the God and Dogstar Planet Sirius	3 July
Ceremony of the Mountain Spirits	4 July
Earth is at the Perphelion to the Sun- the Furthest between the Earth and the Sun 5 July	

Day of the Goddess Hera	6 July
Running of the Bulls in Spain	
Day of the Goddess Hera	
Day of the Goddess Hel Goddess of the Underworld	10 July
Let Fete de la Magdalene (Mary Magdalene) the Sacred harlot	11 July
Day of Justice	
Honouring of all Children	
Day of Forgiveness	
Dr. Margaret Murray HPs and author	13 July 1863 - 13 November 1963
All Souls day Honouring the Spirits of Ancestors	14 July
Festival of the Sacred Rowan Tree	15 July
Day of the Goddess Carmen Healer and Midwife	16 July
Day of the Goddess Freya	17 July
Birthday of the Goddess Nephthys Goddess of Death	18 July
Lady Sheba HPs and author	18 July 1920 - 2 March 2002
The Opet Festival of Egypt the marriage of Isis and Osiris	19 July
Day of the Dragon	20 July
Pope Adrian VI issues the Bull	
Day For Binding the Wreaths for Lovers	
Mayan New Year	21 July
Feast of the Forest Spirits	
Beginning of Leo	22 July
Day of the Goddess Amaterasu	
Max Heindal Author and leader of the Rosicrucians	23 July 1865 - 6 January 1919
Day of Salacia The Goddess of Oceans	23 July

Hekatombaion Noumenia Honouring all deities

Day and the Games of the God Lugh — 24 July

Day of the Serpent Goddess — 25 July

Birthday of Omar Kha

Death of Pope Innocent VIII — 25 July

Feast of St. Anne — 26 July

Sacred day to all Buffalo Gods and Goddesses

Dr Carl Jung Occult psychiatrist — 26 July 1875 - 6 June 1961

Day of the Goddess Hatshepsut Healer Queen and Architect — 27 July

Procession of Witches in Belgium

Day of the God Thor — 28 July

Voudoun Sacred Day for Ceremonies — 29 July

Day of the God Jupiter — 30 July

Eve of Imbolg the Festival — 31 July

AUGUST:

Named after the Emperor Augustus.

Imbolg Festival (southern hemisphere) — 1 August

Lughnasadh Festival (northern hemisphere)

Day of the Goddess Taitu

Fiesta of Our Lady of Angels — 2 August

Day of Saoka

Day of the Dryads dedicated to Maiden Spirits of the Woods and Water 3 August

Day of the Goddess Hathor — 4 August

Day of the Lady of Snow

Day of the Goddess Mara — 5 August

Day of the Benediction of the Sea

Day of the Cherokee Corn Dancers — 6 August

Gaia Consciousness Day	7 August
Breaking of the Nile	
Day of the Goddess Nut	
Birthday of the Virgin Mary	8 August
Festival of the Goddess Venus	9 August
Festival of the Spirits	
Day to Honour the Star Goddesses	10 August
Holy day of St. Claire	11 August
Lychnapsia the Festival of Lights for the Goddess Isis	12 August
Helena Blavatsky occultists and author	12 August 1831 - 8 May 1947
Birthday of the Goddess Aradia Queen of the Witches Born in Volterra in 1313	
13 August	
Celebration of the Goddess Diana and Hecate of the Moon	
Day dedicated to the Goddess Selene	14 August
Day of the Goddess Tiamat	15 August
Birthday of Charles Godfrey Leland	
Celebration of the Goddess Dea Syria	
Day of Giving	16 August
Feast of the Goddess Diana	17 August
Day of Healing the Past	18 August
Vinalia Thanksgiving	19 August
Day of Vinalia Rustica Venus of the Grape Vine	
Birthday of HP Lovecraft	20 August
Sacred Marriage of Heaven and Earth	
Harvest festival	21 August
Metagetnion Noumenia Day to honour all Deities	22 August
Beginning of Virgo	
Festival of the Furies	23 August

Festival of the Goddess of Fate Nemesis

W. E. Butler author and occultist — 23 August 1898 - 1 August 1978

Festival of the Opening of the Mundas — 24 August
Cereris the Womb of the Labyrinth to
the Underworld of Demeter

Opseconsia the Harvest Festival Ritual — 25 August
of Thanksgiving

Feast day of the Goddess Ilmatar — 26 August

Birthday of the Goddesses Isis and Nut — 27 August

Opening the World Parliament of — 28 August
Religions

Birthday of the Goddess Athena

Birthday of the Goddess Hathor — 29 August

Egyptian New Years Day

Charistheria The Thanksgiving — 30 August
ceremony

Raymond Buckland HP and author — 31st August 1934 – 27th September 2017

SEPTEMBER:

Awakening of the Women's Serpent — 1 September
Power Life Force

Ostara - First day of Spring (southern
hemisphere)

Festival of the Vine dedicated to the
Goddess Ariadne and the God Dionysus
2 September

Day of the Goddess Polias and the God
Zeus

Women's Healing Ceremony for the — 3 September
Four Directions

Pilgrimage to test One's Soul — 4 September

Day of the Goddess Cybele — 5 September

Day of the Goddess Artemis — 6 September

Day of the God Bacchus	7 September
Birthday of the Goddess Yemaya	8 September
Feast of the Shepherd	
Birthday of the Goddess Yemaya	
Day of Mercy	
Te Veilat the Gathering of the Fruit	9 September
Reunion Festival	10 September
Marie Laveau Queen of the Voudoun	10 September 1801 - 16 June 1881
Day of Honouring all Queens of Egypt	11 September
Day of the God Bel	12 September
Day of the Goddess Nephthys	13 September
Ceremony for the Lighting of the Fire	
Day of Honouring the Black Madonna	14 September
Day of the Goddess Kore	15 September
The gathering of Initiates .	
International Day of Democracy	
Goddesses Ascent from Annwyn	16 September
Holade Mystai the Ritual bathing in the Sea	
Day of St. Sophia	17 September
Day of Faith, Hope and Charity	
Feast of St. Hildegarde	
Stephen Skinner author	17 September 1932 - 24 September 1997
Giving of Grain and Food to the Poor	18 September
Blessing of the Rain Goddesses	19 September
Boedromion Noumenia Day to Honour all Deities	20 September
Festival of Epopteia the day of Initiation	
Spring Equinox (southern hemisphere)	21 September
Autumn Equinox (northern hemisphere)	
Feast of Honouring the triple Aspect of Maiden, Mother and Crone	

Festival of Mabon the Wicces Thanksgiving	22 September
Day of the Goddess Demeter	
Beginning of Libra	23 September
Genesia Day to make offerings to the Dead	24 September
Day of Mercy	
Birthday of the Goddess Sedna	25 September
Day of Atonement	26 September
Birthday of the Goddess Athena of Knowledge	27 September
Day of Saleeb the Cresting of the Nile at its greatest height	28 September
Feast of Michaelmas (honouring archangel Michael)	29 September
Day of the Goddess Meditrinalia of Medicines and Healing	30 September

OCTOBER:

Day to Forgive Your Enemies	1 October
Neville Drury author	1 October 1947 - 15 October 2013
Isaac Bonawitz Druid and author	
Power Day for Arachnids	
Day of the Goddess Rhiannon	2 October
Feast of the Guardian Spirits	
Rosaleen Norton witch and author	2 October 1917 - 5 December 1979
Arthur Edward Waite witch and author	2 October 1857 - 19 May 1942
St. Dionysis Transformation of the Pagan God of Wine into Christianity 3 October	
Oddudua The Santeria Mother of the Gods and Goddesses	4 October
Fasting day for the Goddess Demeter	
Byzantine day of the Holy Spirit for the Goddess Sophia	5 October

Wine festival for the God Dionysis

Day of the Goddess Artemis 6 October

Day of the God Bau 7 October

Francis Barrett occultist and author 7 October 1872 - 21 February 1941

Oschophoria The bearing of Green Branches to commemorate Theseus Return 8 October

Day of the God Horus 9 October

The Eye of the God Festival

Day of White Buffalo calf Woman 10 October

Thesmophoria of the Goddess Demeter 11 October

Aleister Crowley occultist and author 12 October 1875 - 1 December 1947

Day of Women's Prayers

Day of the God Eros 13 October

Victory day of Good over Evil 14 October

Day of Lady Godiva 15 October

Day of the Goddess Gaia and Nymphs day 16 October

Festival of Fortune

Day of the Goddess Isis 17 October

Day of Clean Water 18 October

St. Luke's day The Great Horn Fair Honouring Horned Gods Day

Day of Good Luck 19 October

Pyanepsion Noumenia Day to honour 20 October
all deities

Birthday of Selena Fox HPs and author

Day of the Virgin Mary

Kite Flying festival

Day of the Goddess Aphrodite 22 October

Sacred day of the Willow Tree

Timothy Leary 22 October 1920 - 31 May 1996

Day of the Goddess Aphrodite

Beginning of Scorpio 23 October

Day of the Goddess Lilith	24 October
Feast of the Spirits of Air	
Day of the God Ge	25 October
Proerosia Festival Harvest	
Festival of the Goddess Hathor	26 October
Honouring the Womb in all Female Life	27 October
Patricia Crowther HPs and author	27 October 1927 - 5 February 2009
Day of the Goddess Isis	28 October
Feast of the Dead	29 October
Day of the God Osiris	30 October
Day to Remember the Burning Times	31 October
Beltane Festival (southern hemisphere)	
Samhain (northern hemisphere)	
Wicces Remembrance Day	

NOVEMBER:

Day of the Banshees	1 November
Rebirth of the God Osiris	3 November
World Communication Day	
Stag Dances	4 November
Birthday of the Goddess Tiamat	6 November
Day of the Goddess Leto	7 November
Sacred day of Elphane	11 November
World Tolerance Day	16 November
Day of the Goddess Ereshkigal	
Israel Regardie author and witch	17 November 1907 - 10 March 1985
Maimakterion Noumenia Day to honour all Deities	18 November
Day of the Goddess Ishtar	21 November
Thanksgiving	23 November
Elders Day of Respect	

Lady Tamara Von Forslun Elder HPs and author	23 November 1956*
Day of the Goddess Cerridwen	26 November
Day of the Goddess Sophia	27 November
Oberon Zell Witch and author	30 November *

DECEMBER:

Franz Bardon occultist and author	1 December 1909 – 10 July 1958
World Aids Day	1 December
Day of the Goddess Pallas Athena	
Day of the Goddess Arachne	2 December
Day of the Goddess Bona Dea	3 December
Day of the Goddess Bride	5 December
Dione Fortune author and occultist	6 December 1890 – 8 January 1946
Day of the Goddess Tara	9 December
Day of the Light Bringer	13 December
Day of the Goddess Sapientia	16 December
Festival of Saturnalia	17 December
Poseidon Poumenia	18 December
Day of Saturnalia	
Day of the Goddess Kwan Yin	
Day of Opalia	19 December
Day of the Goddess Selene and the God Janus	20 December
Festival of Evergreen Trees	21 December
Birthday of the God Mithras	22 December
Mid Summer Solstice (southern hemisphere)	
Mid Winter Solstice (northern hemisphere)	
Day of the Goddess Hathor	23 December
Festival of the Goddess Freyr and the God Freyja	25 December

Festival of the of Poseidon	25 December
Birthday of the God Horus	26 December
Birthday of Buddha	
Birthday of the Goddess Freya	27 December
Day of the Goddess Artemis	29 December
Festival of Father Time	31 December
Day of the Sun God Ra	

BUCKLAND
MUSEUM OF
WITCHCRAFT
AND MAGICK

ADDRESS: 316 Linwood Avenue, Columbus, Ohio. 43205. U.S.A.
WEBSITE: www.bucklandmuseum.org
EMAIL: Toni@bucklandmuseum.org

The <u>Buckland Gallery of Witchcraft and Magick</u> is still a hidden treasure for anyone who wishes to search out some of the most memorable artefacts and relics of our history thanks to Raymond Buckland and other elders of the World Wiccan community who have graciously donated many of the items. But for the most, Raymond Buckland has carefully collected these since 1966, for his personal collected to start with. Ray kept his remarkable collected or artefacts that he collected from his many travels around the world in his basement of his home, originally just for the viewing of friends and fellows Wiccans that were members of his coven.

Ray lived a relative quiet life, but after being outed by local media, he decided to go public and eventually decided to display all his relics in his home on Bay Shore, New York until 1976. This one of a kind collection of rare items started to receive notoriety by public media when he moved to New Hampshire, displaying his artefacts publicly for three years, until again he decided to move onto his dream home ranch in Virginia. Due to Raymond Buckland's heavy schedule with writing of his books, lecturing around the country as the Founder of American Wicca, he again decided to put his beautiful collection in storage.

Through this busy lifestyle, Raymond Buckland had many offers to acquire or purchase his collection, and which he kept declining. But in the late 1990's his collection the Buckland Museum was born again, this time in New Orleans, where it was displayed for nearly a decade but at a disorganized and financially bad period, Raymond and the custodians of the collection had financial fallout from their deal. Raymond legally reclaimed the collection.

It was at this time my good friend and fellow sister whom I had met through the Aquarian Tabernacle Church in Washington at a Spring festival, took over guardianship as their new custodian and displayed them in her garage as an educational tool for the public and for fellow Wiccans in 1999.

It was at a later time that I was invited to attend her Rites of Spring in the latter part of 2007, this was after the devastation that Cyclone Katrina had created on August 15th 2005 with a Category 5 Cyclone. Leaving millions homeless and killing 1833 people. The cost for this devastation was over $108 billion.

When I arrived 2 years later, the devastation was still present, many that left New Orleans never returned. Whilst driving down the streets you could see the water line halfway up the houses where the flooding had reached. Velvets beautiful home were also destroyed and took her 3 years to get rebuilt. After all this devastation, Velvet became quite ill and had to give up her care taking of the museum to look after her health. (Sadly my sister eventually passed away). But she did protect the collection of Raymond Buckland. It was at this time that one of Raymond Buckland's members of his Coven based in Ohio brought the collection in 2015 where again it sat in storage.

Current custodians and caretakers, and husband and wife, Jillian Slane and Steven Intermill who are self proclaimed "Museum Nerds". Jillian originally worked at the Cleveland Museum of natural History and San Francisco's Museum of Modern Art. Her husband Steven was the curator for "a Christmas Story House and Museum". Although they are not Wiccans or even belonging to the Wiccan Community, they were passionate about the collection and were sympathetic to our history. Steven in particular was knowledgeable of the underground Witchcraft scene and of Mystery religions, and so he originally had contact with Raymond Buckland about the collection.

After much diatribe they were granted permission by Raymond to open the Museum in Cleveland, where it stands today tucked away behind a retro record store. Due to the size of the building only about 40% of the artefacts and relics can be shown at any one time, but they are changed and moved around periodically to show as much as possible. They are presently looking for larger premises so that all the treasures can be displayed for all antiquity.

Presently there are over 500 rare artefacts such as Sybil Leek's crystal ball, Gerald Gardner's Broomstick, Morning Glory Zell's High priestess headdress, Raymond Buckland's personal Chalice and ceremonial robes, a bio-mate Bio-rhythm calculator, Anton la Vey's, record of the Black Mass. Plus many tools and artefacts belonging to other famous Witches such as ancient Egyptian Ushabti's, Salem Witch Trial Documents. Relics from Aiden Breac, Israel Regardie, Lady Rowan, Christopher Penczal, Aleister Crowley, Stewart and Janet Farrar, Scott Cunningham and of course myself, where I have left in my will all my artefacts and relics to be left to the Museum.

While I was writing this book for publication, Toni emailed me, from the museum that Raymond Buckland had just passed away. It was such a shock to the Wiccan Community and as my mentor; I was deeply saddened by this great loss. Ray had just had his 83rd birthday only weeks prior to his passing. Not a bad inning for a man that lived life to the full with his devoted wife and family. Raymond was admired and loved by everyone, and he will never be forgotten and has left a huge legacy for the world and for the Wiccan Community as a whole. If you ever get a chance visit the Buckland Museum of Witchcraft and Magick and pay your respects.

None Greater – Hail and Farewell Ray (Robat)
31st August 1934 – 27th September 2017

EPILOGUE

Well here we are at the conclusion of this my first book, which I hope was not only informative but also enjoyable. This is the first part of a series which will elevate the budding Wiccan or affectionately known as the Witchling with the knowledge that they need to see if the Craft is for them on a lesser level, of if they wish to ascend through the ranks to learn the deeper Mysteries of the Old Religion.

This book covers the basic information required to help you advance in your studies and may or may not take you on a journey of self-discovery correctly helping you with the needed information for your Wiccan path ahead. Wicca is not for everyone, as with all religious or spiritual paths many come and many go, finding it not for them. But for those who stay, and research and build a connection with the Earth, Her Mysteries, the Craft and the Magick Circle of their new Spiritual family that you may or may not have found as yet.

All the questionnaires at the end of each chapter are for your own purpose and not for mine, it is to add to your Book of Shadows so you know when and how you answered these questions, because as you learn more and travel the path of Wicca, your answers will change as you change and grow as you become more connected and knowledgeable in these areas.

If you have any queries about these writings, or if you have any questions please feel free to contact me through my website at www.witchofoz.org. Hope you are ready to read my next book *"Complete Teachings of Wicca Book Two - The Wicce"*.